Inside Volatility Arbitrage

Founded in 1807, John Wiley & Sons is the oldest independent publishing company in the United States. With offices in North America, Europe, Australia, and Asia, Wiley is globally committed to developing and marketing print and electronic products and services for our customers' professional and personal knowledge and understanding.

The Wiley Finance series contains books written specifically for finance and investment professionals as well as sophisticated individual investors and their financial advisors. Book topics range from portfolio management to e-commerce, risk management, financial engineering, valuation and financial instrument analysis, as well as much more.

For a list of available titles, visit our Web site at www.WileyFinance.com.

Inside Volatility Arbitrage

The Secrets of Skewness

ALIREZA JAVAHERI

WILEY

John Wiley & Sons, Inc.

Published by John Wiley & Sons, Inc., Hoboken, New Jersey
Published simultaneously in Canada

Library of Congress Cataloging-in-Publication Data

Javaheri, Alireza.
Inside volatility arbitrage : the secrets of skewness / Alireza Javaheri.
p. cm.
Includes bibliographical references and index.
ISBN 0-471-73387-3 (cloth)
1. Stocks–Proces–Mathematical models. 2. Stochastic processes. I. Title.
HG4636.J38 2005
332.63'222'0151922–dc22 2005004696

Printed in the United States of America

10 9 8 7 6 5 4 3 2

Contents

Illustrations

Figures

Tables

Acknowledgments

This book is based upon my Ph.D. dissertation at *École des Mines de Paris*. I would like to thank my advisor, Alain Galli, for his guidance and help. Many thanks go to Margaret Armstrong and Delphine Lautier and the entire CERNA team for their support.

A special thank-you goes to Yves Rouchaleau for helping make all this possible in the first place.

I would like to sincerely thank other committee members, Marco Avellaneda, Lane Hughston, Piotr Karasinski, and Bernard Lapeyre, for their comments and time.

I am grateful to Farshid Asl, Peter Carr, Raphael Douady, Robert Engle, Stephen Figlewski, Espen Haug, Ali Hirsa, Michael Johannes, Simon Julier, Alan Lewis, Dilip Madan, Vlad Piterbarg, Youssef Randjiou, David Wong, and the participants at ICBI 2003 and 2004 for all the interesting discussions and idea exchanges.

I am particularly indebted to Paul Wilmott for encouraging me to speak with Wiley about converting my dissertation into this book.

Finally, I would like to thank my wife, Firoozeh, and my daughters, Neda and Ariana, for their patience and support.

Introduction

SUMMARY

This book focuses on developing methodologies for estimating stochastic volatility (SV) parameters from the stock-price time series under a classical framework. The text contains three chapters structured as follows.

In **Chapter 1**, we shall introduce and discuss the concept of various parametric SV models. This chapter represents a brief survey of the existing literature on the subject of nondeterministic volatility.

We start with the concept of log-normal distribution and historic volatility. We then introduce the Black-Scholes [38] framework. We also mention alternative interpretations as suggested by Cox and Rubinstein [66]. We state how these models are unable to explain the negative skewness and the leptokurticity commonly observed in the stock markets. Also, the famous implied-volatility smile would not exist under these assumptions.

At this point we consider the notion of level-dependent volatility as advanced by researchers, such as Cox and Ross [64] and [65], as well as Bensoussan, Crouhy, and Galai [33]. Either an artificial expression of the instantaneous variance will be used, as is the case for constant elasticity variance (CEV) models, or an implicit expression will be deduced from a firm model, similar to Merton's [189], for instance.

We also bring up the subject of Poisson jumps [190] in the distributions providing a negative skewness and larger kurtosis. These jump-diffusion models offer a link between the volatility smile and credit phenomena.

We then discuss the idea of local volatility [36] and its link to the instantaneous unobservable volatility. Work by researchers such as Dupire [89] and by Derman and Kani [74] will be cited. We also describe the limitations of this idea owing to an ill-poised inversion phenomenon, as revealed by Avellaneda [16] and others.

Unlike nonparametric local volatility models, parametric stochastic volatility (SV) models [140] define a specific stochastic differential equation for the unobservable instantaneous variance. We therefore introduce the notion of two-factor stochastic volatility and its link to one-factor generalized autoregressive conditionally heteroskedastic (GARCH) processes [40]. The SV model class is the one we focus upon. Studies by scholars, such as

Engle [94], Nelson [194], and Heston [134], are discussed at this juncture. We briefly mention related works on stochastic implied volatility by Schonbucher [213], as well as uncertain volatility by Avellaneda [17].

Having introduced SV, we then discuss the two-factor partial differential equations (PDE) and the incompleteness of the markets when only cash and the underlying asset are used for hedging.

We then examine option pricing techniques, such as inversion of the Fourier transform and mixing Monte Carlo, as well as a few asymptotic pricing techniques, as explained, for instance, by Lewis [177].

At this point we tackle the subject of pure-jump models, such as Madan's variance gamma [182] or its variants VG with stochastic arrivals (VGSA) [48]. The latter adds to the traditional VG a way to introduce the volatility clustering (persistence) phenomenon. We mention the distribution of the stock market as well as various option-pricing techniques under these models. The inversion of the characteristic function is clearly the method of choice for option pricing in this context.

In **Chapter 2**, we tackle the notion of inference (or parameter estimation) for parametric SV models. We first briefly analyze cross-sectional inference and then focus upon time-series inference.

We start with a concise description of cross-sectional estimation of SV parameters in a risk-neutral framework. A least-square estimation (LSE) algorithm is discussed. The direction-set optimization algorithm [204] is introduced at this point. The fact that this optimization algorithm does not use the gradient of the input function is important because we shall later deal with functions that contain jumps and are not necessarily differentiable everywhere.

We then discuss the parameter inference from a time series of the underlying asset in the real world. We do this in a classical (non-Bayesian) [240] framework, and in particular we will estimate the parameters via a maximization of likelihood estimation (MLE) [127] methodology. We explain the idea of MLE, its link to the Kullback-Leibler [100] distance, as well as the calculation of the likelihood function for a two-factor SV model.

We see that unlike GARCH models, SV models do not admit an analytic (integrated) likelihood function. This is why we need to introduce the concept of filtering [129].

The idea behind filtering is to obtain the best possible estimation of a hidden state given all the available information up to that point. This estimation is done in an iterative manner in two stages: The first step is a time update in which the prior distribution of the hidden state at a given point in time is determined from all the past information via a Chapman-Kolmogorov equation. The second step would then involve a measurement update where this prior distribution is used together with the conditional likelihood of the newest observation in order to compute the posterior distribution of the hidden state. The Bayes rule is used for this purpose. Once the posterior distribution is determined, it can be exploited for the optimal estimation of the hidden state.

We start with the Gaussian case where the first two moments characterize the entire distribution. For the Gaussian-linear case, the optimal Kalman filter (KF) [129] is introduced. Its nonlinear extension, the extended KF (EKF), is described next. A more suitable version of KF for strongly nonlinear cases, the unscented KF (UKF) [166], is also analyzed. In particular, we see how this filter is related to Kushner's nonlinear filter (NLF) [173] and [174].

The unscented KF uses a first-order Taylor approximation on the nonlinear transition and observation functions, in order to bring us back into a simple KF framework. On the other hand, UKF uses the true nonlinear functions without any approximation. It, however, supposes that the Gaussianity of the distribution is preserved through these functions. The UKF determines the first two moments via integrals that are computed upon a few appropriately chosen "sigma points." The NLF does the same exact thing via a Gauss-Hermite quadrature. However, NLF often introduces an extra centering step, which will avoid poor performance owing to an insufficient intersection between the prior distribution and the conditional likelihood.

As we observe, in addition to their use in the MLE approach, the filters can be applied to a direct estimation of the parameters via a joint filter (JF) [133]. The JF would simply involve the estimation of the parameters together with the hidden state via a dimension augmentation. In other words, one would treat the parameters as hidden states. After choosing initial conditions and applying the filter to an observation data set, one would then disregard a number of initial points and take the average upon the remaining estimations. This initial rejected period is known as the "burn-in" period.

We test various representations or state space models of the stochastic volatility models, such as Heston's [134]. The concept of observability [205] is introduced in this context. We see that the parameter estimation is not always accurate given a limited amount of daily data.

Before a closer analysis of the performance of these estimation methods, we introduce simulation-based particle filters (PF) [79] and [122], which can be applied to non-Gaussian distributions. In a PF algorithm, the importance sampling technique is applied to the distribution. Points are simulated via a chosen proposal distribution, and the resulting weights proportional to the conditional likelihood are computed. Because the variance of these weights tends to increase over time and cause the algorithm to diverge, the simulated points go through a variance reduction technique commonly referred to as *resampling* [14]. During this stage, points with too small a weight are disregarded and points with large weights are reiterated. This technique could cause a sample impoverishment, which can be corrected via a Metropolis-Hastings accept/reject test. Work by researchers such as Doucet [79] and Smith and Gordon [122] are cited and used in this context.

Needless to say, the choice of the proposal distribution could be fundamental in the success of the PF algorithm. The most natural choice would be to take a proposal distribution equal to the prior distribution of the hidden state. Even if this makes the computations simpler, the danger would be a nonalignment between the prior and the conditional likelihood as we previously mentioned. To avoid this, other proposal distributions taking into account the observation should be considered. The extended PF (EPF) and the unscented PF (UPF) [229] precisely do this by adding an extra Gaussian filtering step to the process. Other techniques, such as auxiliary PF (APF), have been developed by Pitt and Shephard [203].

Interestingly, we will see that PF brings only marginal improvement to the traditional KF's when applied to daily data. However, for a larger time step where the nonlinearity is stronger, the PF does help more.

At this point, we also compare the Heston model with other SV models, such as the "3/2" model [177] using real market data, and we see that the latter performs better than the former. This is in line with the findings of Engle and Ishida [95]. We can therefore apply our inference tools to perform model identification.

Various diagnostics [129] are used to judge the performance of the estimation tools. Mean price errors (MPE) and root mean square errors (RMSE) are calculated from the residual errors. The same residuals could be submitted to a Box-Ljung test, which will allow us to see whether they still contain auto correlation. Other tests, such as the chi-square normality test as well as plots of histograms and variograms [110], are performed.

Most importantly, for the inference process, we back-test the tools upon artificially simulated data, and we observe that although they give the correct answer asymptotically, the results remain inaccurate for a smaller amount of data points. It is reassuring to know that these observations are in agreement with work by other researchers, such as Bagchi [19].

Here, we attempt to find an explanation for this mediocre performance. One possible interpretation comes from the fact that in the SV problem, the parameters affect the noise of the observation and not its drift. This is doubly true of volatility-of-volatility and stock-volatility correlation, which affect the noise of the noise. We should, however, note that the *product* of these two parameters enters in the equations at the same level as the drift of the instantaneous variance, and it is precisely this product that appears in the skewness of the distribution.

Indeed, the instantaneous volatility is observable only at the second order of a Taylor (or Ito) expansion of the logarithm of the asset price. This also explains why one-factor GARCH models do not have this problem. In their context, the instantaneous volatility is perfectly known as a function of previous data points. The problem therefore seems to be a low signal-to-noise ratio (SNR). We could improve our estimation by considering additional data points. Using a high frequency (several quotes a day) for the data does help in this context. However, one needs to obtain clean and reliable data first.

Furthermore, we can see why a large time step (e.g., yearly) makes the inference process more robust by improving the observation quality. Still, using a large time step brings up other issues, such as stronger nonlinearity as well as fewer available data points, not to mention the inapplicability of the Girsanov theorem.

We analyze the sampling distributions of these parameters over many simulations and see how unbiased and efficient the estimators are. Not surprisingly, the inefficiency remains significant for a limited amount of data.

One needs to question the performance of the actual optimization algorithm as well. It is known that the greater the number of the parameters we are dealing with, the flatter the likelihood function and therefore the more difficult to find a global optimum. Nevertheless, it is important to remember that the SNR and therefore the performance of the inference tool depend on the actual value of the parameters. Indeed, it is quite possible that the real parameters are such that the inference results *are* accurate.

We then apply our PF to a jump-diffusion model (such as the Bates [28] model), and we see that the estimation of the jump parameters is more robust than the estimation of the diffusion parameters. This reconfirms that the estimation of parameters affecting the drift of the observation is more reliable.

We finally apply the PF to non-Gaussian models such as VGSA [48], and we observe results similar to those for the diffusion-based models. Once again the VG parameters directly affecting the observation are easier to estimate, whereas the arrival rate parameters affecting the noise are more difficult to recover.

Although as mentioned we use a classical approach, we briefly discuss Bayesian methods [34], such as Markov Chain Monte Carlo (MCMC) [163]—including the Gibbs Sampler [55] and the Metropolis-Hastings (MH) [58] algorithm. Bayesian methods consider the parameters not as fixed numbers, but as random variables having a prior distribution. One then updates these distributions from the observations similarly to what is done in the measurement update step of a filter. Sometimes the prior and posterior distributions of the parameters belong to the same family and are referred to as *conjugates*. The parameters are finally estimated via an averaging procedure similar to the one employed in the JF. Whether the Bayesian methods are actually better or worse than the classical ones has been a subject of long philosophical debate [240] and remains for the reader to decide.

Other methodologies that differ from ours are the nonparametric (NP) and the semi-nonparametric (SNP). These methods are based on kernel interpolation procedures and have the obvious advantage of being less restrictive. However, parametric models, such as the ones used by us, offer the possibility of comparing and interpreting parameters such as drift and volatility of the instantaneous variance explicitly. Researchers, such as Gallant and Tauchen [109] and Aït-Sahalia [6], use NP/SNP approaches.

Finally, in **Chapter 3**, we apply the aforementioned parametric inference methodologies to a few assets and will question the consistency of information contained in the options markets on the one hand, and in the stock market on the other hand.

We see that there seems to be an excess negative skewness and kurtosis in the former. This is in contradiction with the Girsanov theorem for a Heston model and could mean either that the model is misspecified or that there is a profitable transaction to be made. Another explanation could come from the peso theory [12] (or crash-o-phobia [155]), where an *expectation* of a so-far absent crash exists in the options markets.

Adding a jump component to the distributions helps to reconcile the volatility-of-volatility and correlation parameters; however, it remains insufficient. This is in agreement with statements made by Bakshi, Cao, and Chen [20].

It is important to realize that, ideally, one should compare the information embedded in the options and the evolution of the underlying asset *during* the life of these options. Indeed, ordinary put or call options are forward (and not backward) looking. However, given the limited amount of available daily data through this period, we make the assumption that the dynamics of the underlying asset do not change before and during the existence of the options. We therefore use time series that start long before the commencement of these contracts.

This assumption allows us to consider a skewness trade [6], in which we would exploit such discrepancies by buying out-of-the-money (OTM) call options and selling OTM put options. We see that the results are not necessarily conclusive. Indeed, even if the trade often generates profits, occasional sudden jumps cause large losses. This transaction is therefore similar to "selling insurance."

We also apply the same idea to the VGSA model in which despite the non-Gaussian features, the volatility of the arrival rate is supposed to be the same under the real and risk-neutral worlds.

Let us be clear on the fact that this chapter does not constitute a thorough empirical study of stock versus options markets. It rather presents a set of examples of application for our previously constructed inference tools. There clearly could be many other applications, such as model identification as discussed in the second chapter.

Yet another application of the separate estimations of the statistical and risk-neutral distributions is the determination of optimal positions in derivatives securities, as discussed by Carr and Madan [52]. Indeed, the expected utility function to be maximized needs the real-world distribution, whereas the initial wealth constraint exploits the risk-neutral distribution. This can be seen via a self-financing portfolio argument similar to the one used by Black and Scholes [38].

Finally, we should remember that in all of the foregoing, we are assuming that the asset and options dynamics follow a known and fixed model, such as Heston or VGSA. This is clearly a simplification of reality. The true markets follow an unknown and, perhaps more importantly, *constantly changing* model. The best we can do is to use the information hitherto available and hope that the future behavior of the assets is not too different from that of the past. Needless to say, as time passes by and new information becomes available, we need to update our models and parameter values. This could be done within either a Bayesian or classical framework.

Also, we apply the same procedures to other asset classes, such as foreign exchange and fixed income. It is noteworthy that although most of the text is centered on equities, almost no change whatsoever is necessary in order to apply the methodologies to these asset classes, which shows again how flexible the tools are.

In the Bibliography, many but not all relevant articles and books are cited. Only some of them are directly referred to in the text.

CONTRIBUTIONS AND FURTHER RESEARCH

The contribution of the book is in presenting a general and systematic way to calibrate any parametric SV model (diffusion based or not) to a time series under a classical (non-Bayesian) framework. Although the concept of filtering has been used for estimating volatility processes before [130], to my knowledge, this has always been for specific cases and was never generalized. The use of particle filtering allows us to do this in a flexible and simple manner. We also study the convergence properties of our tools and show their limitations.

Whether the results of these calibrations are consistent with the information contained in the options markets is a fundamental question. The applications of this test are numerous, among which the skewness trade is only one example.

What else can be done?—a comparative study between our approach and Bayesian approaches on the one hand, and nonparametric approaches on the other hand. Work by researchers such as Johannes, Polson, and Aït-Sahalia would be extremely valuable in this context.

DATA AND PROGRAMS

This book centers on time-series methodologies and exploits either artificially generated inputs or real market data. When real market data is utilized, the source is generally *Bloomberg*. However, most of the data could be obtained from other public sources available on the Internet.

All numeric computations are performed via routines implemented in the C++ programming language. Some algorithms, such as the direction-set optimization algorithm are taken from *Numerical Recipes in C* [204]. No statistical packages, such as *S-Plus* or *R*, have been used.

The actual C++ code for some of the crucial routines (such as EKF or UPF) is provided in this text.

CHAPTER 1

The Volatility Problem

Suppose we use the standard deviation of possible future returns on a stock as a measure of its volatility. Is it reasonable to take that volatility as a constant over time? I think not.

— Fischer Black

INTRODUCTION

It is widely accepted today that an assumption of a constant volatility fails to explain the existence of the volatility smile as well as the leptokurtic character (fat tails) of the stock distribution. The above Fischer Black quote, made shortly after the famous constant-volatility Black-Scholes model was developed, proves the point.

In this chapter, we will start by describing the concept of Brownian motion for the stock price return as well as the concept of historic volatility. We will then discuss the derivatives market and the ideas of hedging and risk neutrality. We will briefly describe the Black-Scholes partial derivatives equation (PDE) in this section. Next, we will talk about jumps and level dependent volatility models. We will first mention the jump diffusion process and introduce the concept of leverage. We will then refer to two popular level dependent approaches: the constant elasticity variance (CEV) model and the Bensoussan-Crouhy-Galai (BCG) model. At this point, we will mention local volatility models developed in the recent past by Dupire and Derman-Kani, and we will discuss their stability.

Following this, we will tackle the subject of stochastic volatility, where we will mention a few popular models, such as the square-root model and the general autoregressive conditional heteroskedasticity (GARCH) model. We will then talk about the pricing PDE under stochastic volatility and the risk-neutral version of it. For this we will need to introduce the concept of market price of risk.

The generalized Fourier transform is the subject of the following section. This technique was used by Alan Lewis extensively for solving stochastic volatility problems. Next, we will discuss the mixing solution, both in correlated and uncorrelated cases. We will mention its link to the fundamental transform and its usefulness for Monte Carlo–based methods. We will then describe the long-term asymptotic case, where we get closed-form approximations for many popular methods, such as the square-root model. Lastly, we will talk about pure-jump models, such as variance gamma and variance gamma with stochastic arrival.

THE STOCK MARKET

The Stock Price Process

The relationship between the stock market and the mathematical concept of Brownian motion goes back to Bachelier [18]. A Brownian motion corresponds to a process, the increments of which are independent stationary normal random variables. Given that a Brownian motion can take negative values, it cannot be used for the stock price. Instead, Samuelson [211] suggested using this process to represent the *return* of the stock price, which will make the stock price a geometric (or exponential) Brownian motion.

In other words, the stock price S follows a log-normal process[1]

$$dS_t = \mu S_t dt + \sigma S_t dB_t \tag{1.1}$$

where dB_t is a Brownian motion process, μ the instantaneous expected total return of the stock (possibly adjusted by a dividend yield), and σ the instantaneous standard deviation of stock price returns, called the *volatility* in financial markets.

Using Ito's lemma,[2] we also have

$$d\ln(S_t) = \left(\mu - \frac{1}{2}\sigma^2\right)dt + \sigma dB_t \tag{1.2}$$

The stock return μ could easily become time dependent without changing any of our arguments. For simplicity, we will often refer to it as μ even if we mean μ_t. This remark holds for other quantities, such as r_t, the interest-rate, or q_t, the dividend yield.

Equation (1.1) represents a continuous process. We can either take this as an approximation of the real discrete tick-by-tick stock movements or

[1]For an introduction to stochastic processes, see Karatzas [167] or Oksendal [197].
[2]See, for example, Hull [146].

consider it the real unobservable dynamics of the stock price, in which case the discrete prices constitute a *sample* from this continuous ideal process. Either way, the use of a continuous equation makes the pricing of financial instruments more analytically tractable.

The discrete equivalent of (1.2) is

$$\ln S_{t+\Delta t} = \ln S_t + \left(\mu - \frac{1}{2}\sigma^2\right)\Delta t + \sigma\sqrt{\Delta t}B_t \tag{1.3}$$

where (B_t) is a sequence of independent normal random variables with zero mean and variance of 1.

Historic Volatility

This suggests a first simple way to estimate the volatility, σ, namely the *historic volatility*. Considering $S_1, ..., S_N$ as a sequence of known historic daily stock close prices, calling $R_n = \ln(S_{n+1}/S_n)$ the stock price return between two days and $\bar{R} = \frac{1}{N}\sum_{n=0}^{N-1} R_n$ the mean return, the historic volatility would be the annualized standard deviation of the returns, namely

$$\sigma_{hist} = \sqrt{\frac{252}{N-1}\sum_{n=0}^{N-1}(R_n - \bar{R})^2} \tag{1.4}$$

Because we work with annualized quantities, and we are using daily stock closing prices, we needed the factor 252, supposing that there are approximately 252 business days in a year.[3]

Note that N, the number of observations, can be more or less than one year; therefore when talking about a historic volatility, it is important to know what time horizon we are considering. We can indeed have three-month historic volatility or three-year historic volatility. Needless to say, taking too few prices would give an inaccurate estimation. Similarly, the begin and end date of the observations matter. It is preferable to take the end date as close as possible to today so that we include recent observations.

An alternative was suggested by Parkinson [200] in which instead of daily closing prices we use the high and the low prices of the stock on that day, and $R_n = \ln(S_n^{high}/S_n^{low})$. The volatility would then be

$$\sigma_{parkinson} = \sqrt{\frac{252}{N-1}\frac{1}{4\ln(2)}\sum_{n=0}^{N-1}(R_n - \bar{R})^2}$$

This second moment estimation derived by Parkinson is based upon the fact that the range R_n of the asset follows a *Feller* distribution.

---

[3]Clearly the observation frequency does not have to be daily.

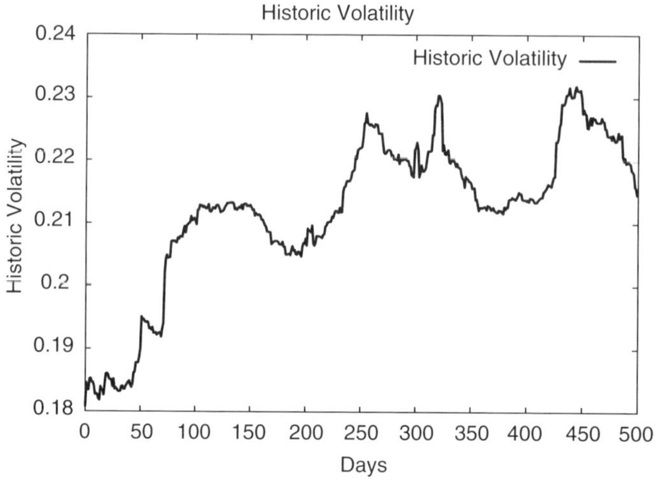

FIGURE 1.1 The SPX Historic Rolling Volatility from 01/03/2000 to 12/31/2001. As we can see, the volatility is clearly nonconstant.

Plotting, for instance, the one-year rolling[4] historic volatility (1.4) of the S&P 500 Stock Index, it is easily seen that this quantity is *not* constant over time (Figure 1.1). This observation was made as early as the 1960s by many financial mathematicians and followers of the *chaos theory*. We therefore need time-varying volatility models.

One natural extension of the constant volatility approach is to make σ_t a deterministic function of time. This is equivalent to giving the volatility a term structure, by analogy with interest rates.

THE DERIVATIVES MARKET

Until now, we have mentioned the stock price movements independently from the derivatives market, but we now are going to include the financial derivatives (especially options) prices as well. These instruments became very popular and as liquid as the stocks themselves after Black and Scholes introduced their risk-neutral pricing formula in [38].

[4]By *rolling* we mean that the one-year interval slides within the total observation period.

The Black-Scholes Approach

The Black-Scholes approach makes a number of reasonable assumptions about markets being frictionless and uses the log-normal model for the stock price movements. It also supposes a constant or deterministically time-dependent stock drift and volatility. Under these conditions, they prove that it is possible to hedge a position in a contingent claim dynamically by taking an offsetting position in the underlying stock and hence become *immune* to the stock movements. This risk neutrality is possible because, as they show, we can replicate the financial derivative (for instance, an option) by taking positions in cash and the underlying security. This condition of the possibility of replication is called *market completeness*.

In this situation, everything happens as if we were replacing the stock drift μ_t with the risk-free rate of interest r_t in (1.1) or $r_t - q_t$ if there is a dividend-yield q_t. The contingent claim $f(S,t)$ having a payoff $G(S_T)$ will satisfy the famous Black-Scholes equation

$$rf = \frac{\partial f}{\partial t} + (r-q)S\frac{\partial f}{\partial S} + \frac{1}{2}\sigma^2 S^2 \frac{\partial^2 f}{\partial S^2} \tag{1.5}$$

Indeed the hedged portfolio $\Pi = f - \frac{\partial f}{\partial S}S$ is immune to the stock random movements and, according to Ito's lemma, verifies

$$d\Pi = \left(\frac{\partial f}{\partial t} + \frac{1}{2}\sigma^2 S^2 \frac{\partial^2 f}{\partial S^2}\right)dt$$

which must also be equal to $r\Pi dt$ or else there would be possibility of Riskless arbitrage.[5]

Note that this equation is closely related to the Feynman-Kac equation satisfied by $F(S,t) = \mathbf{E}_t(h(S_T))$ for any function h under the risk-neutral measure; $F(S,t)$ must be a Martingale[6] under this measure and therefore must be driftless, which implies $dF = \sigma S \frac{\partial F}{\partial S} dB_t$ and

$$0 = \frac{\partial F}{\partial t} + (r-q)S\frac{\partial F}{\partial S} + \frac{1}{2}\sigma^2 S^2 \frac{\partial^2 F}{\partial S^2}$$

This would indeed be a different way to reach the same Black-Scholes equation, by using $f(S,t) = \exp(-rt)F(S,t)$, as was done, for instance, in Shreve [218].

Let us insist again on the fact that the real drift of the stock price does not appear in the preceding equation, which makes the volatility σ_t the only

---

[5]For a detailed discussion, see Hull [146].

[6]For an explanation, see Shreve [218] or Karatzas [167].

unobservable quantity. As we said, the volatility could be a deterministic function of time without changing the foregoing argument, in which case all we need to do is to replace σ^2 with $\frac{1}{t}\int_0^t \sigma_s^2 ds$, and keep everything else the same.

For calls and puts, where the payoffs $G(S_T)$ are respectively $MAX(0, S_T - K)$ and $MAX(0, K - S_T)$ and where K is the strike price and T the maturity of the option, the Black-Scholes partial derivatives equation is solvable and gives the celebrated Black-Scholes formulae

$$call_t = S_t e^{-q(T-t)}\Phi(d_1) - Ke^{-r(T-t)}\Phi(d_2) \tag{1.6}$$

and

$$put_t = -S_t e^{-q(T-t)}\Phi(-d_1) + Ke^{-r(T-t)}\Phi(-d_2) \tag{1.7}$$

where

$$\Phi(x) = \frac{1}{\sqrt{2\pi}}\int_{-\infty}^{x} e^{-\frac{u^2}{2}} du$$

is the cumulative standard normal function and

$$d_1 = d_2 + \sigma\sqrt{T-t} \qquad \text{and} \qquad d_2 = \frac{\ln\left(\frac{S_t}{K}\right) + \left(r - q - \frac{1}{2}\sigma^2\right)(T-t)}{\sigma\sqrt{T-t}}$$

Note that using the well-known symmetry property for normal distributions $\Phi(-x) = 1 - \Phi(x)$ in the above formulae, we could reach the *put-call parity* relationship

$$call_t - put_t = S_t e^{-q(T-t)} - Ke^{-r(T-t)} \tag{1.8}$$

which we can also rearrange as

$$S_t e^{-q(T-t)} - call_t = Ke^{-r(T-t)} - put_t$$

The left-hand side of this last equation is called a *covered call* and is equivalent to a short position in a put combined with a bond.

The Cox-Ross-Rubinstein Approach

Later, Cox, Ross, and Rubinstein [66] developed a simplified approach using the binomial law to reach the same pricing formulae. The approach commonly referred to as the *binomial tree* uses a tree of recombining spot prices, in which at a given time step n we have $n+1$ possible $S[n][j]$ spot prices, with $0 \leq j \leq n$. Calling p the upward transition probability and $1-p$ the downward transition probability, S the stock price today, and $S_u = uS$

and $S_d = dS$ upper and lower possible future spot prices, we can write the expectation equation[7]

$$\mathbf{E}[S] = puS + (1-p)dS = e^{r\Delta t}S$$

which immediately gives us

$$p = \frac{a-d}{u-d}$$

with $a = \exp(r\Delta t)$.

We can also write the variance equation

$$Var[S] = pu^2S^2 + (1-p)d^2S^2 - e^{2r\Delta t}S^2 \approx \sigma^2 S^2 \Delta t$$

which after choosing a centering condition, such as $ud = 1$, will provide us with $u = \exp(\sigma\sqrt{\Delta t})$ and $d = \exp(-\sigma\sqrt{\Delta t})$. Using the values for u, d, and p we can build the tree, and using the final payoff we can calculate the option price by backward induction.[8] We can also build this tree by applying an explicit finite difference scheme to the PDE (1.5), as was done in Wilmott [238]. An important advantage of the tree method is that it can be applied to American options (with early exercise) as well.

It is possible to deduce the *implied* volatility of call and put options by solving a reverse Black-Scholes equation, that is, find the volatility that would equate the Black-Scholes price to the market price of the option. This is a good way to see how derivatives markets *perceive* the underlying volatility. It is easy to see that if we change the maturity and strike prices of options (and keep everything else fixed) the implied volatility will *not* be constant. It will have a linear skew and a convex form as the strike price changes. This famous "smile" cannot be explained by simple time dependence, hence the necessity of introducing new models (Figure 1.2).[9]

JUMP DIFFUSION AND LEVEL-DEPENDENT VOLATILITY

In addition to the volatility smile observable from the implied volatilities of the options, there is evidence that the assumption of a pure normal distribution (also called pure *diffusion*) for the stock return is not accurate. Indeed "fat tails" have been observed away from the mean of the stock return. This

[7]The expectation equation is written under the risk-neutral probability.

[8]For an in-depth discussion on binomial trees, see Cox [67].

[9]It is interesting to note that this smile phenomenon was practically nonexistent prior to the 1987 stock-market crash. Many researchers therefore believe that the markets have *learnt to factor-in* a crash possibility, which creates the volatility smile.

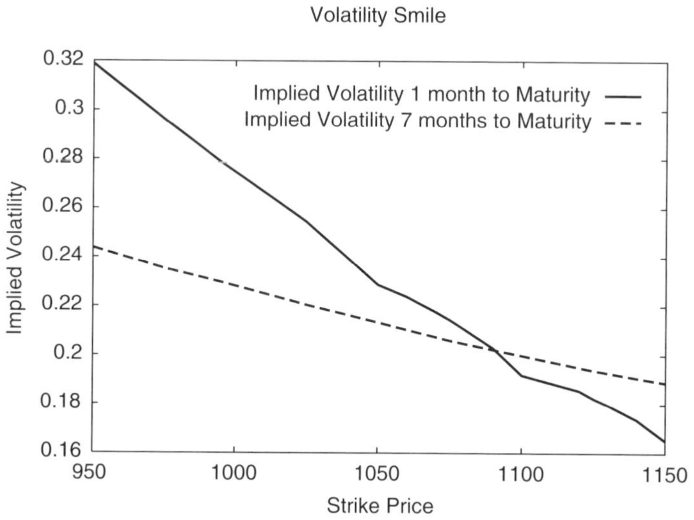

FIGURE 1.2 The SPX Volatility Smile on February 12, 2002 with Index = \$1107.50, 1 Month and 7 Months to Maturity. The negative skewness is clearly visible. Note how the smile becomes *flatter* as time to maturity increases.

phenomenon is called *leptokurticity* and could be explained in many different ways.

Jump Diffusion

Some try to explain the smile and the leptokurticity by changing the underlying stock distribution from a diffusion process to a jump-diffusion process. A jump diffusion is *not* a level-dependent volatility process; however, we are mentioning it in this section to demonstrate the importance of the *leverage effect*. Merton [190] was first to actually introduce jumps in the stock distribution. Kou [172] recently used the same idea to explain both the existence of fat tails and the volatility smile.

The stock price will follow a modified stochastic process under this assumption. If we add to the Brownian motion, dB_t; a Poisson (jump) process[10] dq with an intensity[11] λ, and then calling $k = \mathbf{E}(Y - 1)$ with $Y - 1$

[10]See, for instance, Karatzas [167].

[11]The intensity could be interpreted as the mean number of jumps per time unit.

the random variable percentage change in the stock price, we will have

$$dS_t = (\mu - \lambda k)S_t dt + \sigma S_t dB_t + S_t dq \tag{1.9}$$

or equivalently,

$$S_t = S_0 \exp\left[\left(\mu - \frac{\sigma^2}{2} - \lambda k\right)t + \sigma B_t\right] Y_n$$

where $Y_0 = 1$ and $Y_n = \prod_{j=1}^{n} Y_j$, with Y_j's independently identically distributed random variables and n a Poisson random variable with a parameter λt.

It is worth noting that for the special case where the jump corresponds to total ruin or *default*, we have $k = -1$, which will give us

$$dS_t = (\mu + \lambda)S_t dt + \sigma S_t dB_t + S_t dq \tag{1.10}$$

and

$$S_t = S_0 \exp\left[\left(\mu + \lambda - \frac{\sigma^2}{2}\right)t + \sigma B_t\right] Y_n$$

Given that in this case $\mathbf{E}(Y_n) = \mathbf{E}(Y_n^2) = e^{-\lambda t}$, it is fairly easy to see that in the risk-neutral world

$$\mathbf{E}(S_t) = S_0 e^{rt}$$

exactly as in the pure diffusion case, but

$$Var(S_t) = S_0^2 e^{2rt}\left(e^{(\sigma^2+\lambda)t} - 1\right) \approx S_0^2(\sigma^2 + \lambda)t \tag{1.11}$$

unlike the pure diffusion case, where $Var(S_t) \approx S_0^2\sigma^2 t$.

Proof: Indeed

$$\begin{aligned}
\mathbf{E}(S_t) &= S_0 \exp((r+\lambda)t) \exp\left(-\frac{\sigma^2}{2}t\right)\mathbf{E}[\exp(\sigma B_t)]\mathbf{E}(Y_n) \\
&= S_0 \exp((r+\lambda)t) \exp\left(-\frac{\sigma^2}{2}t\right) \exp\left(\frac{\sigma^2}{2}t\right) \exp(-\lambda t) = S_0 \exp(rt)
\end{aligned}$$

and

$$\begin{aligned}
\mathbf{E}(S_t^2) &= S_0^2 \exp(2(r+\lambda)t) \exp\left(-\sigma^2 t\right)\mathbf{E}[\exp(2\sigma B_t)]\mathbf{E}(Y_n^2) \\
&= S_0^2 \exp(2(r+\lambda)t) \exp\left(-\sigma^2 t\right) \exp\left(\frac{(2\sigma)^2}{2}\right) \exp(-\lambda t) \\
&= S_0^2 \exp((2r+\lambda)t) \exp\left(\sigma^2 t\right)
\end{aligned}$$

and as usual

$$Var(S_t) = \mathbf{E}\left(S_t^2\right) - \mathbf{E}^2(S_t)$$

(QED)

Link to Credit Spread Note that for a zero-coupon risky bond Z with no recovery, a credit spread C and a face value X paid at time t we have

$$Z = e^{-(r+C)t}X = e^{-\lambda t}(e^{-rt}X) + (1 - e^{-\lambda t})(0)$$

consequently $\lambda = C$ and using (1.11) we can write

$$\tilde{\sigma}^2(C) = \sigma^2 + C$$

where σ is the fixed (pure diffusion) volatility and $\tilde{\sigma}$ is the modified jump diffusion volatility. The preceding equation relates the volatility and *leverage*, a concept we will see later in level-dependent models as well.

Also, we could see that everything happens as if we were using the Black-Scholes pricing equation but with a modified "interest rate," which is $r + C$. Indeed the hedged portfolio $\Pi = f - \frac{\partial f}{\partial S}S$ now satisfies

$$d\Pi = \left(\frac{\partial f}{\partial t} + \frac{1}{2}\sigma^2 S^2 \frac{\partial^2 f}{\partial S^2}\right) dt$$

under the no-default case, which occurs with a probability of $e^{-\lambda dt} \approx 1 - \lambda dt$ and

$$d\Pi = -\Pi$$

under the default case, which occurs with a probability of $1 - e^{-\lambda dt} \approx \lambda dt$.

We therefore have

$$\mathbf{E}(d\Pi) = \left(\frac{\partial f}{\partial t} + \frac{1}{2}\sigma^2 S^2 \frac{\partial^2 f}{\partial S^2} - \lambda \Pi\right) dt$$

and using a diversification argument we can always say that $\mathbf{E}(d\Pi) = r\Pi dt$ which provides us with

$$(r + \lambda)f = \frac{\partial f}{\partial t} + (r + \lambda)S\frac{\partial f}{\partial S} + \frac{1}{2}\sigma^2 S^2 \frac{\partial^2 f}{\partial S^2} \tag{1.12}$$

which again is the Black-Scholes PDE with a "risky rate."

A generalization of the jump diffusion process would be the use of the *Levy process*. A Levy process is a stochastic process with independent and stationary increments. Both the Brownian motion and the Poisson process are included in this category. For a description, see Matacz [186].

Level-Dependent Volatility

Many assume that the smile and the fat tails are due to the level dependence of the volatility. The idea would be to make σ_t level dependent or a function of the spot itself; we would therefore have

$$dS_t = \mu_t S_t dt + \sigma(S, t)S_t dB_t \tag{1.13}$$

Note that to be exact, a level-dependent volatility is a function of the spot price alone. When the volatility is a function of the spot price *and* time, it is referred to as *local volatility*, which we shall discuss further.

The Constant Elasticity Variance Approach One of the very first attempts to use this approach was the constant elasticity variance (CEV) method realized by Cox [64] and [65] (Figure 1.3). In this method we would suppose an equation of the type

$$\sigma(S,t) = CS_t^{\gamma} \tag{1.14}$$

where C and γ are parameters to be calibrated either from the stock price returns themselves or from the option prices and their implied volatilities. The CEV method was recently analyzed by Jones [165] in a paper in which he uses two γ exponents.

This level-depending volatility represents an important feature that is observed in options markets as well as in the underlying prices: the negative correlation between the stock price and the volatility, also called the *leverage effect*.

The Bensoussan-Crouhy-Galai Approach Bensoussan, Crouhy, and Galai (BCG) [33] try to find the level dependence of the volatility in a manner that differs from that of Cox and Ross (Figure 1.4). Indeed in the CEV model, Cox and

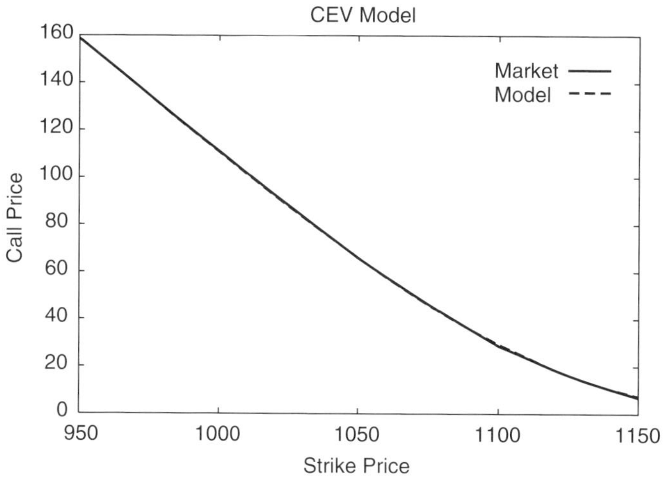

FIGURE 1.3 The CEV Model for SPX on February 12, 2002 with Index = \$1107.50, 1 Month to Maturity. The smile is fitted well, but the model assumes a perfect (negative) correlation between the stock and the volatility.

Ross *first* suppose that $\sigma(S,t)$ has a certain exponential form and only then try to calibrate the model parameters to the market. Alternatively, BCG try to deduce the functional form of $\sigma(S,t)$ by using a firm structure model.

The idea of firm structure is not new and goes back to Merton [189], when he considers that the firm assets follow a log-normal process

$$dV = \mu_V V dt + \sigma_V V dB_t \tag{1.15}$$

where μ_V and σ_V are the asset's return and volatility. One important point is that σ_V is considered *constant*. Merton then argues that the equity S of the firm could be considered a call option on the assets of the firm with a strike price K equal to the face value of the firm liabilities and an expiration T equal to the average liability maturity.

Using Ito's lemma, it is fairly easy to see that

$$\begin{aligned} dS &= \mu S dt + \sigma(S,t) S dB_t \qquad (1.16)\\ &= \left(\frac{\partial S}{\partial t} + \mu_V V\frac{\partial S}{\partial V} + \frac{1}{2}\sigma_V^2 V^2 \frac{\partial^2 S}{\partial V^2}\right)dt + \sigma_V V \frac{\partial S}{\partial V} dB_t \end{aligned}$$

which immediately provides us with

$$\sigma(S,t) = \sigma_V \frac{V}{S}\frac{\partial S}{\partial V} \tag{1.17}$$

which is an implicit functional form for $\sigma(S,t)$.

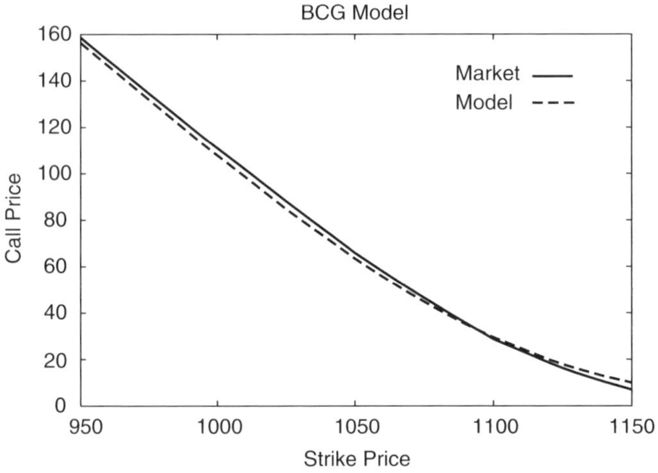

FIGURE 1.4 The BCG Model for SPX on February 12, 2002 with Index = \$1107.50, 1 Month to Maturity. The smile is fitted well.

Next, BCG eliminate the asset term in the preceding functional form and end up with a nonlinear PDE

$$\frac{\partial\sigma}{\partial t}+\frac{1}{2}\sigma^2S^2\frac{\partial^2\sigma}{\partial S^2}+\left(r+\sigma^2\right)S\frac{\partial\sigma}{\partial S}=0 \tag{1.18}$$

This PDE gives the dependence of σ on S and t.

Proof: A quick sketch of the proof is as follows: With S being a contingent claim on V, we have the risk-neutral Black-Scholes PDE

$$\frac{\partial S}{\partial t}+rV\frac{\partial S}{\partial V}+\frac{1}{2}\sigma_V^2V^2\frac{\partial^2S}{\partial V^2}=rS$$

and using $\frac{\partial S}{\partial V}=1/\frac{\partial V}{\partial S}$ as well as $\frac{\partial S}{\partial t}=-\frac{\partial S}{\partial V}\frac{\partial V}{\partial t}$ and $\frac{\partial^2 S}{\partial V^2}=-\frac{\partial^2 V}{\partial S^2}/\left(\frac{\partial V}{\partial S}\right)^3$ we have the reciprocal Black-Scholes equation

$$\frac{\partial V}{\partial t}+rS\frac{\partial V}{\partial S}+\frac{1}{2}\sigma^2S^2\frac{\partial^2V}{\partial S^2}=rV$$

Now posing $\Psi(S,t)=\ln V(S,t)$, we have $\frac{\partial V}{\partial t}=V\frac{\partial\Psi}{\partial t}$ as well as $\frac{\partial V}{\partial S}=V\frac{\partial\Psi}{\partial S}$ and $\frac{\partial^2V}{\partial S^2}=V\left(\frac{\partial^2\Psi}{\partial S^2}+(\frac{\partial\Psi}{\partial S})^2\right)$, and we will have the new PDE

$$r=\frac{\partial\Psi}{\partial t}+rS\frac{\partial\Psi}{\partial S}+\frac{1}{2}\sigma^2S^2\left(\frac{\partial^2\Psi}{\partial S^2}+\left(\frac{\partial\Psi}{\partial S}\right)^2\right)$$

and the equation

$$\sigma=\sigma_V/\left(S\frac{\partial\Psi}{\partial S}\right)$$

This last identity implies that $\frac{\partial\Psi}{\partial S}=\frac{\sigma_V}{S\sigma}$ as well as $\frac{\partial^2\Psi}{\partial S^2}=\frac{-\sigma_V(\sigma+S\frac{\partial\sigma}{\partial S})}{S^2\sigma^2}$, and therefore the PDE becomes

$$r=\frac{\partial\Psi}{\partial t}+r\sigma_V/\sigma+\frac{1}{2}\left(\sigma_V^2-\sigma_V\left(\sigma+S\frac{\partial\sigma}{\partial S}\right)\right)$$

taking the derivative with respect to S and using $\frac{\partial^2\Psi}{\partial S\partial t}=-\frac{\sigma_V}{S\sigma^2}\frac{\partial\sigma}{\partial t}$ we get the final PDE

$$\frac{\partial\sigma}{\partial t}+\frac{1}{2}\sigma^2S^2\frac{\partial^2\sigma}{\partial S^2}+\left(r+\sigma^2\right)S\frac{\partial\sigma}{\partial S}=0$$

as previously stated. *(QED)*

We therefore have an implicit functional form for $\sigma(S,t)$, and, just as for the CEV case, we need to calibrate the parameters to the market data.

LOCAL VOLATILITY

In the early 1990s, Dupire [89], as well as Derman and Kani [74], developed a concept called *local volatility*, in which the volatility smile was retrieved from the option prices.

The Dupire Approach

The Breeden & Litzenberger Identity This approach uses the options prices to get the implied distribution for the underlying stock. To do this we can write

$$V(S_0, K, T) = call(S_0, K, T) = e^{-rT} \int_0^{+\infty} (S-K)^+ p(S_0, S, T)dS \quad (1.19)$$

where S_0 is the stock price at time $t = 0$ and K the strike price of the call, and $p(S_0, S, T)$ is the *unknown* transition density for the stock price. As usual, $x^+ = MAX(x, 0)$

Using Equation (1.19) and differentiating with respect to K twice, we get the Breeden and Litzenberger [44] implied distribution

$$p(S_0, K, T) = e^{rT} \frac{\partial^2 V}{\partial K^2} \quad (1.20)$$

Proof: The proof is straightforward if we write

$$e^{rT} V(S_0, K, T) = \int_K^{+\infty} Sp(S_0, S, T)dS - K \int_K^{+\infty} p(S_0, S, T)dS$$

and take the first derivative

$$e^{rT} \frac{\partial V}{\partial K} = -Kp(S_0, K, T) + Kp(S_0, K, T) - \int_K^{+\infty} p(S_0, S, T)dS$$

and the second derivative in the same manner. *(QED)*

The Dupire Identity Now, according to the Fokker-Planck (or forward Kolmogorov) equation[12] for this density, we have

$$\frac{\partial p}{\partial T} = \frac{1}{2} \frac{\partial^2(\sigma^2(S, t)S^2 p)}{\partial S^2} - r\frac{\partial(Sp)}{\partial S}$$

[12]See, for example, Wilmott [237] for an explanation on Fokker-Planck equation.

and therefore after a little rearrangement have

$$\frac{\partial V}{\partial T} = \frac{1}{2}\sigma^2 K^2 \frac{\partial^2 V}{\partial K^2} - rK\frac{\partial V}{\partial K}$$

which provides us with the local volatility formula

$$\sigma^2(K,T) = \frac{\frac{\partial V}{\partial T} + rK\frac{\partial V}{\partial K}}{\frac{1}{2}K^2\frac{\partial^2 V}{\partial K^2}} \tag{1.21}$$

Proof: For a quick proof of the above let us use the zero interest rates case (the general case could be done similarly). We would then have

$$p(S_0, K, T) = \frac{\partial^2 V}{\partial K^2}$$

as well as Fokker-Planck

$$\frac{\partial p}{\partial T} = \frac{1}{2}\frac{\partial^2(\sigma^2(S,t)S^2 p)}{\partial S^2}$$

Now

$$\begin{aligned}\frac{\partial V}{\partial T} &= \int_0^{+\infty}(S_T - K)^+\frac{\partial p}{\partial T}dS_T \\ &= \int_0^{+\infty}(S_T - K)^+\frac{1}{2}\frac{\partial^2\left(\sigma^2(S,T)S^2 p\right)}{\partial S^2}dS_T\end{aligned}$$

and integrating by parts twice and using the fact that

$$\frac{\partial^2(S_T - K)^+}{\partial K^2} = \delta(S_T - K)$$

with $\delta(.)$, the Dirac function, we will have

$$\frac{\partial V}{\partial T} = \frac{1}{2}\sigma^2(K,T)K^2 p(S_0,K,T) = \frac{1}{2}K^2\sigma^2(K,T)\frac{\partial^2 V}{\partial K^2}$$

as stated. *(QED)*

It is also possible to use the implied volatility, σ_{BS}, from the Black-Scholes formula (1.6) and express the foregoing local volatility in terms of σ_{BS} instead of V. For a detailed discussion, we could refer to Wilmott [237].

Local Volatility vs. Instantaneous Volatility Clearly, the local volatility is related to the instantaneous variance v_t, as Gatheral [113] shows; the relationship could be written as

$$\sigma^2(K, T) = \mathbf{E}[v_T|S_T = K] \tag{1.22}$$

that is, local variance is the risk-neutral expectation of the instantaneous variance conditional on the final stock price being equal to the strike price.[13]

Proof: Let us show the above identity for the case of zero interest rates.[14] As mentioned, we have

$$\sigma^2(K, T) = \frac{\frac{\partial V}{\partial T}}{\frac{1}{2}K^2\frac{\partial^2 V}{\partial K^2}}$$

On the other hand, using the call payoff $V(S_0, K, t = T) = \mathbf{E}[(S_T - K)^+]$ we have

$$\frac{\partial V}{\partial K} = \mathbf{E}[H(S_T - K)]$$

with $H(.)$, the heaviside function and

$$\frac{\partial^2 V}{\partial K^2} = \mathbf{E}[\delta(S_T - K)]$$

with $\delta(.)$, the Dirac function.

Therefore the Ito lemma at $t = T$ would provide

$$d(S_T - K)^+ = H(S_T - K)dS_T + \frac{1}{2}v_T S_T^2 \delta(S_T - K)dT$$

Using the fact that the forward price (here with zero interest rates, the stock price) is a Martingale under the risk-neutral measure

$$dV = d\mathbf{E}[(S_T - K)^+] = \frac{1}{2}\mathbf{E}\left[v_T S_T^2 \delta(S_T - K)\right] dT$$

Now we have

$$\begin{aligned}\mathbf{E}[v_T S_T^2 \delta(S_T - K)] &= \mathbf{E}[v_T|S_T = K]K^2\mathbf{E}[\delta(S_T - K)] \\ &= \mathbf{E}[v_T|S_T = K]K^2\frac{\partial^2 V}{\partial K^2}\end{aligned}$$

[13]Note that this is independent from the process for v_t, meaning that *any* stochastic volatility model satisfies this property, which is an attractive feature of local volatility models.

[14]For the case of nonzero rates, we need to work with the forward price instead of the stock price.

Putting all this together

$$\frac{\partial V}{\partial T} = \frac{1}{2}K^2\frac{\partial^2 V}{\partial K^2}\mathbf{E}[v_T|S_T = K]$$

and by the preceding expression of $\sigma^2(K, T)$, we will have

$$\sigma^2(K, T) = \mathbf{E}[v_T|S_T = K]$$

as claimed. *(QED)*

The Derman-Kani Approach

The Derman-Kani technique is very similar to the above approach, except that it uses the binomial (or trinomial) tree framework instead of the continuous one. Using the binomial tree notations, their upward transition probability p_i from the spot s_i at time t_n to the upper node S_{i+1} at the following time-step t_{n+1}, is obtained from the usual

$$p_i = \frac{F_i - S_i}{S_{i+1} - S_i} \tag{1.23}$$

where F_i is the stock forward price known from the market and S_i the lower spot at the step t_{n+1}.

In addition, we have for a call expiring at time step t_{n+1}

$$C(K, t_{n+1}) = e^{-r\Delta t}\sum_{j=1}^{n}\left[\lambda_j p_j + \lambda_{j+1}\left(1 - p_{j+1}\right)\right]MAX(S_{j+1} - K, 0)$$

where λ_j's are the known Arrow-Debreu prices corresponding to the discounted probability of getting to the point s_j at time t_n from S_0, the initial stock price. These probabilities could easily be derived iteratively.

This allows us after some calculation to obtain S_{i+1} as a function of s_i and S_i, namely

$$S_{i+1} = \frac{S_i[e^{r\Delta t}C(s_i, K, t_{n+1}) - \Sigma] - \lambda_i s_i(F_i - S_i)}{[e^{r\Delta t}C(s_i, K, t_{n+1}) - \Sigma] - \lambda_i(F_i - S_i)}$$

where the term Σ represents the sum $\sum_{j=i+1}^{n}\lambda_j(F_j - s_i)$. This means that after choosing the usual centering condition for the binomial tree

$$s_i^2 = S_i S_{i+1}$$

we have all the elements to build the tree and deduce the implied distribution from the Arrow-Debreu prices.

Stability Issues

The local volatility models are very elegant and theoretically sound; however, they present in practice many stability issues. They are *ill-posed inversion* problems and are extremely sensitive to the input data.[15] This might introduce arbitrage opportunities and in some cases negative probabilities or variances. Derman and Kani suggest overwriting techniques to avoid such problems.

Andersen [13] tries to improve this issue by using an implicit finite difference method; however, he recognizes that the negative variance problem could still happen.

One way to make the results smoother is to use a constrained optimization. In other words, when trying to fit theoretical results C_{theo} to the market prices C_{mrkt}, instead of minimizing

$$\sum_{j=1}^{N}\left(C_{theo}(K_j) - C_{mrkt}(K_j)\right)^2$$

we could minimize

$$\lambda\frac{\partial\sigma}{\partial t} + \sum_{j=1}^{N}\left(C_{theo}(K_j) - C_{mrkt}(K_j)\right)^2$$

where λ is a constraint parameter, which could also be interpreted as a Lagrange multiplier. However, this is an artificial way to smoothen the results and the real issue remains that, once again, we have an inversion problem that is inherently unstable. Furthermore, local volatility models imply that future implied volatility smiles will be flat relative to today's, which is another limitation.[16] As we will see in the following section, stochastic volatility models offer more time-homogeneous volatility smiles.

An alternative approach suggested in [16] would be to choose a prior risk-neutral distribution for the asset (based on a subjective view) and then minimize the relative entropy distance between the desired surface and this prior distribution. This approach uses the Kullback-Leibler distance (which we will discuss in the context of maximum likelihood estimation [MLE]) and performs the minimization via dynamic programming [35] on a tree.

[15] See Tavella [226] or Avellaneda [16].

[16] See Gatheral [114].

Calibration Frequency

One of the most attractive features of local-vol models is their ability to match plain-vanilla puts and calls *exactly*. This will avoid arbitrage situations, or worse, market manipulations by traders to create "phantom" profits. As explained in Hull [147], these arbitrage-free models were developed by researchers with a single calibration (SC) methodology assumption. However, in practice, traders use them with a continual recalibration (CR) strategy. Indeed if they used the SC version of the model, significant errors would be introduced from one week to the following as shown by Dumas et al. [88]. However, once this CR version is used, there is no guarantee that the no-arbitrage property of the original SC model is preserved. Indeed the Dupire equation determines the marginal stock distribution at different points in time, but not the joint distribution of these stock prices. Therefore a path-dependent option could very well be mispriced, and the more path-dependent this option, the greater the mispricing.

Hull [147] takes the example of a bet option, a compound option, and a barrier option. The bet option depends on the distribution of the stock at one point in time and therefore is correctly priced with a continually recalibrated local vol model. The compound option has some path dependency, and hence a certain amount of mispricing compared with a stochastic volatility (SV) model. Finally, the barrier option has a strong degree of path dependency and will introduce large errors. Note that this is due to the discrete nature of the data. Indeed, the maturities we have are limited. If we had all possible maturities in a continuous way, the joint distribution would be determined completely. Also, when interpolating in time, it is customary to interpolate upon the true variance $t\sigma_t^2$ rather than the volatility σ_t given the equation

$$T_2\sigma^2(T_2) = T_1\sigma^2(T_1) + (T_2 - T_1)\sigma^2(T_1, T_2)$$

Interpolating upon the true variance will provide smoother results as shown by Jackel [152].

Proof: Indeed, calling for $0 \le T_1 \le T_2$, the spot return variances

$$Var(0, T_2) = T_2\sigma^2(T_2)$$

$$Var(0, T_1) = T_1\sigma^2(T_1)$$

for a Brownian motion, we have independent increments and therefore a forward variance $Var(T_1, T_2)$ such that

$$Var(0, T_1) + Var(T_1, T_2) = Var(0, T_2)$$

which demonstrates the point. *(QED)*

STOCHASTIC VOLATILITY

Unlike nonparametric local volatility models, parametric stochastic volatility (SV) models define a specific stochastic differential equation for the unobservable instantaneous variance. As we shall see, the previously defined CEV model could be considered a special case of these models.

Stochastic Volatility Processes

The idea would be to use a different stochastic process for σ altogether. Making the volatility a deterministic function of the spot is a special "degenerate" two-factor, a natural generalization of which would precisely be to have two stochastic processes with an imperfect correlation.[17]

Several different stochastic processes have been suggested for the volatility. A popular one is the *Ornstein-Uhlenbeck* (OU) process:

$$d\sigma_t = -\alpha\sigma_t dt + \beta dZ_t \tag{1.24}$$

where α and β are two parameters, remembering the stock equation

$$dS_t = \mu_t S_t dt + \sigma_t S_t dB_t$$

there is a (usually negative) correlation ρ between dZ_t and dB_t, which can in turn be time or level dependent. Heston [134] and Stein [223] were among those who suggested the use of this process. Using Ito's lemma, we can see that the stock-return variance $v_t = \sigma_t^2$ satisfies a *square-root* or Cox-Ingersoll-Ross (CIR) process

$$dv_t = (\omega - \theta v_t)dt + \xi\sqrt{v_t}dZ_t \tag{1.25}$$

with $\omega = \beta^2$, $\theta = 2\alpha$, and $\xi = 2\beta$.

Note that the OU process has a closed-form solution

$$\sigma_t = \sigma_0 e^{-\alpha t} + \beta\int_0^t e^{-\alpha(t-s)}dZ_s$$

[17] Note that here the *instantaneous* volatility is stochastic. Recent work by researchers such as Schonbucher supposes a stochastic implied-volatility process, which is a completely different approach. See, for instance, [213]. On the other hand, Avellaneda et al. [17] use the concept of *uncertain volatility* for pricing and hedging derivative securities. They make the volatility switch between two extreme values based on the convexity of the derivative contract and obtain a nonlinear *Black-Scholes-Barenblatt* equation, which they solve on a grid.

which means that σ_t follows in law $\Phi\left(\sigma_0 e^{-\alpha t}, \frac{\beta^2}{2\alpha}\left(1-e^{-2\alpha t}\right)\right)$, with Φ again the normal distribution. This was discussed in Fouque [104] and Shreve [218].

Heston and Nandi [137] show that this process corresponds to a special case of the general auto regressive conditional heteroskedasticity (GARCH) model, which we will discuss next. Another popular process is the GARCH (1,1) process, where we would have

$$dv_t = (\omega - \theta v_t)dt + \xi v_t dZ_t \tag{1.26}$$

GARCH and Diffusion Limits

The most elementary GARCH process, called GARCH(1,1), was developed originally in the field of econometrics by Engle [94] and Bollerslev [40] in a *discrete* framework. The stock discrete equation (1.3) could be rewritten by taking $\Delta t = 1$ and $v_n = \sigma_n^2$ as

$$\ln S_{n+1} = \ln S_n + \left(\mu - \frac{1}{2}v_{n+1}\right) + \sqrt{v_{n+1}}B_{n+1} \tag{1.27}$$

calling the mean adjusted return

$$u_n = \ln\left(\frac{S_n}{S_{n-1}}\right) - \left(\mu - \frac{1}{2}v_n\right) = \sqrt{v_n}B_n \tag{1.28}$$

the variance process in GARCH(1,1) is supposed to be

$$v_{n+1} = \omega_0 + \beta v_n + \alpha u_n^2 = \omega_0 + \beta v_n + \alpha v_n B_n^2 \tag{1.29}$$

where α and β are weight parameters and ω_0 is a parameter related to the long-term variance.[18]

Nelson [194] shows that as the time interval length decreases and becomes infinitesimal, Equation (1.29) becomes precisely the previously cited Equation (1.26). To be more accurate, there is a *weak convergence* of the discrete GARCH process to the continuous diffusion limit.[19] For a GARCH(1,1) continuous diffusion, the correlation between dZ_t and dB_t is zero.

[18]It is worth mentioning that as explained in [100], a GARCH(1,1) model could be rewritten as an autoregressive moving average model of first order, ARMA(1,1), and therefore an auto regressive model of infinite order, AR($+\infty$). GARCH is therefore a parsimonious model that can fit the data with only a few parameters. Fitting the same data with an ARCH or AR model would require a much larger number of parameters. This feature makes the GARCH model very attractive.

[19]For an explanation on weak convergence, see, for example, Varadhan [230].

It might appear surprising that even if the GARCH(1,1) process has only *one* source of randomness, namely B_n, the continuous version has two independent Brownian motions. This is understandable if we consider B_n a standard normal random variable and $A_n = B_n^2 - 1$ another random variable. It is fairly easy to see that A_n and B_n are uncorrelated even if A_n is a function of B_n. As we go toward the continuous version, we can use Donsker's theorem,[20] by letting the time interval $\Delta t \to 0$, to prove that we end up with two uncorrelated and therefore independent Brownian motions. This is a limitation of the GARCH(1,1) model–hence the introduction of the nonlinear asymmetric GARCH (NGARCH) model.

Duan [83] attempts to explain the volatility smile by using the NGARCH process expressed by

$$v_{n+1} = \omega_0 + \beta v_n + \alpha\left(u_n - c\sqrt{v_n}\right)^2 \tag{1.30}$$

where c is a parameter to be determined.

The NGARCH process was first introduced by Engle [97]. The continuous counterpart of NGARCH is the same equation (1.26), except unlike the equation resulting from GARCH(1,1) there *is* a nonzero correlation between the stock process and the volatility process. This correlation is created precisely because of the parameter c that was introduced, and is once again called the *leverage* effect. The parameter c is sometimes referred to as the *leverage parameter*.

We can find the following relationships between the discrete process and the continuous diffusion limit parameters by letting the time interval become infinitesimal

$$\omega = \frac{\omega_0}{dt^2}$$

$$\theta = \frac{1 - \alpha\left(1 + c^2\right) - \beta}{dt}$$

$$\xi = \alpha\sqrt{\frac{\kappa - 1 + 4c^2}{dt}}$$

and the correlation between dB_t and dZ_t

$$\rho = \frac{-2c}{\sqrt{\kappa - 1 + 4c^2}}$$

where κ represents the Pearson kurtosis[21] of the mean adjusted returns (u_n). As we can see, the sign of the correlation ρ is determined by the parameter c.

[20] For a discussion on Donsker's theorem, similar to the central limit theorem, see, for instance, Whitt [235].

[21] The kurtosis corresponds to the fourth moment. The Pearson kurtosis for a normal distribution is equal to 3.

Proof: A quick proof of the convergence to diffusion limit could be outlined as follows. Let us assume that $c = 0$ for simplicity; we therefore are dealing with the GARCH(1,1) case. As we saw

$$v_{n+1} = \omega_0 + \beta v_n + \alpha v_n B_n^2$$

therefore

$$v_{n+1} - v_n = \omega_0 + \beta v_n - v_n + \alpha v_n - \alpha v_n + \alpha v_n B_n^2$$

or

$$v_{n+1} - v_n = \omega_0 - (1 - \alpha - \beta)v_n + \alpha v_n(B_n^2 - 1)$$

Now, allowing the time-step Δt to become variable and posing $Z_n = (B_n^2 - 1)/\sqrt{\kappa - 1}$

$$v_{n+\Delta t} - v_n = \omega \Delta t^2 - \theta \Delta t v_n + \xi v_n \sqrt{\Delta t} Z_n$$

and annualizing v_n by posing $v_t = v_n/\Delta t$, we shall have

$$v_{t+\Delta t} - v_t = \omega \Delta t - \theta \Delta t v_t + \xi v_t \sqrt{\Delta t} Z_n$$

and as $\Delta t \to 0$, we get

$$dv_t = (\omega - \theta v_t)dt + \xi v_t dZ_t$$

as claimed. *(QED)*

Note that the discrete GARCH version of the square-root process (1.25) is

$$v_{n+1} = \omega_0 + \beta v_n + \alpha(B_n - c\sqrt{v_n})^2 \tag{1.31}$$

as Heston and Nandi show[22] in [137] (Figure 1.5).

Also, note that having a diffusion process $dv_t = b(v_t)dt + a(v_t)dZ_t$ we can apply an Euler approximation[23] to discretize and obtain a Monte Carlo process, such as $v_{n+1} - v_n = b(v_n)\Delta t + a(v_n)\sqrt{\Delta t}Z_n$. It is important to note that if we use a GARCH process and go to the continuous diffusion limit, and then apply an Euler approximation, we will *not necessarily* find the original GARCH process again. Indeed, there are many different ways to discretize the continuous diffusion limit and the GARCH process corresponds to one special way. In particular, if we use (1.31) and allow $\Delta t \to 0$ to get to the continuous diffusion limit, we shall obtain (1.25). As we will see later in

[22]For a detailed discussion on the convergence of different GARCH models toward their diffusion limits, also see Duan [85].
[23]See, for instance, Jones [165].

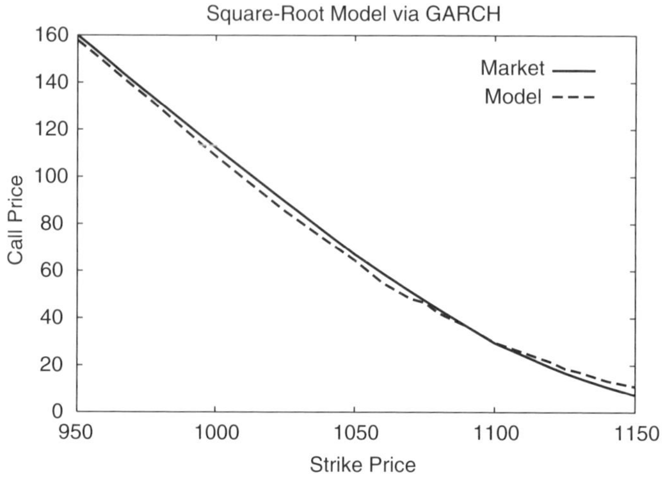

FIGURE 1.5 The GARCH Monte Carlo Simulation with the Square-Root Model for SPX on February 12, 2002 with Index = \$1107.50, 1 Month to Maturity. The Powell optimization method was used for least-square calibration.

the section on *mixing solutions*, we can then apply a discretization to this process and obtain a Monte Carlo simulation

$$v_{n+1} = v_n + (\omega - \theta v_n)\Delta t + \xi\sqrt{v_n}\sqrt{\Delta t}Z_n$$

which is again different from (1.31) but obviously has to be consistent in terms of pricing. However, we should know which method we are working with from the very beginning to perform our calibration on the corresponding specific process.

Corradi [61] explains this in the following manner: The discrete GARCH model could converge either toward a two-factor continuous limit if one chooses the Nelson parameterization, or could very well converge to a one-factor diffusion limit if one chooses another parameterization. Furthermore, an appropriate Euler discretization of the one-factor continuous model will provide a GARCH discrete process, while as previously mentioned the discretization of the two-factor diffusion model provides a two-factor discrete process. This distinction is fundamental and could explain why GARCH and SV behave differently in terms of parameter estimation.

THE PRICING PDE UNDER STOCHASTIC VOLATILITY

A very important issue to underline here is that, because of the unhedgeable second source of randomness, the concept of market completeness is lost.

We can no longer have a straightforward risk-neutral pricing. This is where the *market price of risk* will come into consideration.

The Market Price of Volatility Risk

Indeed, taking a more general form for the variance process

$$dv_t = b(v_t)dt + a(v_t)dZ_t \tag{1.32}$$

as we previously said, using the Black-Scholes risk-neutrality argument, Equation (1.1) could be replaced with

$$dS_t = (r_t - q_t)S_t dt + \sigma_t S_t dB_t \tag{1.33}$$

This is equivalent to changing the probability measure from the real one to the *risk-neutral* one.[24] We therefore need to use (1.33) together with the risk-adjusted volatility process

$$dv_t = \tilde{b}(v_t)dt + a(v_t)dZ_t \tag{1.34}$$

where

$$\tilde{b}(v_t) = b(v_t) - \lambda a(v_t)$$

with λ the market price of volatility risk. This quantity is closely related to the market price of risk for the stock $\lambda_e = (\mu - r)/\sigma$. Indeed, as Hobson [140] and Lewis [177] both show, we have

$$\lambda = \rho\lambda_e + \sqrt{1-\rho^2}\lambda^* \tag{1.35}$$

where λ^* is the market price of risk associated with $dB_t - \rho dZ_t$, which can also be regarded as the market price of risk for the hedged portfolio.

The passage from Equation (1.32) to Equation (1.34) and the introduction of the market price of volatility risk could also be explained by the Girsanov theorem, as was done for instance in Fouque [104].

It is important to underline the difference between the real and the risk-neutral measures here. If we use historic stock prices together with the real stock-return drift μ to estimate the process parameters, we will obtain the real volatility drift $b(v)$. An alternative method would be to estimate $\tilde{b}(v)$ by using current option prices and performing a least-square estimation. These calibration methods will be discussed in detail in the following chapters.

---

[24] See Hull [146] or Shreve [218] for more detail.

The risk-neutral version for a discrete NGARCH model would also involve the market price of risk and instead of the usual

$$\ln S_{n+1} = \ln S_n + \left(\mu - \frac{1}{2}v_{n+1}\right) + \sqrt{v_{n+1}}B_{n+1}$$
$$v_{n+1} = \omega_0 + \beta v_n + \alpha v_n(B_n - c)^2$$

we would have

$$\ln S_{n+1} = \ln S_n + \left(r - \frac{1}{2}v_{n+1}\right) + \sqrt{v_{n+1}}\tilde{B}_{n+1} \tag{1.36}$$
$$v_{n+1} = \omega_0 + \beta v_n + \alpha v_n\left(\tilde{B}_n - c - \lambda_e\right)^2$$

where $\tilde{B}_n = B_n + \lambda_e$, which could be regarded as the discrete version of the Girsanov theorem. Note that the market price of risk for the stock λ_e is *not* separable from the leverage parameter c in the above formulation. Duan shows in [84] and [86] that risk-neutral GARCH system (1.36) will indeed converge toward the continuous risk-neutral GARCH

$$dS_t = S_t r dt + S_t\sqrt{v_t}dB_t$$
$$dv_t = (\omega - \tilde{\theta}v_t)dt + \xi v_t dZ_t$$

as we expected.

The Two-Factor PDE

From here, writing a two-factor PDE for a derivative security f becomes a simple application of the two-dimensional Ito's lemma. The PDE will be[25]

$$rf = \frac{\partial f}{\partial t} + (r-q)S\frac{\partial f}{\partial S} + \frac{1}{2}vS^2\frac{\partial^2 f}{\partial S^2} + \tilde{b}(v)\frac{\partial f}{\partial v} + \frac{1}{2}a^2(v)\frac{\partial^2 f}{\partial v^2} + \rho a(v)\sqrt{v}S\frac{\partial^2 f}{\partial S\partial v} \tag{1.37}$$

Therefore, it is possible, after calibration, to apply a finite difference method[26] to the above PDE to price the derivative $f(S, t, v)$. An alternative would be to use directly the stochastic processes for dS_t and dv_t and apply a two-factor Monte Carlo simulation. Later in the chapter we will also mention other possible methods, such as the mixing solution or asymptotic approximations.

[25] For a proof of the derivation see Wilmott [237] or Lewis [177].

[26] See, for instance, Tavella [227] or Wilmott [237] for a discussion on finite difference methods.

Other possible approaches for incomplete markets and stochastic volatility assumption include *super-replication* and *local risk minimization*.[27] The super-replication strategy is the cheapest self-financing strategy with a terminal value no less than the payoff of the derivative contract. This technique was primarily developed by El-Karoui and Quenez in [91]. Local risk minimization involves a partial hedging of the risk. The risk is reduced to an "intrinsic component" by taking an offsetting position in the underlying security as usual. This method was developed by Follmer and Sondermann in [102].

THE GENERALIZED FOURIER TRANSFORM

The Transform Technique

One useful technique to apply to the PDE (1.37) is the *generalized Fourier transform*.[28] First, we can use the variable $x = \ln S$ in which case, using Ito's lemma, Equation (1.37) could be rewritten as

$$rf = \frac{\partial f}{\partial t} + \left(r - q - \frac{1}{2}v\right)\frac{\partial f}{\partial x} + \frac{1}{2}v\frac{\partial^2 f}{\partial x^2} + \tilde{b}(v)\frac{\partial f}{\partial v} + \frac{1}{2}a^2(v)\frac{\partial^2 f}{\partial v^2} + \rho a(v)\sqrt{v}\frac{\partial^2 f}{\partial x \partial v} \tag{1.38}$$

Calling

$$\hat{f}(k, v, t) = \int_{-\infty}^{+\infty} e^{ikx} f(x, v, t)dx \tag{1.39}$$

where k is a *complex* number,[29] $\hat{f}$ will be defined in a complex *strip* where the imaginary part of k is between two real numbers α and β. Once $\hat{f}$ is suitably defined, meaning that $k_i = \mathcal{I}(k)$ (the imaginary part of k) is within the appropriate strip, we can write the inverse Fourier transform

$$f(x, v, t) = \frac{1}{2\pi}\int_{ik_i-\infty}^{ik_i+\infty} e^{-ikx}\hat{f}(k, v, t)dk \tag{1.40}$$

where we are integrating for a *fixed* k_i parallel to the real axis.

Each derivative satisfying (1.37) or equivalently (1.38) has a known payoff $G(S_T)$ at maturity. For instance, as we said before, a call option has a payoff $MAX(0, S_T - K)$ where K is the call strike price. It is easy to see

[27] For a discussion on both these techniques, see Frey [107].

[28] See Lewis [177] for a detailed discussion on this technique.

[29] As usual we note $i = \sqrt{-1}$.

that for $k_i > 1$ the Fourier transform of a call option exists and the payoff transform is

$$-\frac{K^{ik+1}}{k^2 - ik} \tag{1.41}$$

Proof: Indeed, we can write

$$\begin{aligned}
\int_{-\infty}^{+\infty} e^{ikx}(e^x - K)^+ dx &= \int_{\ln K}^{+\infty} e^{ikx}(e^x - K)dx \\
&= 0 - \left(\frac{K^{ik+1}}{ik+1} - K\frac{K^{ik}}{ik}\right) \\
&= -K^{ik+1}\left(\frac{1}{ik+1} - \frac{1}{ik}\right) = -K^{ik+1}\frac{1}{k^2 - ik}
\end{aligned}$$

as stated. *(QED)*

The same could be applied to a put option or other derivative securities. In particular, a covered call (stock minus call) having a payoff $MIN(S_T, K)$ will have a transform for $0 < k_i < 1$ equal to

$$\frac{K^{ik+1}}{k^2 - ik} \tag{1.42}$$

Applying the transform to the PDE (1.38) and introducing $\tau = T - t$ and

$$\hat{h}(k, v, \tau) = e^{(r+ik(r-q))\tau}\hat{f}(k, v, \tau) \tag{1.43}$$

and posing[30] $c(k) = \frac{1}{2}(k^2 - ik)$, we get the new PDE equation

$$\frac{\partial \hat{h}}{\partial \tau} = \frac{1}{2}a^2(v)\frac{\partial^2 \hat{h}}{\partial v^2} + (\tilde{b}(v) - ik\rho(v)a(v)\sqrt{v})\frac{\partial \hat{h}}{\partial v} - c(k)v\hat{h} \tag{1.44}$$

Lewis calls the *fundamental transform* a function $\hat{H}(k, v, \tau)$ satisfying the PDE (1.44) and satisfying the initial condition $\hat{H}(k, v, \tau = 0) = 1$. If we know this fundamental transform, we can then multiply it by the derivative security's payoff transform and then divide it by $e^{(r+ik(r-q))\tau}$ and apply the inverse Fourier technique by keeping k_i in an appropriate strip and finally get the derivative as a function of $x = \ln S$.

Special Cases

There are cases where the fundamental transform is known. The case of a constant (or deterministic) volatility is the most elementary one. Indeed,

[30]We are following Lewis [177] notations.

using (1.44) together with $dv_t = 0$, we can easily find

$$\hat{H}(k, v, \tau) = e^{-c(k)v\tau}$$

which is analytic in k over the entire complex plane. Using the call payoff transform (1.41), we can rederive the Black-Scholes equation. The same can be done if we have a deterministic volatility $dv_t = b(v_t)dt$ by using the function $Y(v, t)$ where $dY = b(Y)dt$.

The square-root model (1.25) is another important case where $\hat{H}(k, v, \tau)$ is known and analytic. We have for this process

$$dv_t = (\omega - \theta v_t)dt + \xi\sqrt{v_t}dZ_t$$

or under the risk-neutral measure

$$dv_t = (\omega - \tilde{\theta} v_t)dt + \xi\sqrt{v_t}dZ_t$$

with $\tilde{\theta} = (1-\gamma)\rho\xi + \sqrt{\theta^2 - \gamma(1-\gamma)\xi^2}$, where $\gamma \leq 1$ represents the risk-aversion factor.

For the fundamental transform, we get

$$\hat{H}(k, v, \tau) = \exp\left[f_1(t) + f_2(t)v\right] \tag{1.45}$$

with

$$t = \frac{1}{2}\xi^2\tau \quad \tilde{\omega} = \frac{2}{\xi^2}\omega \quad \tilde{c} = \frac{2}{\xi^2}c(k) \qquad \text{and}$$

$$f_1(t) = \left[tg - \ln\left(\frac{1 - he^{td}}{1-h}\right)\right]\tilde{\omega}$$

$$f_2(t) = \left[\frac{1 - e^{td}}{1 - he^{td}}\right]g$$

where

$$d = \sqrt{\bar{\theta}^2 + 4\tilde{c}} \quad g = \frac{1}{2}(\bar{\theta} + d) \quad h = \frac{\bar{\theta} + d}{\bar{\theta} - d} \qquad \text{and}$$

$$\bar{\theta} = \frac{2}{\xi^2}\left[(1 - \gamma + ik)\rho\xi + \sqrt{\theta^2 - \gamma(1-\gamma)\xi^2}\right]$$

The above transform has a cumbersome expression, but it can be seen that it is analytic in k and therefore always exists. For a proof of the foregoing refer to Lewis [177].

TABLE 1.1 SPX Implied Surface as of 03/09/2004. T is the maturity and $M = K/S$ the inverse of the moneyness

T / M	0.70	0.80	0.85	0.90	0.95	1.00	1.05	1.10	1.15	1.20	1.30
1.000	24.61	21.29	19.73	18.21	16.81	15.51	14.43	13.61	13.12	12.94	13.23
2.000	21.94	18.73	18.68	17.65	16.69	15.79	14.98	14.26	13.67	13.22	12.75
3.000	20.16	18.69	17.96	17.28	16.61	15.97	15.39	14.86	14.38	13.96	13.30
4.000	19.64	18.48	17.87	17.33	16.78	16.26	15.78	15.33	14.92	14.53	13.93
5.000	18.89	18.12	17.70	17.29	16.88	16.50	16.13	15.77	15.42	15.11	14.54
6.000	18.46	17.90	17.56	17.23	16.90	16.57	16.25	15.94	15.64	15.35	14.83
7.000	18.32	17.86	17.59	17.30	17.00	16.71	16.43	16.15	15.88	15.62	15.15
8.000	17.73	17.54	17.37	17.17	16.95	16.72	16.50	16.27	16.04	15.82	15.40

The inversion of the Fourier transform for the square-root (Heston) model is a very popular and powerful approach. It is appealing because of its robustness and speed. The following example is based on SPX options as of 03/09/2004 expiring in 1 to 8 years from the calibration date (Tables 1.1 and 1.2).

As we shall see further, the optimal Heston parameter set to fit this surface could be found via a least-square estimation approach and for the index at $S = \$1156.86$ we find the optimal parameters $\hat{v}_0 = 0.1940$ and

$$\hat{\Psi} = (\hat{\omega}, \hat{\theta}, \hat{\xi}, \hat{\rho}) = (0.052042332, 1.8408, 0.4710, -0.4677)$$

THE MIXING SOLUTION

The Romano-Touzi Approach

The idea of *mixing solutions* was probably presented for the first time by Hull and White [149] for a zero correlation case. Later, Romano and Touzi

TABLE 1.2 Heston Prices Fitted to the 03/09/2004 Surface

T / M	0.70	0.80	0.85	0.90	0.95	1.00	1.05	1.10	1.15	1.20	1.30
1.000	30.67	21.44	17.09	13.01	9.33	6.18	3.72	2.03	1.03	0.50	0.13
2.000	31.60	22.98	18.98	15.25	11.87	8.89	6.37	4.35	2.83	1.78	0.66
3.000	32.31	24.18	20.44	16.98	13.82	11.00	8.55	6.47	4.77	3.43	1.66
4.000	33.21	25.48	21.93	18.66	15.63	12.91	10.50	8.39	6.61	5.10	2.93
5.000	33.87	26.54	23.20	20.09	17.22	14.63	12.30	10.21	8.39	6.82	4.36
6.000	34.56	27.55	24.34	21.36	18.60	16.08	13.79	11.73	9.89	8.26	5.64
7.000	35.35	28.61	25.52	22.64	19.96	17.49	15.24	13.19	11.35	9.70	6.97
8.000	35.77	29.34	26.39	23.64	21.07	18.69	16.51	14.51	12.68	11.04	8.24

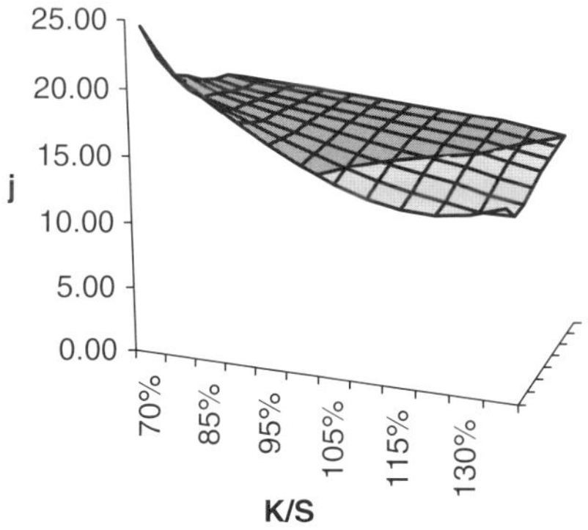

FIGURE 1.6 The SPX implied surface as of 03/09/2004. We can observe the negative skewness as well as the flattening of the slope with maturity.

[209] generalized this approach for a correlated case. The basic idea is to *separate* the random processes of the stock and the volatility, integrate the stock process conditionally upon a given volatility, and finally end up with a one-factor problem. Let us be reminded of the two processes we had:

$$dS_t = (r_t - q_t)S_t dt + \sigma_t S_t dB_t$$

and

$$dv_t = \tilde{b}(v_t)dt + a(v_t)dZ_t$$

under a risk-neutral measure.

Given a correlation ρ_t between dB_t and dZ_t, we can introduce the Brownian motion dW_t independent of dZ_t and write the usual Cholesky[31] factorization:

$$dB_t = \rho_t dZ_t + \sqrt{1 - \rho_t^2} dW_t$$

We can then introduce the same $X_t = \ln S_t$ and write the new system of equations:

$$dX_t = (r - q)dt + dY_t - \frac{1}{2}(1 - \rho_t^2)\sigma_t^2 dt + \sqrt{1 - \rho_t^2}\sigma_t dW_t \qquad (1.46)$$

$$dY_t = -\frac{1}{2}\rho_t^2\sigma_t^2 dt + \rho_t\sigma_t dZ_t$$

$$dv_t = \tilde{b}_t dt + a_t dZ_t$$

where, once again, the two Brownian motions are independent.

[31] See, for example, Press [204].

It is now possible to integrate the stock process for a given volatility and end up with an expectation on the volatility process only. We can think of (1.46) as the limit of a discrete process, while the time step $\Delta t \to 0$.

For a derivative security $f(S_0, v_0, T)$ with a payoff[32] $G(S_T)$, using the bivariate normal density for two uncorrelated variables, we can write

$$
\begin{aligned}
f(S_0, v_0, T) &= e^{-rT}\mathbf{E}_0[G(S_T)] && (1.47)\\
&= e^{-rT} \lim_{\Delta t \to 0} \int_{-\infty}^{\infty} \ldots \int_{-\infty}^{\infty} G(S_T) \prod_{t=0}^{T-\Delta t} \exp\left[-\frac{1}{2}(Z_t^2 + W_t^2)\right] \frac{dZ_t dW_t}{2\pi}
\end{aligned}
$$

If we know how to integrate the above over dW_t for a given volatility and we know the result $f^*(S, v, T)$ (for instance, for a European call option, we know the Black-Scholes formula (1.6), there are many other cases where we have closed-form solutions), then we can introduce the auxiliary variables[33]

$$
S^{eff} = S_0 e^{Y_T} = S_0 \exp\left(-\frac{1}{2}\int_0^T \rho_t^2 \sigma_t^2 dt + \int_0^T \rho_t \sigma_t dZ_t\right) \tag{1.48}
$$

and

$$
v^{eff} = \frac{1}{T}\int_0^T (1 - \rho_t^2)\sigma_t^2 dt \tag{1.49}
$$

and as Romano and Touzi prove in [209], we will have

$$
f(S_0, v_0, T) = \mathbf{E}_0[f^*(S^{eff},\ v^{eff},\ T)] \tag{1.50}
$$

where this last expectation is being taken on dZ_t only. Note that in the zero correlation case discussed by Hull and White [149] we have $S^{eff} = S_0$ and $v^{eff} = v_T = \frac{1}{T}\int_0^T \sigma_t^2 dt$, which makes the expression (1.50) a natural weighted average.

A One-Factor Monte Carlo Technique

As Lewis suggests, this will enable us to run a single-factor Monte Carlo simulation on the dZ_t and apply the known closed form for each simulated path. The method does suppose, however, that the payoff $G(S_T)$ does *not* depend on the volatility. Indeed, going back to (1.46) we can do a simulation on Y_t and v_t using the random sequence of (Z_t); then, after one path is generated, we can calculate $S^{eff} = S_0 \exp(Y_T)$ and $v^{eff} = \frac{1}{T}\sum_{t=0}^{T-\Delta t}(1 - \rho_t^2)v_t \Delta t$

[32]The payoff should *not* depend on the volatility process.

[33]Again, all notations are taken from Lewis [177].

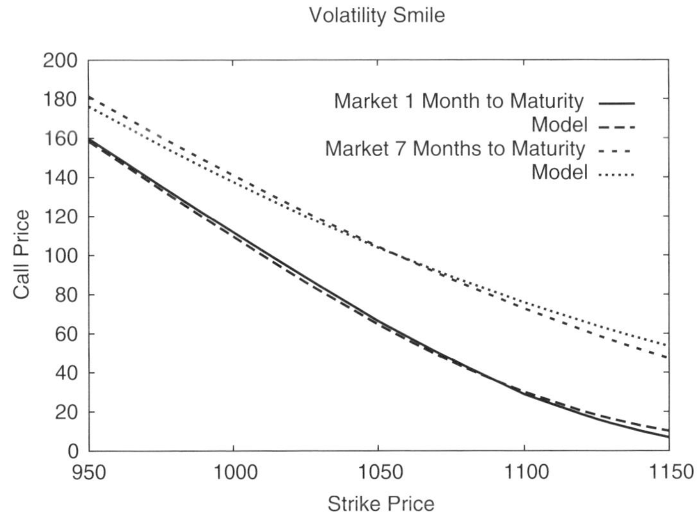

FIGURE 1.7 Mixing Monte Carlo Simulation with the Square-Root Model for SPX on February 12, 2002 with Index = \$1107.50, 1 month and 7 months to Maturity. The Powell optimization method was used for least-square calibration. As we can see, both maturities are fitted fairly well.

and then apply the known closed form (e.g. Black-Scholes for a call or put) with S^{eff} and v^{eff}. Repeating this procedure for a large number of times and averaging over the paths, as we usually do in Monte-Carlo methods, we will have $f(S_0, v_0, T)$. This will give us a way to calibrate the model parameters to the market data. For instance, using the square-root model

$$dv_t = (\omega - \theta v_t)dt + \xi\sqrt{v_t}dZ_t$$

we can estimate ω, θ, ξ, and ρ from the market prices via a least-square estimation applied to theoretical prices obtained from the preceding Monte Carlo method (Figure 1.7). We can either use a single calibration and suppose we have time-independent parameters or perform one calibration per maturity. The single calibration method is known to provide a bad fit, hence the idea of adding jumps to the stochastic volatility process as described by Matytsin [187]. However, this method will introduce new parameters for calibration.[34]

[34]Eraker et al. [98] claim that a model containing jumps in the return *and* the volatility process will fit the options and the underlying data well, and will have no misspecification left.

THE LONG-TERM ASYMPTOTIC CASE

In this section we will discuss the case in which the contract time to maturity is very large, $t \to \infty$. We will focus on the special case of a square-root process because this is the model we will use in many cases.

The Deterministic Case

We shall start with the case of deterministic volatility and use that for the more general case of the stochastic volatility.

We know that under the square-root model the variance follows

$$dv_t = (\omega - \theta v_t)dt + \xi\sqrt{v_t}dZ_t$$

As an *approximation*, we can drop the stochastic term and obtain

$$\frac{dv_t}{dt} = \omega - \theta v_t$$

which is an ordinary differential equation providing us immediately with

$$v_t = \frac{\omega}{\theta} + \left(v - \frac{\omega}{\theta}\right)e^{-\theta t} \tag{1.51}$$

where v is the initial variance for $t = 0$.

Using the results from the fundamental transform for a covered call option and put-call parity, we have for $0 < k_i < 1$

$$call(S, v, \tau) = Se^{-q\tau} - Ke^{-r\tau}\frac{1}{2\pi}\int_{ik_i-\infty}^{ik_i+\infty} e^{-ikX}\frac{\hat{H}(k, v, \tau)}{k^2 - ik}dk \tag{1.52}$$

where $\tau = T - t$ and $X = \ln\left(\frac{Se^{-q\tau}}{Ke^{-r\tau}}\right)$ represent the adjusted moneyness of the option. For the special "at-the-money"[35] case, where $X = 0$, we have

$$call(S, v, \tau) = Ke^{-r\tau}\left[1 - \frac{1}{2\pi}\int_{ik_i-\infty}^{ik_i+\infty}\frac{\hat{H}(k, v, \tau)}{k^2 - ik}dk\right] \tag{1.53}$$

As we previously said for a deterministic volatility case, we know the fundamental transform

$$\hat{H}(k, v, \tau) = \exp[-c(k)U(v, \tau)]$$

[35]This is different from the usual definition of at-the-money calls, where $S = K$. This vocabulary is borrowed from Alan Lewis.

With $U(v,\tau)=\int_0^\tau v(t)dt$ and as before $c(k)=\frac{1}{2}(k^2-ik)$, which in the special case of the square-root model (1.51), will provide us with

$$U(v,\tau)=\frac{\omega}{\theta}\tau+\left(v-\frac{\omega}{\theta}\right)\left(\frac{1-e^{-\theta\tau}}{\theta}\right)$$

This shows once again that $\hat{H}(k)$ is analytic in k over the entire complex plane.

Now if we let $\tau\to\infty$, we can write the approximation

$$\frac{call(S,v,\tau)}{Ke^{-r\tau}}\approx 1-\frac{1}{2\pi}\int_{ik_i-\infty}^{ik_i+\infty}\exp\left[-c(k)\frac{\omega}{\theta}\tau-c(k)\frac{1}{\theta}\left(v-\frac{\omega}{\theta}\right)\right]\frac{dk}{k^2-ik} \tag{1.54}$$

We can either calculate the above integral exactly using the Black-Scholes theory, or take the minimum where $c'(k_0)=0$, meaning $k_0=\frac{i}{2}$, and perform a Taylor approximation parallel to the real axis around the point $k=k_r+\frac{i}{2}$, which will give us

$$\frac{call(S,v,\tau)}{Ke^{-r\tau}}\approx 1-\frac{2}{\pi}\exp\left(-\frac{\omega}{8\theta}\tau\right)\exp\left[-\frac{1}{8\theta}\left(v-\frac{\omega}{\theta}\right)\right]\int_{-\infty}^{\infty}\exp\left(-k_r^2\frac{\omega}{2\theta}\tau\right)dk_r$$

the integral being a Gaussian we will get the result

$$\frac{call(S,v,\tau)}{Ke^{-r\tau}}\approx 1-\sqrt{\frac{8\theta}{\pi\omega\tau}}\exp\left[-\frac{1}{8\theta}\left(v-\frac{\omega}{\theta}\right)\right]\exp\left(-\frac{\omega}{8\theta}\tau\right) \tag{1.55}$$

which finishes our deterministic approximation case.

The Stochastic Case

For the stochastic volatility case, Lewis uses the same Taylor expansion. He notices that for the deterministic case we had

$$\hat{H}(k,v,\tau)=\exp\left[-c(k)U(v,\tau)\right]\approx\exp[-\lambda(k)\tau]u(k,v)$$

for $\tau\to\infty$, where

$$\lambda(k)=c(k)\frac{\omega}{\theta}$$

and

$$u(k,v)=\exp\left[-c(k)\frac{1}{\theta}\left(v-\frac{\omega}{\theta}\right)\right]$$

If we *suppose* that this identity holds for the stochastic volatility case as well, we can use the PDE (1.44) and interpret the result as an *eigenvalue-eigenfunction* identity with the eigenvalue $\lambda(k)$ and the eigenfunction $u(k,v)$.

This assumption is reasonable because the first Taylor approximation term for the stochastic process *is* deterministic. Indeed, introducing the operator

$$\Lambda(u) = -\frac{1}{2}a^2(v)\frac{d^2u}{dv^2} - \left[\tilde{b}(v) - ik\rho(v)a(v)\sqrt{v}\right]\frac{du}{dv} + c(k)vu$$

we have

$$\Lambda(u) = \lambda(k)u \tag{1.56}$$

Now the idea would be to perform a Taylor expansion around the minimum k_0 where $\lambda'(k_0) = 0$. Lewis shows that such k_0 is always situated on the imaginary axis. This property is referred to as the "ridge" property.

The Taylor expansion along the real axis could be written as

$$\lambda(k) = \lambda(k_0 + k_r) \approx \lambda(k_0) + \frac{1}{2}k_r^2\lambda''(k_0)$$

Note that we are dealing with a *minimum*, and therefore $\lambda''(k_0) > 0$. Using the above second-order approximation for $\lambda(k)$, we get

$$\frac{call(S, v, \tau)}{Ke^{-r\tau}} \approx 1 - \frac{u(k_0, v)}{k_0^2 - ik_0}\frac{1}{\sqrt{2\pi\lambda''(k_0)\tau}}\exp[-\lambda(k_0)\tau]$$

We can then move from the special "at-the-money" case to the general case by reintroducing $X = \ln\left(\frac{Se^{-q\tau}}{Ke^{-r\tau}}\right)$, and we will finally obtain

$$\frac{call(S, v, \tau)}{Ke^{-r\tau}} \approx e^X - \frac{u(k_0, v)}{k_0^2 - ik_0}\frac{1}{\sqrt{2\pi\lambda''(k_0)\tau}}\exp[-\lambda(k_0)\tau - ik_0X] \tag{1.57}$$

which completes our determination of the asymptotic closed form in the general case.

For the special case of the square-root model, taking the risk-neutral case $\gamma = 1$, we have[36]

$$\lambda(k) = -\omega g^*(k) = \frac{\omega}{\xi^2}\left[\sqrt{(\theta + ik\rho\xi)^2 + (k^2 - ik)\xi^2} - (\theta + ik\rho\xi)\right]$$

which also allows us to calculate $\lambda''(k)$. Also

$$u(k, v) = \exp[g^*(k)v]$$

[36]We can go back to the general case $\gamma \leq 1$ by replacing θ with $\sqrt{\theta^2 - \gamma(1-\gamma)\xi^2} + (1-\gamma)\rho\xi$ because this transformation is independent from k altogether.

where we use the notations from (1.45) and we pose

$$g^* = g - d$$

The k_0 such that $\lambda'(k_0) = 0$ is

$$k_0 = \frac{i}{1-\rho^2}\left(\frac{1}{2} - \frac{\rho}{\xi}\left[\theta - \frac{1}{2}\sqrt{4\theta^2 + \xi^2 - 4\rho\theta\xi}\right]\right)$$

which together with (1.57) provides us with the result for $call(S, v, \tau)$ in the asymptotic case under the square-root stochastic volatility model.

Note that for $\xi \to 0$ and $\rho \to 0$, we find again the deterministic result $k_0 \to \frac{i}{2}$.

A Series Expansion on Volatility-of-Volatility

Another asymptotic approach for the stochastic volatility model suggested by Lewis [177] is a Taylor expansion on the volatility-of-volatility. There are two possibilities for this: We can perform the expansion *either* for the option price *or* for the implied volatility directly. In what follows, we consider the former approach. Once again, we use the fundamental transform $H(k, V, \tau)$ with $H(k, V, 0) = 1$ and

$$\frac{\partial H}{\partial \tau} = \frac{1}{2}a^2(v)\frac{\partial^2 H}{\partial v^2} + \left(\tilde{b}(v) - ik\rho(v)a(v)\sqrt{v}\right)\frac{\partial H}{\partial v} - c(k)vH$$

and $c(k) = \frac{1}{2}(k^2 - ik)$. We then pose $a(v) = \xi\eta(v)$ and expand $H(k, V, \tau)$on powers of ξ and finally apply the inverse Fourier transform to obtain an expansion on the call price.
With our usual notations $\tau = T - t$, $X = \ln(\frac{S}{K}) + (r - q)\tau$and $Z(V) = V\tau$, the series will be

$$\begin{aligned} C(S, V, \tau) &= c_{BS}(S, v, \tau) + \xi\tau^{-1}J_1\tilde{R}_{11}\frac{\partial c_{BS}(S, v, \tau)}{\partial V} \\ &+\xi^2\left[\tau^{-2}J_3\tilde{R}_{20} + \tau^{-1}J_4\tilde{R}_{12} + \frac{1}{2}\tau^{-2}J_1^2\tilde{R}_{22}\right]\frac{\partial c_{BS}(S, v, \tau)}{\partial V} + O(\xi^3) \end{aligned}$$

where $v(V, \tau)$ is the deterministic variance

$$v(V, \tau) = \frac{\omega}{\theta} + \left(V - \frac{\omega}{\theta}\right)\left(\frac{1 - e^{-\theta\tau}}{\theta\tau}\right)$$

and $\tilde{R}_{pq} = R_{pq}(X, v(V, \tau), \tau)$ with R_{pq} given polynomials of (X, Z) of degree four at most, and J_n's known functions of (V, τ).

The explicit expressions for all these functions are given in the third chapter of the Lewis book [177].

The obvious advantages of this approach are its speed and stability. The issue of lack of time homogeneity of the parameters $\Psi = (\omega, \theta, \xi, \rho)$ could be addressed by performing one calibration per time interval. In this case, for each time interval $[t_n, t_{n+1}]$ we will have one set of parameters $\Psi_n = (\omega_n, \theta_n, \xi_n, \rho_n)$ and depending on what maturity T we are dealing with, we will use one or the other parameter set.

We compare the values obtained from this series-based approach with those from a mixing Monte Carlo method in Figure 1.8. We are taking the example that Heston studied in [134]. The graph shows the difference $C(S, V, \tau) - c_{BS}(S, V, \tau)$ for a fixed $K = \$100$ and $\tau = 0.50$ year. The other inputs are $\omega = 0.02$, $\theta = 2.00$, $\xi = 0.10$, $\rho = -0.50$, $V = 0.01$, and $r = q = 0$. As we can see, the true value of the call is *lower* than the Black-Scholes value for the out-of-the-money (OTM) region. The higher ξ and $|\rho|$ are, the larger this difference will be.

In Figures 1.9 and 1.10, we reset the correlation ρ to zero to have a symmetric distribution, but we use a volatility-of-volatility of $\xi = 0.10$ and $\xi = 0.20$ respectively. As discussed, the parameter ξ is the one creating the leptokur-

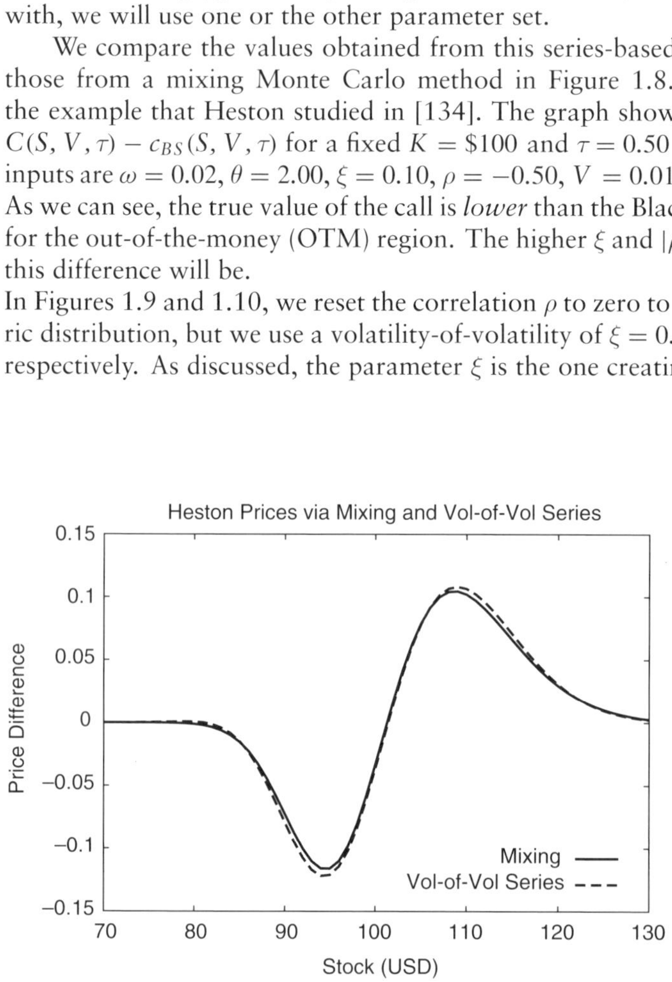

FIGURE 1.8 Comparing the Volatility-of-Volatility Series Expansion with the Monte Carlo Mixing Model. The graph shows the price difference $C(S, V, \tau) - c_{BS}(S, V, \tau)$. We are taking $\xi = 0.10$ and $\rho = -0.50$. This example was used in the original Heston paper.

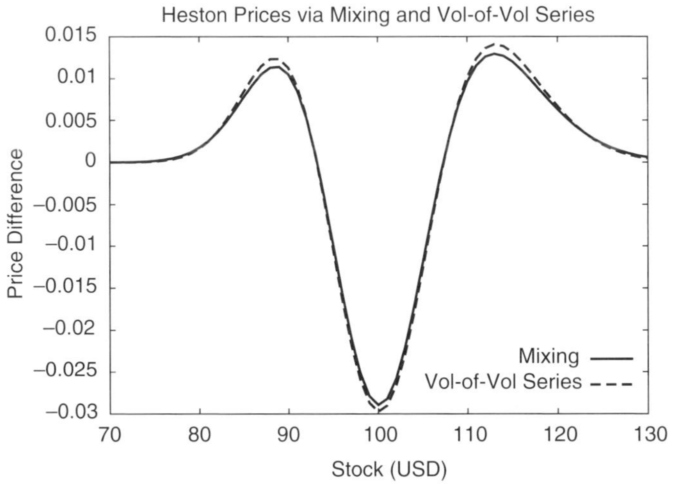

FIGURE 1.9 Comparing the Volatility-of-Volatility Series Expansion with the Monte Carlo Mixing Model. The graph shows the price difference $C(S, V, \tau) - c_{BS}(S, V, \tau)$. We are taking $\xi = 0.10$ and $\rho = 0$. This example was used in the original Heston paper.

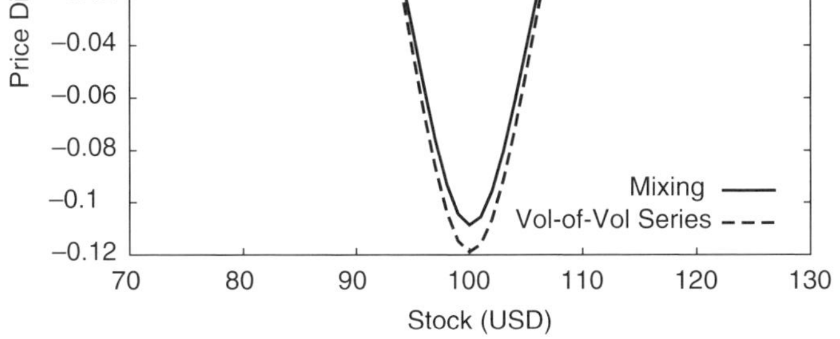

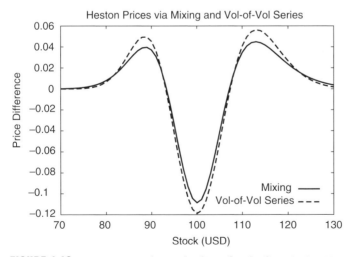

FIGURE 1.10 Comparing the Volatility-of-Volatility Series Expansion with the Monte Carlo Mixing Model. The graph shows the price difference $C(S, V, \tau) - c_{BS}(S, V, \tau)$. We are taking $\xi = 0.20$ and $\rho = 0$. This example was used in the original Heston paper.

ticity phenomenon. A higher volatility-of-volatility causes higher valuation for far-from-the-money options.[37]

Unfortunately, the foregoing series approximation becomes poor as soon as the volatility-of-volatility becomes larger than 0.40 and the maturity becomes of the order of 1 year. This case is not unusual at all and therefore makes the use of this method limited. This is why the method of choice remains the inversion of the Fourier transform, as previously described.

PURE-JUMP MODELS

Variance Gamma

An alternative point of view is to drop the diffusion assumption altogether and replace it with a pure-jump process. Note that this is different from the jump-diffusion process previously discussed. Madan et al. suggested the following framework, called *variance-gamma* (VG) in [182]. We would have the log-normal-like stock process

$$d\ln S_t = (\mu_S + \omega)dt + X(dt; \sigma, \nu, \theta)$$

where as before μ_S is the real-world statistical drift of the stock log return and $\omega = \frac{1}{\nu}\ln(1 - \theta\nu - \sigma^2\nu/2)$.

As for $X(dt; \sigma, \nu, \theta)$, it has the following meaning:

$$X(dt; \sigma, \nu, \theta) = B(\gamma(dt, 1, \nu); \theta, \sigma)$$

where $B(dt; \theta, \sigma)$ would be a Brownian motion with drift θ and volatility σ. In other words

$$B(dt; \theta, \sigma) = \theta dt + \sigma\sqrt{dt}N(0, 1)$$

and $N(0, 1)$ is a standard Gaussian realization.

The time interval at which the Brownian motion is considered is not dt but $\gamma(dt, 1, \nu)$ which is a random realization following a gamma distribution with a mean 1 and variance rate ν. The corresponding probability density function is

$$f_\nu(dt, \tau) = \frac{\tau^{\frac{dt}{\nu}-1}e^{-\frac{\tau}{\nu}}}{\nu^{\frac{dt}{\nu}}\Gamma(\frac{dt}{\nu})}$$

where $\Gamma(x)$ is the usual gamma function.

Note that the stock log-return density could actually be *integrated* for the VG model, and the density of $\ln(S_t/S_0)$ is known and could be implemented

[37]Also note that the gap between the closed-form series and the Monte Carlo model increases with ξ. Indeed, the accuracy of the expansion decreases as ξ becomes larger.

via $K_\alpha(x)$, the modified Bessel function of the second kind. Indeed, calling $z = \ln(S_k/S_{k-1})$ and $h = t_k - t_{k-1}$ and posing $x_h = z - \mu_S h - \frac{h}{\nu}\ln(1 - \theta\nu - \sigma^2\nu/2)$ we have

$$p(z|h) = \frac{2\exp(\theta x_h/\sigma^2)}{\nu^{\frac{h}{\nu}}\sqrt{2\pi}\sigma\Gamma(\frac{h}{\nu})}\left(\frac{x_h^2}{2\sigma^2/\nu + \theta^2}\right)^{\frac{h}{2\nu}-\frac{1}{4}} K_{\frac{h}{\nu}-\frac{1}{2}}\left(\frac{1}{\sigma^2}\sqrt{x_h^2(2\sigma^2/\nu + \theta^2)}\right)$$

Moreover, as Madan et al. show, the option valuation under VG is fairly straightforward and admits an analytically tractable closed form that can be implemented via the above modified Bessel function of second kind and a degenerate hypergeometric function. All details are available in [182].

Remark on the Gamma Distribution The gamma cumulative distribution function (CDF) could be defined as

$$P(a, x) = \frac{1}{\Gamma(a)}\int_0^x e^{-t}t^{a-1}dt$$

Note that with our notations

$$F_\nu(h, x) = F(h, x, \mu = 1, \nu)$$

with

$$F(h, x, \mu, \nu) = \frac{1}{\Gamma(\frac{\mu^2 h}{\nu})}\left(\frac{\mu}{\nu}\right)^{\frac{\mu^2 h}{\nu}}\int_0^x e^{-\frac{\mu t}{\nu}}t^{\frac{\mu^2 h}{\nu}-1}dt$$

In other words

$$F(h, x, \mu, \nu) = P\left(\frac{\mu^2 h}{\nu}, \frac{\mu x}{\nu}\right)$$

The behavior of this CDF is displayed in Figure 1.11 for different values of the parameter $a > 0$ and for $0 < x < +\infty$.

Using the inverse of this CDF, we can have a simulated data set for the gamma law:

$$x^{(i)} = F_\nu^{-1}(h, \mathcal{U}^{(i)}[0, 1])$$

with $1 \leq i \leq N_{sims}$ and $\mathcal{U}^{(i)}[0, 1]$ a uniform random realization between zero and one.

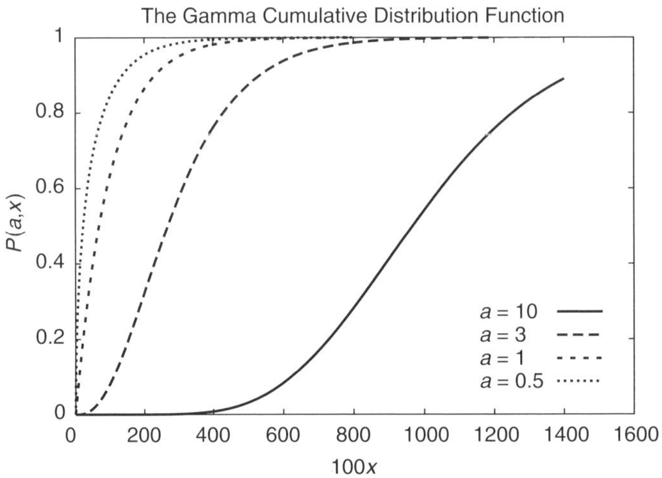

FIGURE 1.11 The Gamma Cumulative Distribution Function $P(a, x)$ for Various Values of the Parameter a. The implementation is based on code available in *Numerical Recipes in C* [204].

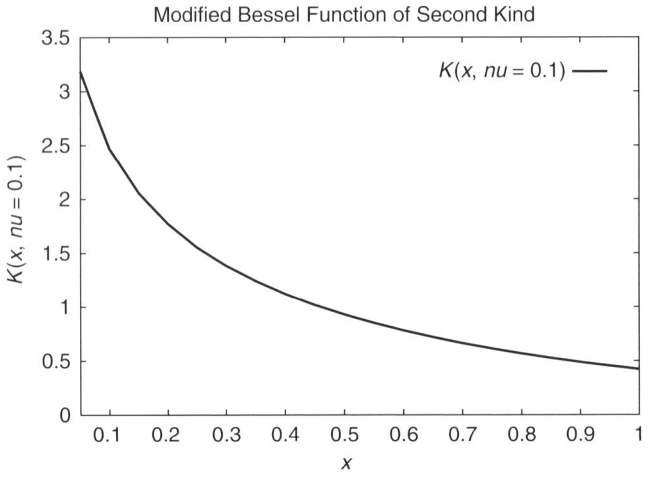

FIGURE 1.12 The Modified Bessel Function of Second Kind for a Given Parameter. The implementation is based on code available in *Numerical Recipes in C* [204].

Stochastic Volatility vs. Time-Changed processes As mentioned in [23], this alternative formulation leading to time-changed processes is closely related to the previously discussed stochastic volatility approach in the following way.

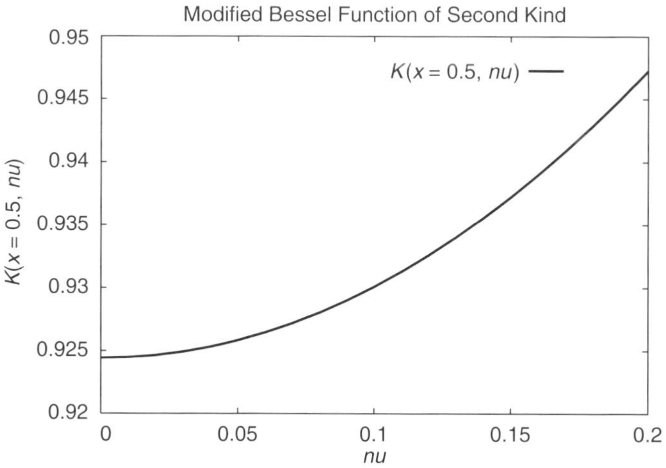

FIGURE 1.13 The Modified Bessel Function of Second Kind as a Function of the Parameter. The implementation is based on code available in *Numerical Recipes in C* [204].

Taking the foregoing VG stochastic differential equation

$$d \ln S_t = (\mu_S + \omega)dt + \theta\gamma(dt, 1, \nu) + \sigma\sqrt{\gamma(dt, 1, \nu)}N(0, 1)$$

one could consider $\sigma^2\gamma(t, 1, \nu)$ as the integrated variance and define $v_t(\nu)$, the instantaneous variance, as

$$\sigma^2\gamma(dt, 1, \nu) = v_t(\nu)dt$$

in which case, we would have

$$\begin{aligned} d \ln S_t &= (\mu_S + \omega)dt + (\theta/\sigma^2)v_t(\nu)dt + \sqrt{v_t(\nu)dt}N(0, 1) \\ &= (\mu_S + \omega + (\theta/\sigma^2)v_t(\nu))dt + \sqrt{v_t(\nu)}dZ_t \end{aligned}$$

where dZ_t is a Brownian motion. This last expression is a traditional stochastic volatility equation.

Variance Gamma with Stochastic Arrival

An extension of the VG model would be a variance gamma model with stochastic arrival (VGSA), which would include the volatility *clustering* effect. This phenomenon (also represented by GARCH) means that a high (low) volatility will be followed by a series of high (low) volatilities. In this approach, we replace the dt in the previously defined $f_\nu(dt, \tau)$ with $y_t dt$, where y_t follows a square-root (CIR) process

$$dy_t = \kappa(\eta - y_t)dt + \lambda\sqrt{y_t}dW_t$$

where the Brownian motion dW_t is independent from other processes in the model. This is therefore a VG process in which the arrival time itself is stochastic. The mean reversion of the square-root process will cause the volatility persistence effect that is empirically observed. Note that (not counting μ_S) the new model parameter set is $\Psi = (\kappa, \eta, \lambda, \nu, \theta, \sigma)$.

Option Pricing under VGSA The option pricing could be carried out via a Monte Carlo simulation algorithm under the risk-neutral measure, where, as before, μ_S is replaced with $r - q$. We first would simulate the path of y_t by writing

$$y_k = y_{k-1} + \kappa(\eta - y_{k-1})\Delta t + \lambda\sqrt{y_{k-1}}\sqrt{\Delta t}Z_k$$

then calculate

$$Y_T = \sum_{k=0}^{N-1} y_k \Delta t$$

and finally apply *one-step* simulations

$$T^* = F_\nu^{-1}\left(Y_T, \mathcal{U}[0,1]\right)$$

and[38]

$$\ln S_T = \ln S_0 + (r - q + \omega)T + \theta T^* + \sigma\sqrt{T^*}B_k$$

Note that we have two normal random variables B_k, Z_k as well as a gamma-distributed random variable T^*, and that they are all uncorrelated. Once the stock price S_T is properly simulated, we can calculate the option price as usual.

The Characteristic Function As previously discussed, another way to tackle the option-pricing issue would be to use the characteristic functions. For VG, the characteristic function is

$$\Psi(u,t) = \mathbf{E}[e^{iuX(t)}] = \left(\frac{1}{1 - i\frac{\nu}{\mu}u}\right)^{\frac{\mu 2}{\nu}t}$$

Therefore the log-characteristic function could be written as

$$\psi(u,t) = \ln(\Psi(u,t)) = t\psi(u,1)$$

[38]This means that T in VG is replaced with Y_T. The rest remains identical.

In other words

$$\mathbf{E}[e^{iuX(t)}] = \Psi(u,t) = \exp(t\psi(u,1))$$

Using which, the VGSA characteristic function becomes

$$\mathbf{E}\left[e^{iuX(Y(t))}\right] = \mathbf{E}[\exp(Y(t)\psi(u,1))] = \phi(-i\psi(u,1))$$

with $\phi()$ the CIR characteristic function, namely

$$\phi(u_t) = \mathbf{E}[\exp(iuY_t)] = A(t,u)\exp(B(t,u)y_0)$$

where

$$A(t,u) = \frac{\exp(\kappa^2\eta t/\lambda^2)}{[\cosh(\gamma t/2) + \kappa/\gamma \sinh(\gamma t/2)]^{\frac{2\kappa\eta}{\lambda^2}}}$$

$$B(t,u) = \frac{2iu}{\kappa + \gamma\coth(\gamma t/2)}$$

and

$$\gamma = \sqrt{\kappa^2 - 2\lambda^2 iu}$$

This allows us to determine the VGSA characteristic function, which we can use to calculate options prices via numeric Fourier inversion as described in [48] and [51].

Variance Gamma with Gamma Arrival Rate

For the variance gamma with gamma arrival rate (VGG), as before, the stock process under the risk-neutral framework is

$$d\ln S_t = (r - q + \omega)dt + X(h(dt); \sigma, \nu, \theta)$$

with $\omega = \frac{1}{\nu}\ln(1 - \theta\nu - \sigma^2\nu/2)$ and

$$X(h(dt); \sigma, \nu, \theta) = B(\gamma(h(dt), 1, \nu); \theta, \sigma)$$

and the general gamma cumulative distribution function for $\gamma(h, \mu, \nu)$ is

$$F(\mu, \nu; h, x) = \frac{1}{\Gamma\left(\frac{\mu^2 h}{\nu}\right)}\left(\frac{\mu}{\nu}\right)^{\frac{\mu^2 h}{\nu}} \int_0^x e^{-\frac{\mu t}{\nu}} t^{\frac{\mu^2 h}{\nu}-1} dt$$

and here $h(dt) = dY_t$ with Y_t is also gamma-distributed

$$dY_t = \gamma(dt, \mu_a, \nu_a)$$

The parameter set is therefore $\Psi = (\mu_a, \nu_a, \nu, \theta, \sigma)$.

CHAPTER 2

The Inference Problem

In applying option pricing models, one always encounters the difficulty that the spot volatility and the structural parameters are unobservable.

— Gurdip Bakshi, Charles Cao, and Zhiwu Chen

INTRODUCTION

Regardless of which specific model we are using, it seems that we cannot avoid the issue of calibration. There are two possible sets of data that we can use for estimating the model parameters: options prices and historic stock prices.[1]

Using options prices via a least-square estimator (LSE) has the obvious advantage of guaranteeing that we will match the used option market prices within a certain tolerance. However, the availability of option data is typically limited, which would force us to use interpolation and extrapolation methods. These data manipulation approaches might deteriorate the quality and the smoothness of our inputs. More importantly, matching a set of plain-vanilla option prices does not necessarily mean that we would obtain the correct price for an exotic derivative.

Using stock prices has the disadvantage of offering no guarantee of matching option prices. However, *supposing* that the model is right, we do have a great quantity of data input for calibration, which is a powerful argument in favor of this approach.

It is important, however, to note that in using historic stock prices we are assuming that our time step Δt is small enough that we are almost in

[1] Recently some researchers have also tried to use historic option prices. See, for instance, Elliott [93] or Van der Merwe [229].

a continuous setting. Further, we are assuming the validity of the Girsanov theorem, which is applicable to a diffusion-based model. This also means we are implicitly assuming that the market price of volatility risk is stable and so are the risk-neutral volatility-drift parameters.

More accurately, having for instance a *real-world* model

$$dv_t = (\omega - \theta v_t)dt + \xi v_t^p dZ_t$$

with $p = 0.5$ corresponding to the Heston model, we know that the *risk-neutral* volatility-drift parameter is

$$\theta^{(r)} = \theta + \lambda \xi v_t^{p-1}$$

As a result, supposing that $\theta^{(r)}$ is a stable (or even constant) parameter is equivalent to supposing that λ the market-price-of-volatility-risk[2] verifies

$$\lambda = \phi v_t^{1-p}$$

with ϕ a constant coefficient. The implication of this assumption for a model with a real-world parameter set $\Psi = (\omega, \theta, \xi, \rho)$ and a risk-neutral counterpart $\Psi^{(r)} = (\omega^{(r)}, \theta^{(r)}, \xi^{(r)}, \rho^{(r)})$ is

$$\begin{aligned}
\xi &= \xi^{(r)} \\
\rho &= \rho^{(r)} \\
\omega &= \omega^{(r)} \\
\theta &= \theta^{(r)} - \phi
\end{aligned}$$

Let us insist on the fact that the above assumption[3] is valid *only* for a diffusion-based model. For some non-Gaussian pure-jump models, such as VGG, we lose the comparability between the statistical and the risk-neutral parameters. We could instead use the stock-price time series to determine the statistical density $p(z)$ on the one hand, use the options prices to determine the risk-neutral density $q(z)$ on the other, and calculate the ratio

---

[2]Note that many call the market-price-of-volatility-risk the quantity $\lambda \xi v_t^p$.

[3]Also as stated by Bakshi, Cao, and Chen [20]: *When the risk-aversion coefficient of the representative agent is bounded within a reasonable range, the parameters of the true distributions will not differ significantly from their risk-neutral counterparts.* The direct implication of this is $\theta \approx \theta^{(r)}$. More importantly, for daily data we have $\Delta t = o(\sqrt{\Delta t})$ and therefore using either the real-world asset drift μ_S or the dividend-adjusted risk-free rate $r - q$ would not make a difference in parameter estimation. Some [10] even ignore the stock drift term altogether.

$r(z) = p(z)/q(z)$ corresponding to the Radon-Nikodym derivative of the two measures for this model.

The central question of this chapter is therefore the *inference* of the parameters embedded in a stochastic volatility model. The logical subdivisions of the problem are summarized as follows.

1. **Cross-Sectional vs. Time Series:** The former uses options prices at a given point in time, and the latter a series of the underlying prices for a given period. As mentioned earlier, the former provides an estimation of the parameters in the risk-neutral universe and the latter estimation takes place in the statistical universe.
2. **Classical vs. Bayesian:** Using *time series*, one could suppose that there exists an unknown but fixed set of parameters and try to estimate them as closely as possible. This is a classical (frequentist) approach. Alternatively, one could use a Bayesian approach, in which the parameters are supposed to be random variables and have their prior distributions that one can update via the observations.
3. **Learning vs. Likelihood Maximization:** Under the *classical* hypothesis, one could try to estimate the instantaneous variance together with the fixed parameters, which corresponds to a learning process. A more robust way would be to estimate the likelihood function and maximize it over all the possible values of the parameters.
4. **Gaussian vs. Non-Gaussian:** In any of the preceding approaches, the stochastic volatility (SV) model could be diffusion based or not. As we will see further, this will affect the actual estimation methodology. Among the Gaussian SV models we consider are Heston, GARCH, and 3/2. Among the Non-Gaussian ones are Bates, VGSA, and VGG.
5. **State-Space Representation:** For each of the above approaches and for each SV model, we have a number of ways of choosing a state and represent the instantaneous variance as well as the spot price. Needless to say, a more parsimonious and lower-dimension state is preferable.
6. **Diagnostics and Sampling Distribution:** Once the inference process is finished, one has to verify its accuracy via various tests. Quantities such as MPE, RMSE, Box-Ljung, or χ^2 numbers correspond to some of the possible diagnostics. Observing the sampling distribution over various paths is another way of checking the validity of the inference methodology.

Finally, it is worth noting that our entire approach is based on *parametric* stochastic volatility models. This model class is more restrictive than the non- or semiparametric; however, it has the advantage of offering the possibility of a direct interpretation of the resulting parameters.

USING OPTION PRICES

Using a set of current vanilla option prices, we can perform an LSE and assess the risk-neutral model parameters. Taking a set of J strike prices K_j's with their corresponding option prices $C_{mkt}(K_j)$ for a given maturity, we would try to minimize

$$\sum_{j=1}^{J}(C_{model}(K_j) - C_{mkt}(K_j))^2$$

The minimization[4] could, for example, be done via the direction set (Powell) method, the conjugate gradient (Fletcher-Reeves-Polak-Ribiere) method, or the Levenberg-Marquardt (LM) method. We will now briefly describe the Powell optimization algorithm.

Direction Set (Powell) Method

The optimization method we will use later is the direction set (Powell) method and does *not* require any gradient or Hessian computation.[5] This is a quadratically convergent method producing mutually conjugate directions.

Most multi dimensional optimization algorithms require a one-dimensional *line minimization* routine that does the following: Given as input the vectors $\mathbf{P}$ and $\mathbf{n}$ and the function f, find the scalar λ that minimizes $f(\mathbf{P}+\lambda\mathbf{n})$, and then replace $\mathbf{P}$ with $\mathbf{P}+\lambda\mathbf{n}$ and $\mathbf{n}$ with $\lambda\mathbf{n}$. The idea would be to take a set of directions that are as noninterfering as possible in order to avoid spoiling one minimization with the subsequent one. This way an interminable cycling through the set of directions will not occur. This is why we seek *conjugate directions*. Calling the function to be minimized $f(\mathbf{x})$, with $\mathbf{x}$ a vector of dimension N, we can write the second-order Taylor expansion around a particular point $\mathbf{P}$

$$f(\mathbf{x}) \approx f(\mathbf{P}) + \nabla f(\mathbf{P})\mathbf{x} + \frac{1}{2}\mathbf{x}\mathbf{H}\mathbf{x}$$

where $\mathbf{H}_{ij} = \frac{\partial^2 f}{\partial x_i \partial x_j}$ is the Hessian matrix of the function at point $\mathbf{P}$. We therefore have for the variation of the gradient $\delta(\nabla f) = \mathbf{H}\delta\mathbf{x}$, and, in order to

[4] Some consider that this minimization will give more importance to the ATM options, and they try therefore to correct by introducing weights into the summation. There are also entropy-based techniques as discussed in [16] applied to local volatility models, which are different from our parametric models.

[5] This is an important feature when the function to be optimized contains discontinuities.

have a noninterfering new direction, we choose **v** such that the motion along **v** remains perpendicular to our previous direction **u**

$$\mathbf{u}\delta(\nabla f) = \mathbf{uHv} = 0$$

In this case, the directions **u** and **v** are said to be *conjugate*.

Powell suggests a quadratically convergent method that produces a set of N mutually conjugate directions. The following description is taken from Press [204], where the corresponding source code could be found as well.

1. Initialize the set of directions $\mathbf{u}_i$ to the basis vectors for $i = 1, ..., N$
2. Save the starting point as $\mathbf{P}_0$
3. Move $\mathbf{P}_{i-1}$ to the minimum along direction $\mathbf{u}_i$ and call it $\mathbf{P}_i$
4. Set $\mathbf{u}_i$ to $\mathbf{u}_{i+1}$ for $i = 1, ..., N-1$ and set $\mathbf{u}_N$ to $\mathbf{P}_N - \mathbf{P}_0$
5. Move $\mathbf{P}_N$ to the minimum along $\mathbf{u}_N$ and call this point $\mathbf{P}_0$, and go back to Step 2

For a quadratic form, k iterations of this algorithm will produce a set of directions whose last k members are mutually conjugate. The idea is to repeat the steps until the function stops decreasing. However, this procedure tends to produce directions that are linearly dependent and therefore provides us with the minimum only over a sub space —hence—the idea of discarding the direction along which f makes the largest decrease. This seems paradoxical; we are dropping our best direction in the new iteration. However, this is the best chance of avoiding a buildup of linear dependence.

In what follows we apply the Powell algorithm to SPX options valued via the mixing Monte Carlo method.

Numeric Tests

We apply the Powell algorithm to SPX options valued via the mixing Monte Carlo method. The optimization is performed across close-to-the-money strike prices as of $t_0 = 05/21/2002$ with the index $S_0 = 1079.88$ and maturities $T = 08/17/2002$, $T = 09/21/2002$, $T = 12/21/2002$, and $T = 03/22/2003$ (Figures 2.1 through 2.5).

As we see in Table 2.1, the estimated parameters are fairly stable for different maturities and therefore the stochastic volatility model seems to be fairly *time homogeneous*.

The Distribution of the Errors

Because the parameter set Ψ contains only a few elements and we can have many options prices, it is clear that the matching of the model and market

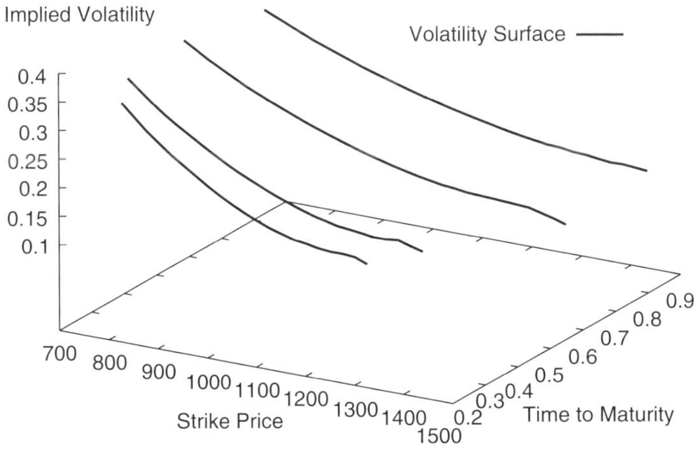

FIGURE 2.1 The S&P 500 Volatility Surface as of 05/21/2002 with Index = \$1079.88. The surface will be used for fitting via the direction set (Powell) optimization algorithm applied to a square-root model implemented with a one-factor Monte Carlo mixing method.

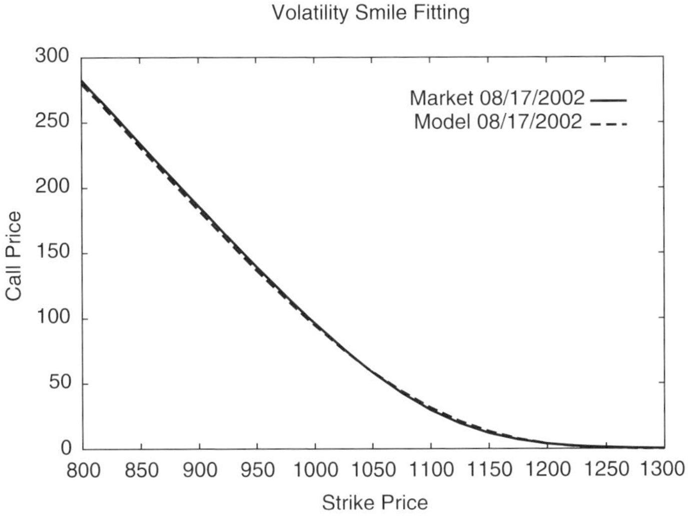

FIGURE 2.2 Mixing Monte Carlo Simulation with the Square-Root Model for SPX on 05/21/2002 with Index = \$1079.88, Maturity 08/17/2002. Powell (direction set) optimization method was used for least-square calibration. Optimal parameters $\hat{\omega} = 0.081575$, $\hat{\theta} = 3.308023$, $\hat{\xi} = 0.268151$, $\hat{\rho} = -0.999999$.

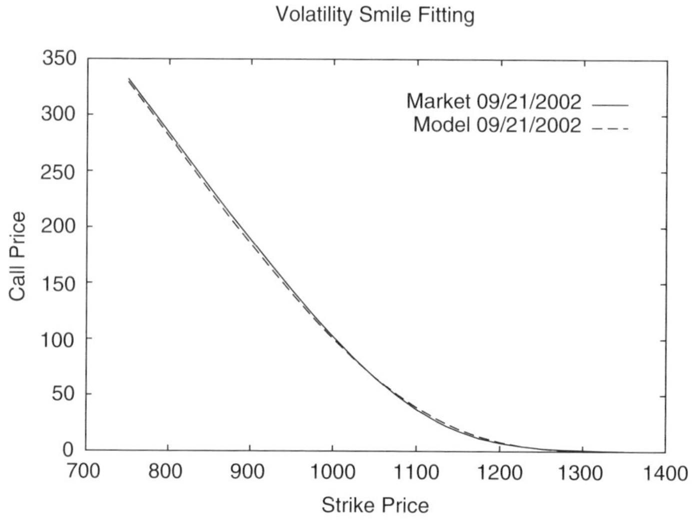

FIGURE 2.3 Mixing Monte Carlo Simulation with the Square-Root Model for SPX on 05/21/2002 with Index = \$1079.88, Maturity 09/21/2002. Powell (direction set) optimization method was used for least-square calibration. Optimal parameters $\hat{\omega} = 0.108359$, $\hat{\theta} = 3.798900$, $\hat{\xi} = 0.242820$, $\hat{\rho} = -0.999830$.

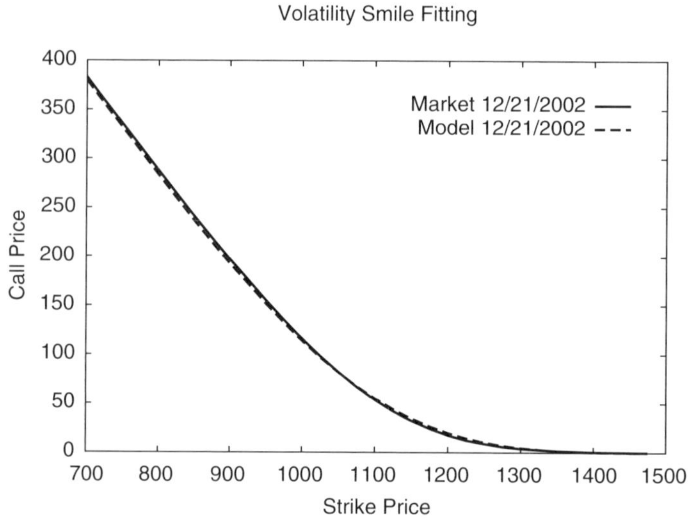

FIGURE 2.4 Mixing Monte Carlo Simulation with the Square-Root Model for SPX on 05/21/2002 with Index = \$1079.88, Maturity 12/21/2002. Powell (direction set) optimization method was used for least-square calibration. Optimal parameters $\hat{\omega} = 0.126519$, $\hat{\theta} = 3.473910$, $\hat{\xi} = 0.222532$, $\hat{\rho} = -0.999991$.

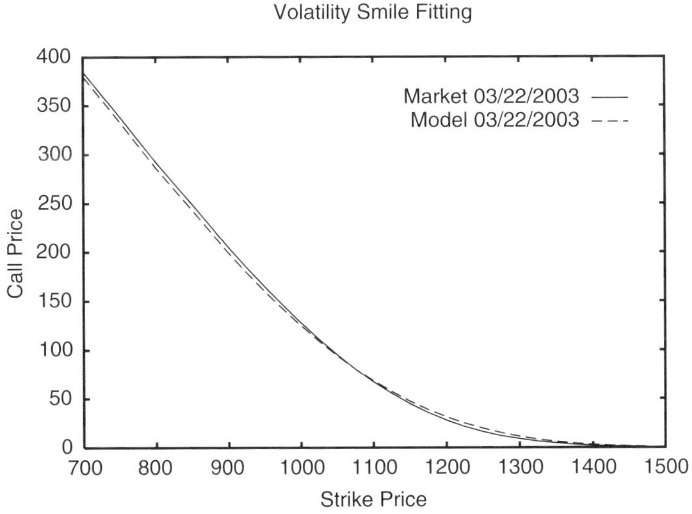

FIGURE 2.5 Mixing Monte-Carlo Simulation with the Square-Root Model for SPX on 05/21/2002 with Index = \$1079.88, Maturity 03/22/2003. Powell (direction set) optimization method was used for least-square calibration. Optimal parameters $\hat{\omega} = 0.138687$, $\hat{\theta} = 3.497779$, $\hat{\xi} = 0.180010$, $\hat{\rho} = -1.000000$.

prices is not perfect. Thus, we observe the distribution of the errors

$$C_{mkt}(K_j) = C_{model}(K_j, \hat{\Psi}) \exp\left\{-\frac{1}{2}\Upsilon^2 + \Upsilon\mathcal{N}^{(j)}(0, 1)\right\}$$

with $1 \leq j \leq J$ and Υ the error standard deviation and $\hat{\Psi}$ the optimal parameter set. As usual, $\mathcal{N}(0, 1)$ is the standard normal distribution. Note that our previously discussed LSE approach is not exactly equivalent to the maximization of a likelihood function based on the above distribution

TABLE 2.1 The Estimation is Performed for SPX on $t = 05/21/2002$ with Index = \$1079.88 for Different Maturities T.

T	$\hat{\omega}$	$\hat{\theta}$	$\hat{\xi}$	$\hat{\rho}$
08172002	0.081575	3.308023	0.268151	−0.999999
09212002	0.108359	3.798900	0.242820	−0.999830
12212002	0.126519	3.473910	0.222532	−0.999991
03222003	0.138687	3.497779	0.180010	−1.000000

because the latter would correspond to the minimization of the sum of the squared *log* returns.

A good *bias test* would be to check for the predictability of the errors. For this, one could run a regression of the error

$$e_j = C_{mkt}(K_j) - C_{model}(K_j, \hat{\Psi})$$

on a few factors corresponding, for instance, to moneyness or maturity. A low R^2 for the regression would prove that the model errors are not predictable and there is no major bias. For a detailed study, see [182] for instance.

USING STOCK PRICES

The Likelihood Function

If, as in the previous section, we use European options with a given maturity T and with different strike prices, then we will be estimating

$$q(S_T|S_0; \Psi)$$

which corresponds to the risk-neutral density, given a known current stock price S_0 and given a *constant* parameter set Ψ. As discussed, least-squares estimation (LSE) is used to find the best guess for the unknown ideal parameter set. Alternatively, if we use a time series of stock prices $(S_t)_{0 \leq t \leq T}$, we would be dealing with the *joint* probability

$$p(S_1, ..., S_T|S_0; \Psi)$$

which we can rewrite as

$$p(S_1, ..., S_T|S_0; \Psi) = \prod_{t=1}^{T} p(S_t|S_{t-1}, ..., S_0; \Psi)$$

It is this joint probability that is commonly referred to as the *likelihood function* $L_{0:T}(\Psi)$. Maximizing the likelihood over the parameter set Ψ would provide us with the best parameter set for the statistical density $p(S_T|S_0; \Psi)$. Note that we are using a classical (frequentist) approach, in which we assume that the parameters are unknown but are fixed over $[0, T]$. In other words, we would be dealing with the *same* parameter set for any of the $p(S_t|S_{t-1}, ..., S_0; \Psi)$ with $1 \leq t \leq T$.

It is often convenient to work with the log of the likelihood function since this will produce a sum

$$\ln L_{0:T}(\Psi) = \sum_{t=1}^{T} \ln p(S_t|S_{t-1}, ..., S_0; \Psi)$$

The Justification for the MLE As explained, for instance, in [100], one justification of the maximization of the (log) likelihood function comes from the *Kullback-Leibler* (KL) distance. The KL distance is defined as[6]

$$d(p^*, p) = \int p^*(x)\left(\ln p^*(x) - \ln p(x)\right) dx$$

where $p^*(x)$ is the ideal density, and $p(x)$ is the density under estimation. We can write

$$d(p^*, p) = \mathbf{E}^* \ln\left(p^*(x)/p(x)\right)$$

Note that using the Jensen (log convexity) inequality

$$d(p^*, p) = -\mathbf{E}^* \ln\left(p(x)/p^*(x)\right) \geq -\ln\left(\mathbf{E}^*(p(x)/p^*(x))\right)$$

so

$$d(p^*, p) \geq -\ln \int p^*(x)p(x)/p^*(x)dx = 0$$

and $d(p, p^*) = 0$ if and only if $p = p^*$, which confirms that $d(.,.)$ is a distance. Now minimizing $d(p, p^*)$ over $p()$ would be equivalent to minimizing the term

$$-\int p^*(x)\ln p(x)dx$$

since the rest of the expression depends on $p^*()$ only. This latter expression could be written in the discrete framework, having T observations $S_1, \ldots, S_T$ as

$$-\sum_{t=1}^{T} \ln p(S_t)$$

because the observations are by assumption distributed according to the ideal $p^*()$. This justifies our maximizing

$$\prod_{t=1}^{T} p(S_t)$$

Note that in a pure parameter estimation, this would be the MLE approach. However, the minimization of the KL distance is more general and can allow for model identification.

Maximum likelihood estimation has many desirable asymptotic attributes as explained, for example, in [127]. Indeed, ML estimators are *consistent* and converge to the right parameter set as the number of observations

[6]Hereafter when the bounds are not specified, the integral is taken on the entire space of the integrand argument.

increases. They actually reach the lower bound for the error, referred to as the *Cramer-Rao bound*, which corresponds to the inverse of the *Fisher information matrix*.

Calling the first derivative of the log likelihood the *score* function

$$h(\Psi) = \frac{\partial \ln L_{0:T}(\Psi)}{\partial \Psi}$$

it is known that MLE could be interpreted as a special case of the general method of moments (GMM), where the moment $g(\Psi)$ such that

$$\mathbf{E}[g(\Psi)] = 0$$

is simply taken to be the above score function. Indeed we would then have

$$\mathbf{E}[h(\Psi)] = \int \frac{\partial \ln L_{0:T}(\Psi)}{\partial \Psi} L_{0:T}(\Psi) dz_{0:T} = 0$$

which means that

$$\int \frac{\partial L_{0:T}(\Psi)}{\partial \Psi} dz_{0:T} = 0$$

as previously discussed in the MLE.

Note that taking the derivative of the above with respect to the parameter set (using one-dimensional notations for simplicity)

$$\int \frac{\partial}{\partial \Psi} \left(h(\Psi) L_{0:T}(\Psi) \right) dz_{0:T} = 0$$

which will give us

$$\begin{aligned} \int \frac{\partial^2 \ln L_{0:T}(\Psi)}{\partial \Psi^2} L_{0:T}(\Psi) dz_{0:T} &= -\int \frac{\frac{\partial L_{0:T}(\Psi)}{\partial \Psi}}{L_{0:T}(\Psi)} \frac{\partial L_{0:T}(\Psi)}{\partial \Psi} dz_{0:T} \\ &= -\int \left(\frac{\partial \ln L_{0:T}(\Psi)}{\partial \Psi} \right)^2 L_{0:T}(\Psi) dz_{0:T} \end{aligned}$$

meaning that

$$\mathcal{J} = -E\left[\frac{\partial^2 \ln L_{0:T}(\Psi)}{\partial \Psi^2} \right] = E\left[\left(\frac{\partial \ln L_{0:T}(\Psi)}{\partial \Psi} \right)^2 \right]$$

which is referred to as the *information matrix identity*. As previously stated, asymptotically we have for the optimal parameter set $\hat{\Psi}$ and the ideal Ψ^*

$$\hat{\Psi} - \Psi^* \sim \mathcal{N}\left(0, \mathcal{J}^{-1}\right)$$

Likelihood Evaluation and Filtering For GARCH models, the likelihood is known under an integrated form. Indeed, calling u_t the mean-adjusted stock return, v_t the variance, and (B_t) a Gaussian sequence, we have for any GARCH model

$$u_t = h(v_t, B_t)$$

and

$$v_t = f(v_{t-1}, u_{t-1}; \Psi)$$

where $f()$ and $h()$ are two deterministic functions. This will allow us to directly determine and optimize[7]

$$L_{1:T}(\Psi) \propto -\sum_{t=1}^{T} \ln(v_t) + \frac{u_t^2}{v_t}$$

This is possible because GARCH models have one source of randomness and there is a time shift between the variance and the spot equations.

Unlike GARCH, most stochastic volatility models have two (imperfectly correlated) sources of randomness (B_t) and (Z_t) and have equations of the form

$$u_t = h(v_t, B_t)$$

$$v_t = f(v_{t-1}, Z_t; \Psi)$$

which means that the likelihood function is *not* directly known under an integrated form, and we need *filtering* techniques for its estimation and optimization.

Another justification for filtering is its application to parameter learning. As we shall see, in this approach we use the joint distribution of the hidden state and the parameters. In order to obtain the optimal value of the hidden state v_t given all the observations $z_{1:t}$, we need to use a filter.

Filtering

The idea here is to use the filtering theory for the estimation of stochastic volatility model parameters. What we are trying to do is to find the probability density function (pdf) corresponding to a state x_k at time step k given all the observations $z_{1:k}$ up to that time. Looking for the pdf $p(x_k|z_{1:k})$, we can proceed in two stages.

[7]We generally drop constant terms in the likelihood function because they do not affect the optimal arguments, hence the notation $L_{1:T}(\Psi) \propto \ldots$.

1. First we can write the time update iteration by applying the Chapman-Kolmogorov equation[8]

$$p(x_k|z_{1:k-1}) = \int p(x_k|x_{k-1}, z_{1:k-1})p(x_{k-1}|z_{1:k-1})dx_{k-1}$$
$$= \int p(x_k|x_{k-1})p(x_{k-1}|z_{1:k-1})dx_{k-1}$$

   by using the Markov property.
2. Following this, for the measurement update we use the Bayes rule

$$p(x_k|z_{1:k}) = \frac{p(z_k|x_k)p(x_k|z_{1:k-1})}{p(z_k|z_{1:k-1})}$$

   where the denominator $p(z_k|z_{1:k-1})$ could be written as

$$p(z_k|z_{1:k-1}) = \int p(z_k|x_k)p(x_k|z_{1:k-1})dx_k$$

   and corresponds to the likelihood function for the time-step k.

Proof: Indeed we have

$$\begin{aligned} p(x_k|z_{1:k}) &= \frac{p(z_{1:k}|x_k)p(x_k)}{p(z_{1:k})} \\ &= \frac{p(z_k, z_{1:k-1}|x_k)p(x_k)}{p(z_k, z_{1:k-1})} \\ &= \frac{p(z_k|z_{1:k-1}, x_k)p(z_{1:k-1}|x_k)p(x_k)}{p(z_k|z_{1:k-1})p(z_{1:k-1})} \\ &= \frac{p(z_k|z_{1:k-1}, x_k)p(x_k|z_{1:k-1})p(z_{1:k-1})p(x_k)}{p(z_k|z_{1:k-1})p(z_{1:k-1})p(x_k)} \\ &= \frac{p(z_k|x_k)p(x_k|z_{1:k-1})}{p(z_k|z_{1:k-1})} \end{aligned}$$

(QED)

Note that we use the fact that at time step k the value of $z_{1:k}$ is perfectly known.

The Kalman Filter (detailed below) is a special case where the distributions are normal and could be written as

$$p(x_k|z_{k-1}) = \mathcal{N}(\hat{x}_k^-, P_k^-)$$
$$p(x_k|z_k) = \mathcal{N}(\hat{x}_k, P_k)$$

[8]See Shreve [218], for instance.

In the special Gaussian case, each distribution could be entirely characterized via its first two moments. However, it is important to remember that the Kalman filter (KF) is optimal in the Gaussian *linear* case. In the nonlinear case, it will always be suboptimal.

Interpretation of the Kalman Gain The basic idea behind the KF is the following observation. Having x a normally distributed random variable with a mean m_x and variance S_{xx}, having z a normally distributed random variable with a mean m_z and variance S_{zz}, as well as $S_{zx} = S_{xz}$ the covariance between x and z, the conditional distribution of $x|z$ is also normal with

$$m_{x|z} = m_x + K(z - m_z)$$

with

$$K = S_{xz}S_{zz}^{-1}$$

Interpreting x as the hidden-state and z as the observation, the above matrix K would correspond to the Kalman filter in the linear case. We also have

$$S_{x|z} = S_{xx} - KS_{xz}$$

An alternative interpretation of the Kalman filter could be based on linear regression. Indeed, if we knew the time-series of (z_k) and (x_k), then the regression could be written as

$$x_k = \beta z_k + \alpha + \epsilon_k$$

with β the slope, α the intercept, and (ϵ_k) the residuals. It is known that under a least-square regression, we have

$$\beta = S_{xz}S_{zz}^{-1}$$

which again is the expression for the Kalman gain.

We now will describe various nonlinear extensions of the Kalman filter.

The Simple and Extended Kalman Filters

The first algorithms we choose here are the simple and extended Kalman filters,[9] owing to their well-known flexibility and ease of implementation. The simple or traditional Kalman filter (KF) applies to *linear* Gaussian cases, whereas the extended KF (EKF) could be used for nonlinear Gaussian cases via a first-order linearization. We shall therefore describe EKF and consider

---

[9]For a description see, for instance, Welch [233] or Harvey [129].

the simple KF as a special case. In order to clarify the notations, let us briefly rewrite the EKF equations. Given a dynamic process $\mathbf{x}_k$ following a possibly nonlinear *transition equation*

$$\mathbf{x}_k = \mathbf{f}(\mathbf{x}_{k-1}, \mathbf{w}_k) \tag{2.1}$$

we suppose we have a measurement $\mathbf{z}_k$ via a possibly nonlinear *observation equation*

$$\mathbf{z}_k = \mathbf{h}(\mathbf{x}_k, \mathbf{u}_k) \tag{2.2}$$

where $\mathbf{w}_k$ and $\mathbf{u}_k$ are two mutually uncorrelated sequences of temporally uncorrelated normal random variables with zero means and covariance matrices $\mathbf{Q}_k$, $\mathbf{R}_k$, respectively.[10] Moreover, $\mathbf{w}_k$ is uncorrelated with $\mathbf{x}_{k-1}$ and $\mathbf{u}_k$ uncorrelated with $\mathbf{x}_k$.

We define the *linear a priori* process estimate as

$$\hat{\mathbf{x}}_k^- = \mathbf{E}[\mathbf{x}_k] \tag{2.3}$$

which is the estimation at time step $k-1$ prior to measurement. Similarly, we define the *linear a posteriori* estimate

$$\hat{\mathbf{x}}_k = \mathbf{E}[\mathbf{x}_k|\mathbf{z}_k] \tag{2.4}$$

which is the estimation at time step k after the measurement.

We also have the corresponding estimation errors $\mathbf{e}_k^- = \mathbf{x}_k - \hat{\mathbf{x}}_k^-$ and $\mathbf{e}_k = \mathbf{x}_k - \hat{\mathbf{x}}_k$ and the estimate error covariances

$$\mathbf{P}_k^- = \mathbf{E}[\mathbf{e}_k^- \mathbf{e}_k^{-t}] \tag{2.5}$$

$$\mathbf{P}_k = \mathbf{E}[\mathbf{e}_k \mathbf{e}_k^t] \tag{2.6}$$

where the superscript t corresponds to the transpose operator.

We now define the Jacobian matrices of $\mathbf{f}$ with respect to the system process and the system noise as $\mathbf{A}_k$ and $\mathbf{W}_k$ respectively. Similarly, we define the gradient matrices of $\mathbf{h}$ with respect to the system process and the measurement noise as $\mathbf{H}_k$ and $\mathbf{U}_k$ respectively. More accurately, for every row i and column j we have

$$\mathbf{A}_{ij} = \partial \mathbf{f}_i / \partial \mathbf{x}_j \, (\hat{\mathbf{x}}_{k-1}, 0) \qquad \mathbf{W}_{ij} = \partial \mathbf{f}_i / \partial \mathbf{w}_j \, (\hat{\mathbf{x}}_{k-1}, 0)$$

$$\mathbf{H}_{ij} = \partial \mathbf{h}_i / \partial \mathbf{x}_j \, (\hat{\mathbf{x}}_k^-, 0) \qquad \mathbf{U}_{ij} = \partial \mathbf{h}_i / \partial \mathbf{u}_j \, (\hat{\mathbf{x}}_k^-, 0)$$

---

[10] Some prefer to write $\mathbf{x}_k = \mathbf{f}(\mathbf{x}_{k-1}, \mathbf{w}_{k-1})$. Needless to say, the two notations are equivalent.

We therefore have the following *time update* equations

$$\hat{\mathbf{x}}_k^- = \mathbf{f}(\hat{\mathbf{x}}_{k-1}, 0) \tag{2.7}$$

and

$$\mathbf{P}_k^- = \mathbf{A}_k \mathbf{P}_{k-1} \mathbf{A}_k^t + \mathbf{W}_k \mathbf{Q}_{k-1} \mathbf{W}_k^t \tag{2.8}$$

We define the Kalman gain as the matrix $\mathbf{K}_k$ used in the *measurement update* equations

$$\hat{\mathbf{x}}_k = \hat{\mathbf{x}}_k^- + \mathbf{K}_k(\mathbf{z}_k - \mathbf{h}(\hat{\mathbf{x}}_k^-, 0)) \tag{2.9}$$

and

$$\mathbf{P}_k = (\mathbf{I} - \mathbf{K}_k \mathbf{H}_k)\mathbf{P}_k^- \tag{2.10}$$

where $\mathbf{I}$ represents the identity matrix.

The optimal Kalman gain corresponds to the mean of the conditional distribution of $\mathbf{x}_k$ upon the observation $\mathbf{z}_k$ or, equivalently, the matrix that would minimize the mean square error $\mathbf{P}_k$ within the class of linear estimators. This optimal gain is

$$\mathbf{K}_k = \mathbf{P}_k^- \mathbf{H}_k^t (\mathbf{H}_k \mathbf{P}_k^- \mathbf{H}_k^t + \mathbf{U}_k \mathbf{R}_k \mathbf{U}_k^t)^{-1} \tag{2.11}$$

The foregoing equations complete the Kalman filter algorithm.

Another Interpretation of the Kalman Gain Note that an easy way to observe that K_k minimizes the a posteriori error covariance P_k is to consider the one-dimensional linear case

$$\hat{x}_k = \hat{x}_k^- + K_k(z_k - H_k \hat{x}_k^-) = \hat{x}_k^- + K_k(z_k - H_k x_k + H_k e_k^-)$$

so

$$e_k = x_k - \hat{x}_k = e_k^- - K_k(u_k + H_k e_k^-)$$

Therefore

$$P_k = \mathbf{E}(e_k^2) = P_k^- + K_k^2(R_k + H_k^2 P_k^- + 0) - 2K_k H_k P_k^-$$

and taking the derivative with respect to K_k and setting it to zero, we get

$$K_k = \frac{P_k^- H_k}{H_k^2 P_k^- + R_k}$$

which is the one-dimensional expression for the linear Kalman gain.

Residuals, Mean Price Error (MPE) and Root Mean Square Error (RMSE) In what follows we shall call the estimated observations $\hat{z}_k^-$. For the simple and extended Kalman filters, we have

$$\hat{z}_k^- = h(\hat{x}_k^-, 0)$$

The *residuals* are the observation errors, defined as

$$\tilde{z}_k = z_k - \hat{z}_k^-$$

Needless to say, the smaller these residuals, the higher the quality of the filter. Therefore, to measure the performance, we define the mean price error (MPE) and root mean square error (RMSE) as the mean and standard deviation of the residuals

$$MPE = \frac{1}{N}\sum_{k=1}^{N} \tilde{z}_k$$

$$RMSE = \sqrt{\frac{1}{N}\sum_{k=1}^{N}(\tilde{z}_k - MPE)^2}$$

The Unscented Kalman Filter

Recently, Julier and Uhlmann [166] proposed a new extension of the Kalman filter to nonlinear systems, one that is completely different from the EKF. They argue that EKF could be difficult to implement and, more importantly, difficult to tune and that it would be reliable only for systems that are almost linear within the update intervals. The new method, called the *unscented Kalman filter* (UKF), will calculate the mean to a higher order of accuracy than the EKF and the covariance to the same order of accuracy. Unlike the EKF, this method does not require any Jacobian calculation since it *does not approximate the nonlinear functions* of the process and the observation. Therefore, it uses the true nonlinear models but *approximates the distribution* of the state random variable $\mathbf{x}_k$ by applying an *unscented transformation* to it. As we will see in the following, we construct a set of *sigma points* that capture the mean and covariance of the original distribution and, when propagated through the true nonlinear system, capture the posterior mean and covariance accurately to the third order.

Similarly to the EKF, we start with an initial choice for the state vector $\hat{\mathbf{x}}_0 = \mathbf{E}[\mathbf{x}_0]$ and its covariance matrix $\mathbf{P}_0 = \mathbf{E}[(\mathbf{x}_0 - \hat{\mathbf{x}}_0)(\mathbf{x}_0 - \hat{\mathbf{x}}_0)^t]$. We then concatenate the space vector with the system noise and the observation noise[11] and create an *augmented* state vector for each step k greater than one

$$\mathbf{x}^a_{k-1} = \begin{pmatrix} \mathbf{x}_{k-1} \\ \mathbf{w}_{k-1} \\ \mathbf{u}_{k-1} \end{pmatrix}$$

and therefore

$$\hat{\mathbf{x}}^a_{k-1} = \begin{pmatrix} \hat{\mathbf{x}}_{k-1} \\ \mathbf{0} \\ \mathbf{0} \end{pmatrix}$$

and

$$\mathbf{P}^a_{k-1} = \begin{pmatrix} \mathbf{P}_{k-1} & \mathbf{P}_{xw}(k-1|k-1) & \mathbf{0} \\ \mathbf{P}_{xw}(k-1|k-1) & \mathbf{P}_{ww}(k-1|k-1) & \mathbf{0} \\ \mathbf{0} & \mathbf{0} & \mathbf{P}_{uu}(k-1|k-1) \end{pmatrix}$$

for each iteration k. The augmented state will therefore have a dimension $n_a = n_x + n_w + n_u$.

We then need to calculate the corresponding *sigma points* through the unscented transformation:

$$\chi^a_{k-1}(0) = \hat{\mathbf{x}}^a_{k-1}$$

For $i = 1, ..., n_a$

$$\chi^a_{k-1}(i) = \hat{\mathbf{x}}^a_{k-1} + \left(\sqrt{(n_a + \lambda)\mathbf{P}^a_{k-1}}\right)_i$$

and for $i = n_a + 1, ..., 2n_a$

$$\chi^a_{k-1}(i) = \hat{\mathbf{x}}^a_{k-1} - \left(\sqrt{(n_a + \lambda)\mathbf{P}^a_{k-1}}\right)_{i-n_a}$$

where the above subscripts i and $i - n_a$ correspond to the ith and $i - n_a^{th}$ columns of the square-root matrix.[12] This prepares us for the time update and the measurement update equations, similarly to the EKF.

The *time update* equations are

$$\chi_{k|k-1}(i) = \mathbf{f}(\chi^x_{k-1}(i), \chi^w_{k-1}(i))$$

---

[11] This space augmentation will not be necessary if we have *additive* noises as in $x_k = f(x_{k-1}) + w_{k-1}$ and $z_k = h(x_k) + u_k$.

[12] The square-root matrix is calculated via singular value decomposition (SVD) and Cholesky factorization [204]. In case $\mathbf{P}^a_{k-1}$ is not positive-definite, one could, for example, use a truncation procedure.

for $i = 0, \ldots, 2n_a + 1$ and

$$\hat{\mathbf{x}}_k^- = \sum_{i=0}^{2n_a} W_i^{(m)} \chi_{k|k-1}(i)$$

and

$$\mathbf{P}_k^- = \sum_{i=0}^{2n_a} W_i^{(c)} (\chi_{k|k-1}(i) - \hat{\mathbf{x}}_k^-)(\chi_{k|k-1}(i) - \hat{\mathbf{x}}_k^-)^t$$

where the superscripts x and w respectively correspond to the state and system-noise portions of the augmented state.

The $W_i^{(m)}$ and $W_i^{(c)}$ weights are defined as

$$W_0^{(m)} = \frac{\lambda}{n_a + \lambda}$$

and

$$W_0^{(c)} = \frac{\lambda}{n_a + \lambda} + (1 - \alpha^2 + \beta)$$

and for $i = 1, \ldots, 2n_a$

$$W_i^{(m)} = W_i^{(c)} = \frac{1}{2(n_a + \lambda)}$$

The scaling parameters α, β, κ and $\lambda = \alpha^2(n_a + \kappa) - n_a$ will be chosen for tuning.

We also define within the time update equations

$$\mathbf{Z}_{k|k-1}(i) = \mathbf{h}(\chi_{k|k-1}(i), \chi_{k-1}^u(i))$$

and

$$\hat{\mathbf{z}}_k^- = \sum_{i=0}^{2n_a} W_i^{(m)} \mathbf{Z}_{k|k-1}(i)$$

where the superscript u corresponds to the observation-noise portion of the augmented state.

As for the *measurement update* equations, we have

$$\mathbf{P}_{z_k z_k} = \sum_{i=0}^{2n_a} W_i^{(c)} (\mathbf{Z}_{k|k-1}(i) - \hat{\mathbf{z}}_k^-)(\mathbf{Z}_{k|k-1}(i) - \hat{\mathbf{z}}_k^-)^t$$

and

$$\mathbf{P}_{x_k z_k} = \sum_{i=0}^{2n_a} W_i^{(c)} (\chi_{k|k-1}(i) - \hat{\mathbf{x}}_k^-)(\mathbf{Z}_{k|k-1}(i) - \hat{\mathbf{z}}_k^-)^t$$

which gives us the Kalman gain

$$\mathbf{K}_k = \mathbf{P}_{x_k z_k} \mathbf{P}_{z_k z_k}^{-1}$$

and we get as before

$$\hat{\mathbf{x}}_k = \hat{\mathbf{x}}_k^- + \mathbf{K}_k(\mathbf{z}_k - \hat{\mathbf{z}}_k^-)$$

where again $\mathbf{z}_k$ is the observation at time (iteration) k. Also, we have

$$\mathbf{P}_k = \mathbf{P}_k^- - \mathbf{K}_k \mathbf{P}_{z_k z_k} \mathbf{K}_k^t$$

which completes the measurement update equations.

Kushner's Nonlinear Filter

It would be instructive to compare this algorithm to the nonlinear filtering algorithm based on an approximation of the conditional distribution by Kushner et al. [174]. In this approach, the authors suggest using a Gaussian quadrature in order to calculate the integral at the measurement update (or the time update) step.[13] As the Kushner paper indicates, having an N-dimensional normal random variable $\mathbf{X} = \mathcal{N}(\mathbf{m}, \mathbf{P})$, with $\mathbf{m}$ and $\mathbf{P}$ the corresponding mean and covariance, for a polynomial G of degree $2M - 1$, we can write[14]

$$\mathbf{E}[G(\mathbf{X})] = \frac{1}{(2\pi)^{\frac{N}{2}} |\mathbf{P}|^{\frac{1}{2}}} \int G(\mathbf{y}) \exp\left[-\frac{(\mathbf{y}-\mathbf{m})^t \mathbf{P}^{-1} (\mathbf{y}-\mathbf{m})}{2}\right] d\mathbf{y}$$

which is equal to

$$\mathbf{E}[G(\mathbf{X})] = \sum_{i_1=1}^{M} \ldots \sum_{i_N=1}^{M} w_{i_1} \ldots w_{i_N} G\left(\mathbf{m} + \sqrt{\mathbf{P}}\zeta\right)$$

where $\zeta^t = (\zeta_{i_1}, \ldots, \zeta_{i_N})$ is the vector of the Gauss-Hermite roots of order M and $w_{i_1}, \ldots, w_{i_N}$ are the corresponding weights. Note that even if both Kushner's NLF and UKF use Gaussian qadratures, UKF only uses $2N + 1$ sigma points, whereas NLF needs M^N points for the integral computation.

Kushner and Budhiraja suggest using this technique primarily for the measurement update (filtering) step. They claim that provided this step is properly implemented, the time update (prediction) step can be carried out via a linearization similar to the EKF.

---

[13]The analogy between Kushner's nonlinear filter and the unscented Kalman filter, has already been studied in Ito & Xiong [151].

[14]A description of the Gaussian quadrature can be found in Press et al. [204].

Details of the Kushner algorithm Let us use the same notations as for the UKF algorithm. We therefore have the augmented state $\mathbf{x}^a_{k-1}$ and its covariance $\mathbf{P}^a_{k-1}$ as before. Here, for a quadrature order of M on an N-dimensional variable, the sigma points are defined for $j = 1, ..., N$ and $i_j = 1, ..., M$ as

$$\chi^a_{k-1}(i_1, ..., i_N) = \hat{\mathbf{x}}^a_{k-1} + \sqrt{\mathbf{P}^a_{k-1}}\zeta(i_1, ..., i_N)$$

where the square root here corresponds to the Cholesky factorization, and again $\zeta(i_1, \ldots, i_N)[j] = \zeta_{i_j}$ for each j between 1 and the dimension N and each i_j between 1 and the quadrature order M. Similarly to the UKF, we have the time update equations

$$\chi_{k|k-1}(i_1, ..., i_N) = \mathbf{f}\left(\chi^x_{k-1}(i_1, ..., i_N), \chi^w_{k-1}(i_1, ..., i_N)\right)$$

but now

$$\hat{\mathbf{x}}^-_k = \sum_{i_1=1}^{M} ... \sum_{i_N=1}^{M} w_{i_1}...w_{i_N}\chi_{k|k-1}(i_1, ..., i_N)$$

and

$$\mathbf{P}^-_k = \sum_{i_1=1}^{M} ... \sum_{i_N=1}^{M} w_{i_1}...w_{i_N}(\chi_{k|k-1}(i_1, ..., i_N) - \hat{\mathbf{x}}^-_k)(\chi_{k|k-1}(i_1, ..., i_N) - \hat{\mathbf{x}}^-_k)^t$$

Again, we have

$$\mathbf{Z}_{k|k-1}(i_1, ..., i_N) = \mathbf{h}\left(\chi_{k|k-1}(i_1, ..., i_N), \chi^u_{k-1}(i_1, ..., i_N)\right)$$

and

$$\hat{\mathbf{z}}^-_k = \sum_{i_1=1}^{M} ... \sum_{i_N=1}^{M} w_{i_1}...w_{i_N}\mathbf{Z}_{k|k-1}(i_1, ..., i_N)$$

Therefore, the measurement update equations will be

$$\mathbf{P}_{z_k z_k} = \sum_{i_1=1}^{M} ... \sum_{i_N=1}^{M} w_{i_1}...w_{i_N}(\mathbf{Z}_{k|k-1}(i_1, ..., i_N) - \hat{\mathbf{z}}^-_k)(\mathbf{Z}_{k|k-1}(i_1, ..., i_N) - \hat{\mathbf{z}}^-_k)^t$$

and

$$\mathbf{P}_{x_k z_k} = \sum_{i_1=1}^{M} ... \sum_{i_N=1}^{M} w_{i_1}...w_{i_N}(\chi_{k|k-1}(i_1, ..., i_N) - \hat{\mathbf{x}}^-_k)(\mathbf{Z}_{k|k-1}(i_1, ..., i_N) - \hat{\mathbf{z}}^-_k)^t$$

which gives us the Kalman gain

$$\mathbf{K}_k = \mathbf{P}_{x_k z_k}\mathbf{P}^{-1}_{z_k z_k}$$

and we get as before

$$\hat{\mathbf{x}}_k = \hat{\mathbf{x}}^-_k + \mathbf{K}_k(\mathbf{z}_k - \hat{\mathbf{z}}^-_k)$$

where again $\mathbf{z}_k$ is the observation at time (iteration) k.

Also, we have

$$\mathbf{P}_k = \mathbf{P}^-_k - \mathbf{K}_k\mathbf{P}_{z_k z_k}\mathbf{K}^t_k$$

which completes the measurement update equations.

When $N = 1$ and $\lambda = 2$, the numeric integration in the UKF will correspond to a Gauss-Hermite quadrature of order $M = 3$. However, in the UKF we can tune the filter and reduce the higher term errors via the previously mentioned parameters α and β.

Note that when $h(x, u)$ is strongly nonlinear, the Gauss Hermite integration is not efficient for evaluating the moments of the measurement update equation, since the term $p(z_k|x_k)$ contains the exponent $z_k - h(x_k, u_k)$. The iterative methods based on the idea of importance sampling proposed in [174] correct this problem at the price of a strong increase in computation time. As suggested in [151], one way to avoid this integration would be to make the additional hypothesis that $x_k, h(x_k, u_k)|z_{1:k-1}$ is Gaussian.

Parameter Learning

One important issue to realize is that the Kalman filter can be used either for state estimation (filtering) or for parameter estimation (machine learning). When we have both state estimation *and* parameter estimation, we are dealing with a dual estimation or a joint estimation. The latter case is the one concerning us because we are estimating the state volatility as well as the model parameters. As explained in Haykin's book [133], in a dual filter we separate the state vector from the parameters and we apply two intertwined filters to them. By contrast, in a joint filter, we concatenate the state vector and the parameters and apply one filter to this augmented state. Note that in the dual filter we need to compute recurrent derivatives with respect to parameters, whereas in a joint filter no such step is needed.

It is possible to interpret the joint filter in the following way. In a regular filter, that is, filtering of the state x_k for a fixed set of parameters Ψ_0, we are maximizing the conditional density

$$p(x_{1:k}|z_{1:k}, \Psi_0)$$

and as we said, to do that we write

$$p(x_{1:k}|z_{1:k},\Psi_0) = \frac{p(z_{1:k}|x_{1:k},\Psi_0)p(x_{1:k}|\Psi_0)}{p(z_{1:k}|\Psi_0)}$$

so we maximize the above with respect to the state x_k for a given set of parameters. This means that the optimal state $\hat{x}_{1:k}$ for a given parameter set is given by

$$\hat{x}_{1:k} = argmax[p(z_{1:k}, x_{1:k}|\Psi_0)]$$

As we will see, in an MLE approach we use this optimal state filtering for *each* iteration of the likelihood maximization over the parameter set Ψ.

In a joint filter, we are directly optimizing the joint conditional density

$$p(x_{1:k}, \Psi|z_{1:k})$$

which we can also write as

$$p(x_{1:k}, \Psi|z_{1:k}) = \frac{p(z_{1:k}|x_{1:k},\Psi)p(x_{1:k}|\Psi)p(\Psi)}{p(z_{1:k})}$$

given that the denominator is functionally independent of $x_{1:k}$ and Ψ, and given that $p(\Psi)$ contains no prior information,[15] the maximization will be upon

$$p(z_{1:k}|x_{1:k},\Psi)p(x_{1:k}|\Psi) = p(z_{1:k}, x_{1:k}|\Psi)$$

That is to say, in a joint filter, the optimal state $\hat{x}_{1:k}$ and parameter set $\hat{\Psi}$ are found by writing

$$(\hat{x}_{1:k}, \hat{\Psi}) = argmax\,[p(z_{1:k}, x_{1:k}|\Psi)]$$

In what follows, we apply the joint EKF methodology to a few examples.

An Illustration Before using this technique for the stochastic volatility model, let us take a simple example

$$\xi_k = \xi_{k-1} + \pi + 0.10w_k$$

and

$$z_k = \xi_k + 0.10u_k$$

where $\pi \approx 3.14159$ and w_k, u_k are independent Gaussian random variables. The linear state-space system could be written as

$$\mathbf{x}_k = \begin{pmatrix} \xi_k \\ \pi_k \end{pmatrix} = \begin{pmatrix} 1 & 1 \\ 0 & 1 \end{pmatrix} \mathbf{x}_{k-1} + 0.10 \begin{pmatrix} w_k \\ 0 \end{pmatrix}$$

[15] Again, we are in a frequentist framework, not Bayesian.

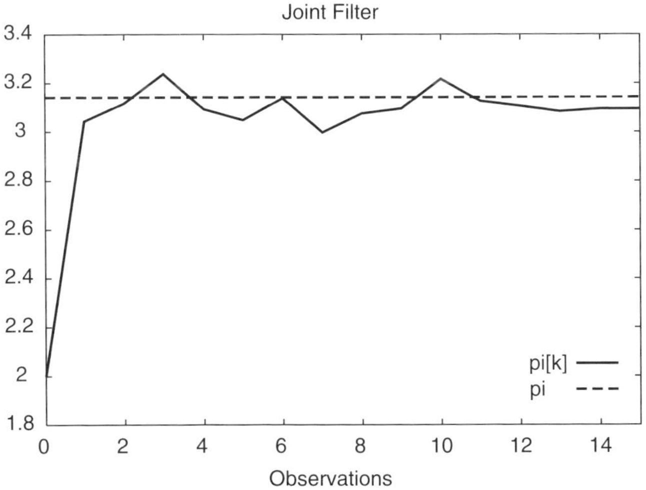

FIGURE 2.6 A Simple Example for the Joint Filter. The convergence toward the constant parameter π happens after a few iterations.

and

$$z_k = (1 \quad 0)\,\mathbf{x}_k + 0.10u_k$$

We choose the initial values $\xi_0 = z_0 = 0$ and $\pi_0 = 1.0$. We also take $\mathbf{Q} = 0.1\mathbf{I}_2$ and $R = 0.10$. Applying the Kalman filter to an artificially generated data set, we plot the resulting π_k in Figure 2.6. As we can see, the parameter converges very quickly to its true value.

Even if we associated a noise of 0.10 to the constant parameter π, we can see that for 5000 observations, taking the mean of the filtered state between observations 20 and 5000 we get

$$\hat{\pi} = 3.141390488$$

which is very close to the value 3.14159 used in data generation process.

Joint Filtering Examples After going through this simple example, we now apply the JF technique to our stochastic volatility problem. We shall study a few examples in order to find the best state-space representation.

Example 1 Our first example would be the square-root stochastic volatility model

$$\ln S_k = \ln S_{k-1} + \left(\mu_S - \frac{1}{2}v_{k-1}\right)\Delta t + \sqrt{v_{k-1}}\sqrt{\Delta t}B_{k-1}$$

$$v_k = v_{k-1} + (\omega - \theta v_{k-1})\Delta t + \xi\sqrt{v_{k-1}}\sqrt{\Delta t}Z_{k-1}$$

To simplify we suppose that the value of μ_S is known. We can now define the state variable[16]

$$\mathbf{x}_k = \begin{pmatrix} \ln S_k \\ v_k \\ \omega \\ \theta \\ \xi \\ \rho \end{pmatrix}$$

and the system noise

$$\mathbf{w}_k = \begin{pmatrix} B_k \\ Z_k \end{pmatrix}$$

with its covariance matrix

$$\mathbf{Q}_k = \begin{pmatrix} 1 & \rho \\ \rho & 1 \end{pmatrix}$$

and therefore

$$\mathbf{x}_k = \mathbf{f}(\mathbf{x}_{k-1}, \mathbf{w}_{k-1}) = \begin{pmatrix} \ln S_{k-1} + (\mu_S - \frac{1}{2}v_{k-1})\Delta t + \sqrt{v_{k-1}}\sqrt{\Delta t}B_{k-1} \\ v_{k-1} + (\omega - \theta v_{k-1})\Delta t + \xi\sqrt{v_{k-1}}\sqrt{\Delta t}Z_{k-1} \\ \omega \\ \theta \\ \xi \\ \rho \end{pmatrix}$$

and therefore the Jacobian $\mathbf{A}_k$ is

$$\mathbf{A}_k = \begin{pmatrix} 1 & -\frac{1}{2}\Delta t & 0 & 0 & 0 & 0 \\ 0 & 1 - \theta\Delta t & \Delta t & -v_{k-1}\Delta t & 0 & 0 \\ 0 & 0 & 1 & 0 & 0 & 0 \\ 0 & 0 & 0 & 1 & 0 & 0 \\ 0 & 0 & 0 & 0 & 1 & 0 \\ 0 & 0 & 0 & 0 & 0 & 1 \end{pmatrix}$$

and

$$\mathbf{W}_k = \begin{pmatrix} \sqrt{v_{k-1}}\sqrt{\Delta t} & 0 \\ 0 & \xi\sqrt{v_{k-1}}\sqrt{\Delta t} \\ 0 & 0 \\ 0 & 0 \\ 0 & 0 \\ 0 & 0 \end{pmatrix}$$

[16]In reality we should write the estimation parameters ω_k, θ_k, ξ_k, and ρ_k. However, we drop the indexes for simplifying the notations.

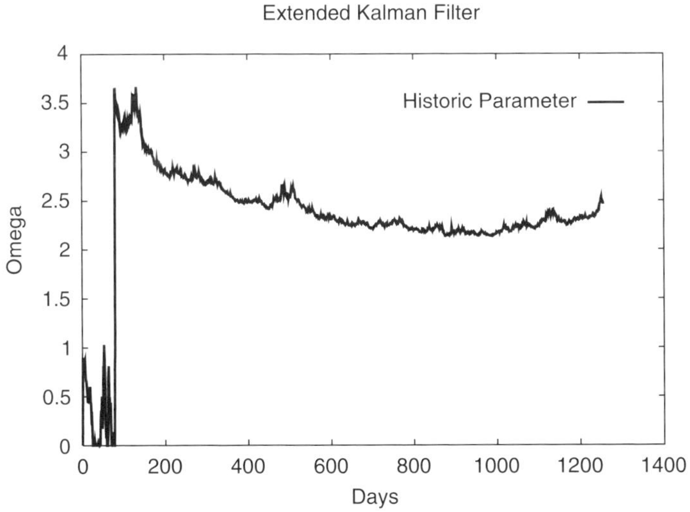

FIGURE 2.7 The EKF Estimation (Example 1) for the Drift Parameter ω. The SPX index daily close prices were used over five years from 10/01/1996 to 09/28/2001. The convergence is fairly good.

having the measurement $z_k = \ln S_k$ we can write

$$\mathbf{H}_k = \begin{pmatrix} 1 & 0 & 0 & 0 & 0 & 0 \end{pmatrix}$$

and $U_k = 0$.

We could, however, introduce a measurement noise R corresponding to the intraday stock price movements and the bid-ask spread, in which case we would have $z_k = \ln S_k + R\epsilon_k$, where ϵ_k represents a sequence of uncorrelated standard normal random variables. This means that $R_k = R$ and $U_k = 1$. We can then *tune* the value of R in order to get more stable results (Figures 2.7 through 2.10).

Example 2 The same exact methodology could be used in the GARCH framework. We define the state variable $\mathbf{x}_k^t = (\ln S_k, v_k, \omega_0, \alpha, \beta, c)$ and take for observation the logarithm of the actual stock price S_k. The system could be written as

$$\mathbf{x}_k = \mathbf{f}(\mathbf{x}_{k-1}, \mathbf{w}_{k-1})$$

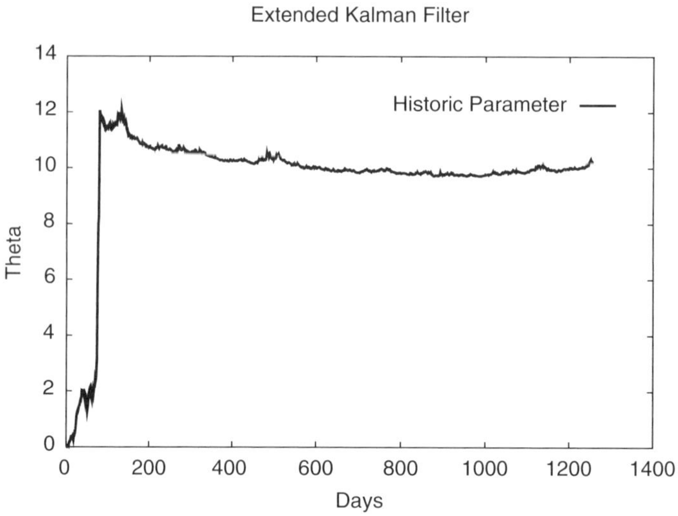

FIGURE 2.8 The EKF Estimation (Example 1) for the Drift Parameter θ. The SPX index daily close prices were used over five years from 10/01/1996 to 09/28/2001. The convergence is fairly good.

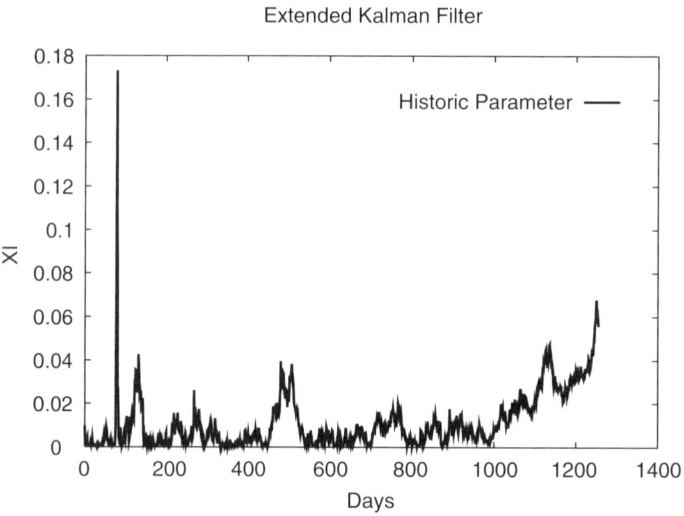

FIGURE 2.9 The EKF Estimation (Example 1) for the Volatility-of-Volatility Parameter ξ. The SPX index daily close prices were used over five years from 10/01/1996 to 09/28/2001. The convergence is rather poor. We shall explain this via the concept of observability.

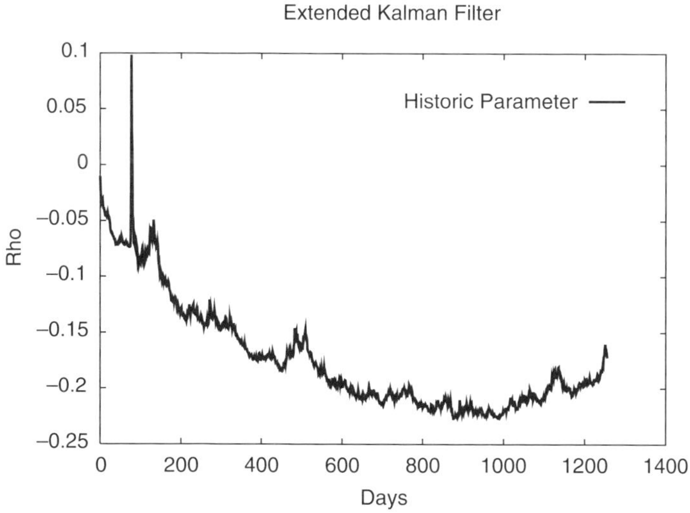

FIGURE 2.10 The EKF Estimation (Example 1) for the correlation parameter ρ. The SPX index daily close prices were used over five years from 10/01/1996 to 09/28/2001. The convergence is rather poor. We shall explain this via the concept of observability.

with $\mathbf{w}_k = B_k$ a one-dimensional source of noise with a variance $Q_k = 1$ and

$$\mathbf{f}(\mathbf{x}_{k-1}, \mathbf{w}_{k-1}) = \begin{pmatrix} \ln S_{k-1} + \left(\mu_S - \frac{1}{2}v_{k-1}\right) + \sqrt{v_{k-1}}B_{k-1} \\ \omega_0 + \beta v_{k-1} + \alpha(B_{k-1} - c\sqrt{v_{k-1}})^2 \\ \omega_0 \\ \alpha \\ \beta \\ c \end{pmatrix}$$

and the Jacobian

$$\mathbf{A}_k = \begin{pmatrix} 1 & -\frac{1}{2} & 0 & 0 & 0 & 0 \\ 0 & \beta + \alpha c^2 & 1 & c^2 v_{k-1} & v_{k-1} & 2\alpha c v_{k-1} \\ 0 & 0 & 1 & 0 & 0 & 0 \\ 0 & 0 & 0 & 1 & 0 & 0 \\ 0 & 0 & 0 & 0 & 1 & 0 \\ 0 & 0 & 0 & 0 & 0 & 1 \end{pmatrix}$$

and

$$\mathbf{W}_k = \begin{pmatrix} \sqrt{v_{k-1}} \\ -2\alpha c\sqrt{v_{k-1}} \\ 0 \\ 0 \\ 0 \\ 0 \end{pmatrix}$$

The observation z_k will be

$$\mathbf{z}_k = \mathbf{h}(\mathbf{x}_k) = \ln(S_k)$$

exactly as in the previous example. The rest of the algorithm would therefore be identical to the one included in Example 1.

Example 3 In Examples 1 and 2, we included all the variables in the system process and we observed part of the system. It is also possible to separate the measurement and the system variables as follows.

Taking a general discrete stochastic volatility process as[17]

$$\ln S_k = \ln S_{k-1} + \left(\mu_S - \frac{1}{2}v_k\right)\Delta t + \sqrt{v_k}\sqrt{\Delta t}B_k$$

$$v_k = v_{k-1} + b(v_{k-1})\Delta t + a(v_{k-1})\sqrt{\Delta t}Z_k$$

with B_k and Z_k two Normal random sequences with a mean of zero and variance one, with a correlation equal to ρ.

Posing $y_k = \sqrt{v_k}Z_k$ and performing the usual Cholesky factorization $B_k = \rho Z_k + \sqrt{1-\rho^2}X_k$, where Z_k and X_k are uncorrelated, we can now take the case of a square-root process and write

$$\mathbf{x}_k = \begin{pmatrix} v_k \\ y_k \\ \omega \\ \theta \\ \xi \\ \rho \end{pmatrix}$$

and $\mathbf{x}_k = \mathbf{f}(\mathbf{x}_{k-1}, Z_k)$ with

$$\mathbf{f}(x_{k-1}, Z_k) = \begin{pmatrix} v_{k-1} + (\omega - \theta v_{k-1})\Delta t + \xi\sqrt{v_{k-1}}\sqrt{\Delta t}Z_k \\ \left(v_{k-1} + (\omega - \theta v_{k-1})\Delta t + \xi\sqrt{v_{k-1}}\sqrt{\Delta t}Z_k\right)^{\frac{1}{2}} Z_k \\ \omega + QZ_k \\ \theta + QZ_k \\ \xi + QZ_k \\ \rho + QZ_k \end{pmatrix}$$

[17]Note that the indexing here is slightly different from the previous examples.

which provides us with the Jacobian

$$\mathbf{A}_k = \begin{pmatrix} 1-\theta\Delta t & 0 & \Delta t & -v_{k-1}\Delta t & 0 & 0 \\ 0 & 0 & 0 & 0 & 0 & 0 \\ 0 & 0 & 1 & 0 & 0 & 0 \\ 0 & 0 & 0 & 1 & 0 & 0 \\ 0 & 0 & 0 & 0 & 1 & 0 \\ 0 & 0 & 0 & 0 & 0 & 1 \end{pmatrix}$$

and

$$\mathbf{W}_k = \begin{pmatrix} \xi\sqrt{v_{k-1}}\sqrt{\Delta t} \\ (v_{k-1} + (\omega - \theta v_{k-1})\Delta t)^{\frac{1}{2}} \\ Q \\ Q \\ Q \\ Q \end{pmatrix}$$

The measurement equation is

$$z_k = \ln\left(\frac{S_k}{S_{k-1}}\right) = \left(\mu_S - \frac{1}{2}v_k\right)\Delta t + \rho\sqrt{\Delta t}y_k + \sqrt{1-\rho^2}\sqrt{v_k}\sqrt{\Delta t}X_k$$

and therefore

$$\mathbf{H}_k = \begin{pmatrix} -\frac{1}{2}\Delta t & \rho\sqrt{\Delta t} & 0 & 0 & 0 & 0 \end{pmatrix}$$

with $u_k = X_k$ and $U_k = \sqrt{1-\rho^2}\sqrt{v_k}\sqrt{\Delta t}$, which completes our set of equations. Again we could tune the system noise Q in order to obtain more stable results.

Observability From the preceding tests, it seems that the EKF provides us with a nonrobust calibration methodology. Indeed the results are very sensitive to the choice of system noise Q and observation noise R. We chose for this case $Q = 10^{-3}$ and $R \approx 0$.

This brings to attention the issue of *observability*. A nonlinear system with a state vector $\mathbf{x}_k$ of dimension n is observable if

$$\mathbf{O} = \begin{pmatrix} \mathbf{H} \\ \mathbf{HA} \\ \mathbf{HA}^2 \\ \dots \\ \mathbf{HA}^{n-1} \end{pmatrix}$$

has a full rank of n. For an explanation, refer to Reif et al. [205].

It is fairly easy to see that among the foregoing examples, the first and third (corresponding to the stochastic volatility formulation) have for the observation matrix **O** a rank of four and therefore are *not* observable. This explains why they do not converge well and are so sensitive to the tuning parameters Q and R. This means that the choices of the state variables for Examples 1 and 3 were rather poor. One reason is that in our state-space choice, we considered

$$z_k = h(v_{k-1}, ...)$$

and

$$x_k = (..., v_k, ...) = f(x_{k-1}, ...)$$

which implies that

$$\frac{\partial h}{\partial v_k} = 0$$

We shall see how to correct this in the next section by choosing a more appropriate state-space representation.

The One-Dimensional State within the Joint Filter Considering the state equation

$$\begin{aligned} v_k = {} & v_{k-1} + (\omega - \theta v_{k-1})\Delta t + \xi\sqrt{v_{k-1}}\sqrt{\Delta t}Z_{k-1} \\ & - \rho\xi\left[\ln S_{k-1} + \left(\mu_S - \frac{1}{2}v_{k-1}\right)\Delta t + \sqrt{v_{k-1}}\sqrt{\Delta t}B_{k-1} - \ln S_k\right] \end{aligned}$$

posing for every k

$$\tilde{Z}_k = \frac{1}{\sqrt{1-\rho^2}}(Z_k - \rho B_k)$$

we will have as expected $\tilde{Z}_k$ *uncorrelated* with B_k. Therefore, considering the augmented state

$$\mathbf{x}_k = \begin{pmatrix} v_k \\ \omega \\ \theta \\ \xi \\ \rho \end{pmatrix}$$

we will have the state transition equation

$$\mathbf{f}(\mathbf{x}_{k-1}, \tilde{Z}_{k-1}) = \begin{pmatrix} v_{k-1} + [(\omega - \rho\xi\mu_S) - \left(\theta - \frac{1}{2}\rho\xi\right)v_{k-1}]\Delta t + \rho\xi\ln\left(\frac{S_k}{S_{k-1}}\right) + \xi\sqrt{1-\rho^2}\sqrt{v_{k-1}}\sqrt{\Delta t}\tilde{Z}_{k-1} \\ \omega \\ \theta \\ \xi \\ \rho \end{pmatrix}$$

and the measurement equation would be

$$z_k = \ln S_{k+1} = \ln S_k + \left(\mu_S - \frac{1}{2}v_k\right)\Delta t + \sqrt{v_k}\sqrt{\Delta t}B_k$$

The corresponding EKF Jacobians for this system are

$$\mathbf{A}_k = \begin{pmatrix} 1-\left(\theta-\frac{1}{2}\rho\xi\right)\Delta t & \Delta t & -v_{k-1}\Delta t & \rho\left(\ln\left(\frac{S_k}{S_{k-1}}\right)-\left(\mu_S-\frac{1}{2}v_{k-1}\right)\Delta t\right) & \xi\left(\ln\left(\frac{S_k}{S_{k-1}}\right)-\left(\mu_S-\frac{1}{2}v_{k-1}\right)\Delta t\right) \\ 0 & 1 & 0 & 0 & 0 \\ 0 & 0 & 1 & 0 & 0 \\ 0 & 0 & 0 & 1 & 0 \\ 0 & 0 & 0 & 0 & 1 \end{pmatrix}$$

$$\mathbf{W}_k = \begin{pmatrix} \xi\sqrt{1-\rho^2}\sqrt{v_{k-1}}\sqrt{\Delta t} \\ 0 \\ 0 \\ 0 \\ 0 \end{pmatrix}$$

$$\mathbf{H}_k = \left(-\tfrac{1}{2}\Delta t \quad 0 \quad 0 \quad 0 \quad 0\right)$$

$$\mathbf{U}_k = \sqrt{v_k}\sqrt{\Delta t}$$

It is easy to check that this system is observable since the observation matrix $\mathbf{O}_k$ is of full rank. This shows that our state-space choice is better than the previous ones.

The UKF would be implemented in a fashion similar to that of the transition and observation equations above. Again, for the UKF, we would *not* need to compute any Jacobians.

An important issue to consider is that of *tuning*. We could add extra noise to the observation and hence lower the weight associated with the observations. In which case, after choosing a tuning parameter R, we would write

$$\mathbf{U}_k = \left(\sqrt{v_k}\sqrt{\Delta t} \quad R\right)$$

and

$$\mathbf{U}_k\mathbf{U}_k^t = v_k\Delta t + R^2$$

The choice of the initial conditions and the tuning parameters could make the algorithm fail or succeed. It therefore seems that there is little robustness in this procedure.

We consider the example of 5000 data points artificially produced via a Heston stochastic volatility process with a parameter set

$$\Psi^* = (\omega = 0.10, \theta = 10.0, \xi = 0.03, \rho = -0.50)$$

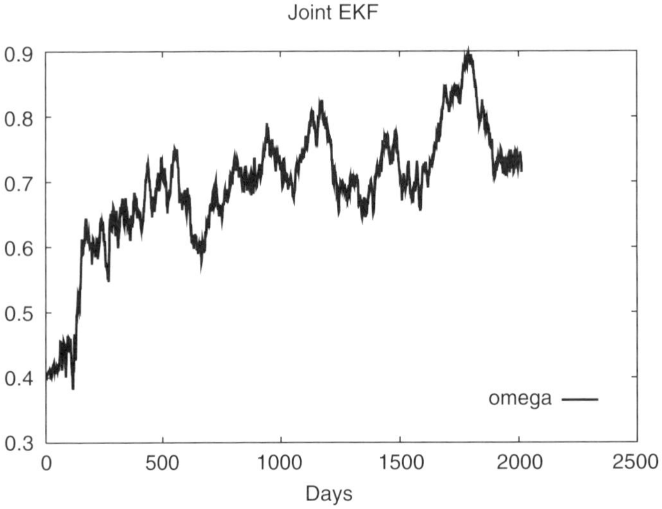

FIGURE 2.11 Joint EKF Estimation for the Parameter ω. Prices were simulated with $\Psi^* = (0.10, 10.0, 0.03, -0.50)$. The convergence remains mediocre. We shall explain this in the following section.

with a given $\mu_S = 0.025$. We then choose a tuning parameter $R = 0.10$ and take a reasonable guess for the initial conditions

$$\Psi_0 = (\omega_0 = 0.15, \theta_0 = 10.0, \xi_0 = 0.02, \rho_0 = -0.51)$$

and apply the joint filter. The results are displayed in Figures 2.11 to 2.14. As we can see, the convergence for ω and θ is better than it was for the two others. We shall see later why this is.

Allowing a *burn-in* period of 1000 points, we can calculate the mean (and the standard deviation) of the generated parameters, after the simulation 1000.

Joint Filters and Time Interval One difficulty with the application of the joint filter (JF) to the stochastic volatility problem is the following: Unless we are dealing with a longer time interval, such as $\Delta t = 1$, the observation error $\sqrt{v_k}\sqrt{\Delta t}B_k$ is too large compared with the sensitivity of the filter with respect to the state through $-0.5v_k\Delta t$. Indeed, for a $\Delta t = 1/252$ we have[18]

$$\Delta t = o(\sqrt{\Delta t})$$

[18]Hereafter $x_h = o(y_h)$ means $x_h/y_h \to 0$ as $h \to 0$, or, more intuitively, x_h is much smaller than y_h for a tiny h.

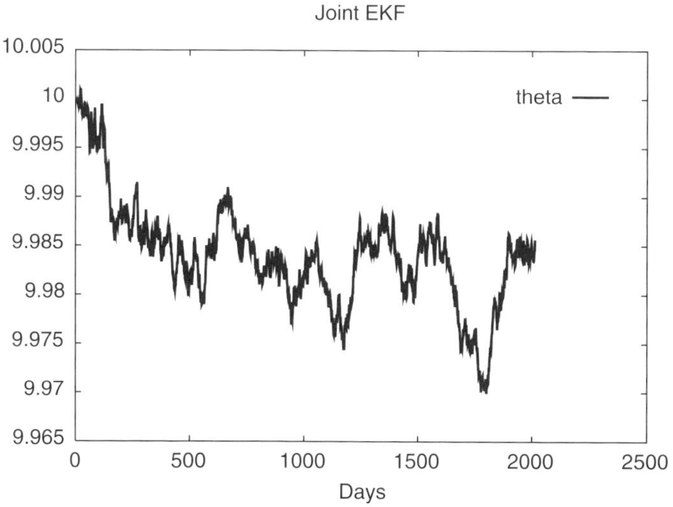

FIGURE 2.12 Joint EKF Estimation for the Parameter θ. Prices were simulated with $\Psi^* = (0.10, 10.0, 0.03, -0.50)$. The convergence remains mediocre. We shall explain this in the following section.

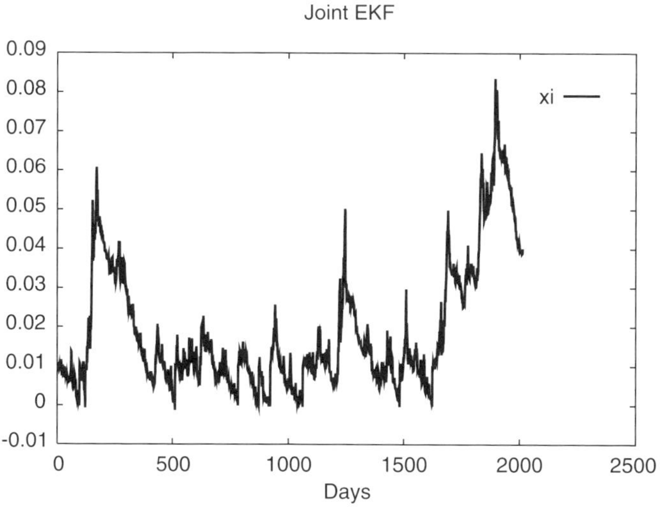

FIGURE 2.13 Joint EKF Estimation for the Parameter ξ. Prices were simulated with $\Psi^* = (0.10, 10.0, 0.03, -0.50)$. The convergence remains mediocre. We shall explain this in the following section.

A simple Monte Carlo test will allow us to verify this. We simulate a Heston model and another model in which we multiply both Brownian

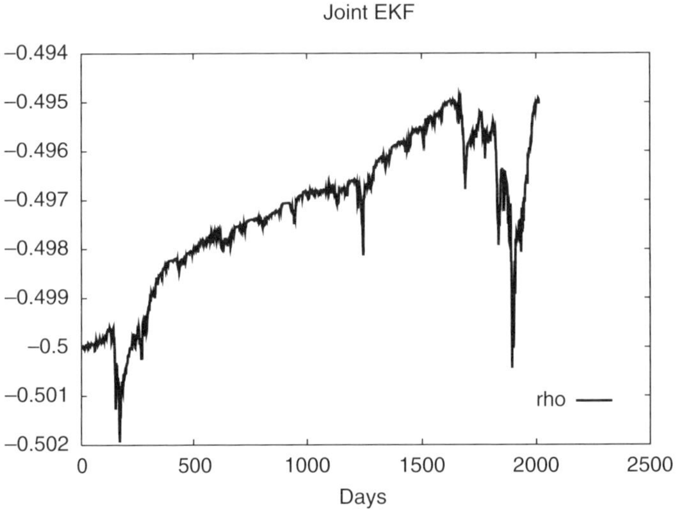

FIGURE 2.14 Joint EKF Estimation for the Parameter ρ. Prices were simulated with $\Psi^* = (0.10, 10.0, 0.03, -0.50)$. The convergence remains mediocre. We shall explain this in the following section.

motions by a factor Δt. This will make the errors smaller by a factor of 252 for the daily case. We call this model the *modified model*. After generating 5000 data points with a parameter set ($\omega^* = 0.10, \theta^* = 10.0, \xi^* = 0.03, \rho^* = -0.50$) and a drift $\mu_S = 0.025$, we suppose we know all parameters except ω.

We then apply the JKF to find the estimate $\hat{\omega}$. We can observe in Figure 2.15 that the filter diverges when applied to the Heston model but converges fast when applied to the modified model. However, in reality we have no control over the observation error, which is precisely the volatility! In a way, this brings up a more fundamental issue regarding the stochastic volatility estimation problem: By definition, volatility represents the noise of the stock process. If we had taken the spot price S_k as the observation and the variance v_k as the state, we would have

$$S_k = S_{k-1} + S_{k-1}\mu_S \Delta t + S_{k-1}\sqrt{v_k}\sqrt{\Delta t}B_k$$

we would then have an observation function gradient $H = 0$ and the system would be *unobservable*! It is precisely because we use a Taylor second-order

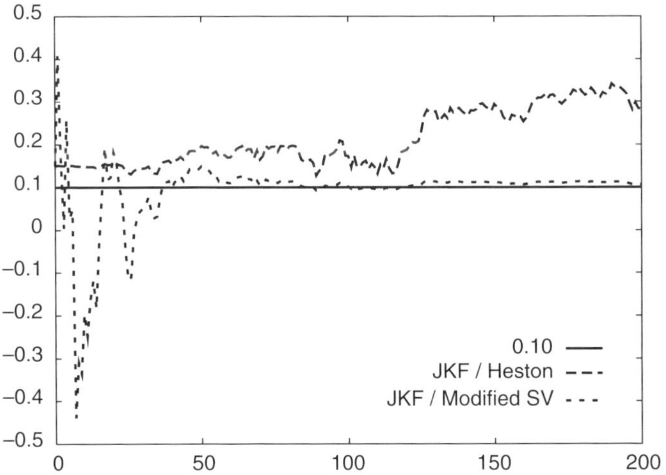

FIGURE 2.15 Joint EKF Estimation for the Parameter ω Applied to the Heston Model as Well as to a Modified Model Where the Noise is Reduced by a Factor 252. As we can see, the convergence for the modified model is improved dramatically. This justifies our comments on large observation error.

expansion

$$\ln(1 + R) \approx R - \frac{1}{2}R^2$$

that we obtain access to v_k through the observation function. However, the error remains *dominant* as the first order of the expansion.

Some [130] have tried

$$\ln\left(\ln^2\left(\frac{S_k}{S_{k-1}}\right)\right) \approx \ln(v_k) + \ln(\Delta t) + \ln(B_k^2)$$

and

$$\ln(B_k^2) \sim -1.27 + \frac{\pi}{\sqrt{2}}\mathcal{N}(0, 1)$$

but the latter approximation may or may not be valid depending on the problem under study.

Parameter Estimation via MLE

As previously stated, one of the principal methods of estimation under the classical framework is the maximization of the likelihood. Indeed this estimation method has many desirable asymptotic properties. Therefore, instead of using the filters alone, we could separate the parameter set $\Psi = (\omega, \theta, \xi, \rho)$ from the state vector $(\ln S_k, v_k)$ and use the Kalman filter for state filtering *within each* MLE iteration[19] and estimate the parameters iteratively.

An Illustration Let us first consider the case of the previous illustration

$$\xi_k = \xi_{k-1} + \pi + 0.10 w_k$$

and

$$z_k = \xi_k + 0.10 u_k$$

where $\pi \approx 3.14159$ and w_k, u_k are independent Gaussian random variables. Here we take

$$x_k = \xi_k$$

and

$$A_k = H_k = 1$$

$$W_k = U_k = 0.1$$

The maximization of the Gaussian likelihood with respect to the parameter π is equivalent to minimizing

$$L_{1:N} = \sum_{k=1}^{N} \left[\ln(F_k) + \frac{\tilde{z}_k^2}{F_k} \right]$$

with residuals

$$\tilde{z}_k = z_k - \hat{z}_k^- = z_k - \hat{x}_k^-$$

and

$$F_k = P_{z_k z_k} = H_k P_k^- H_k^t + U_k R_k U_k^t$$

Note that we used *scalar* notations here, and in vectorial notations we would have

$$L_{1:N} = \sum_{k=1}^{N} \left[\ln(|\mathbf{F}_k|) + \tilde{\mathbf{z}}_k^t \mathbf{F}_k^{-1} \tilde{\mathbf{z}}_k \right]$$

where $|\mathbf{F}_k|$ is the determinant of $\mathbf{F}_k$. We use the scalar notations for simplicity and also because in the stochastic volatility problem we usually deal with one-dimensional observations (namely, the stock price).

[19]To be more accurate, since the noise process is *conditionally* Gaussian, we are dealing with a quasi-maximum-likelihood (QML) Estimation. More detail can be found, for instance, in Gourieroux [124].

The minimization via a direction set (Powell) method over 500 artificially generated observation points will provide

$$\hat{\pi} = 3.145953$$

very quickly.

Stochastic Volatility Examples For Example 1, the system state vector now becomes

$$\mathbf{x}_k = \begin{pmatrix} \ln S_k \\ v_k \end{pmatrix}$$

which means the dimension of our state is now two, and

$$\mathbf{x}_k = \mathbf{f}(\mathbf{x}_{k-1}, \mathbf{w}_{k-1}) = \begin{pmatrix} \ln S_{k-1} + \left(\mu_S - \frac{1}{2}v_{k-1}\right)\Delta t + \sqrt{v_{k-1}}\sqrt{\Delta t}B_{k-1} \\ v_{k-1} + (\omega - \theta v_{k-1})\Delta t + \xi\sqrt{v_{k-1}}\sqrt{\Delta t}Z_{k-1} \end{pmatrix}$$

The system noise is still

$$\mathbf{w}_k = \begin{pmatrix} B_k \\ Z_k \end{pmatrix}$$

and the corresponding covariance matrix is

$$\mathbf{Q}_k = \begin{pmatrix} 1 & \rho \\ \rho & 1 \end{pmatrix}$$

We have the measurement $z_k = \ln S_k$, and therefore we can write

$$\mathbf{H}_k = \begin{pmatrix} 1 & 0 \end{pmatrix}$$

Now for a *given* set of parameters $(\omega, \theta, \xi, \rho)$ we can filter this system with the EKF (or the UKF) using

$$\mathbf{A}_k = \begin{pmatrix} 1 & -\frac{1}{2}\Delta t \\ 0 & 1 - \theta\Delta t \end{pmatrix}$$

and

$$\mathbf{W}_k = \begin{pmatrix} \sqrt{v_{k-1}}\sqrt{\Delta t} & 0 \\ 0 & \xi\sqrt{v_{k-1}}\sqrt{\Delta t} \end{pmatrix}$$

Note that the observation matrix is

$$\mathbf{O}_k = \begin{pmatrix} 1 & 0 \\ 1 & -\frac{1}{2}\Delta t \end{pmatrix}$$

which is of full rank. Our system is therefore observable.

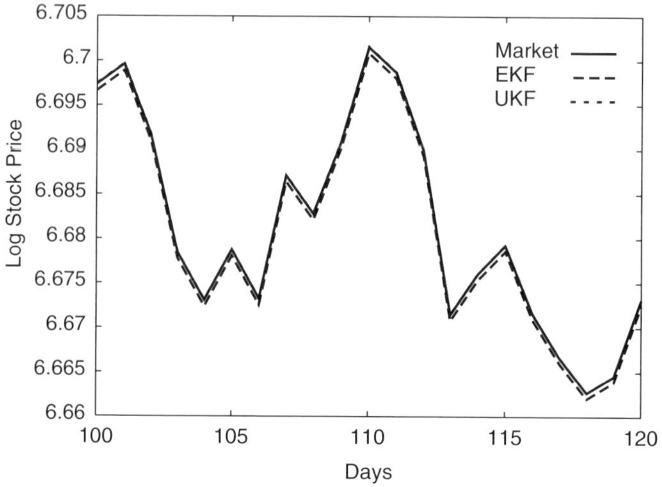

FIGURE 2.16 The SPX Historic Data (1996–2001) is Filtered via EKF and UKF. The results are very close, however, the estimated parameters $\hat{\Psi} = (\hat{\omega}, \hat{\theta}, \hat{\xi}, \hat{\rho})$ differ. Indeed we find ($\hat{\omega} = 0.073028, \hat{\theta} = 1.644488, \hat{\xi} = 0.190461, \hat{\rho} = -1.000000$) for the EKF and ($\hat{\omega} = 0.540715, \hat{\theta} = 13.013577, \hat{\xi} = 0.437523, \hat{\rho} = -1.000000$) for the UKF. This might be due to the relative insensitivity of the filters to the parameter set Ψ or the non-uniqueness of the optimal parameter set. We shall explain this low sensitivity in more detail.

After filtering for this set of parameters, we calculate the sum to be minimized

$$\phi(\omega, \theta, \xi, \rho) = \sum_{k=1}^{N} \left[\ln(F_k) + \frac{\tilde{z}_k^2}{F_k} \right]$$

with

$$\tilde{\mathbf{z}}_k = \mathbf{z}_k - \mathbf{h}(\hat{\mathbf{x}}_k^-, 0)$$

and

$$\mathbf{F}_k = \mathbf{H}_k \mathbf{P}_k^- \mathbf{H}_k^t + \mathbf{U}_k \mathbf{R}_k \mathbf{U}_k^t$$

The minimization could once again be done via a direction set (Powell) method, as described previously. This will avoid a calculation of the gradient $\nabla\phi$.

It is interesting to observe (cf. Figures 2.16 and 2.17) that the results of the EKF and UKF are very close and the filter errors are comparable.

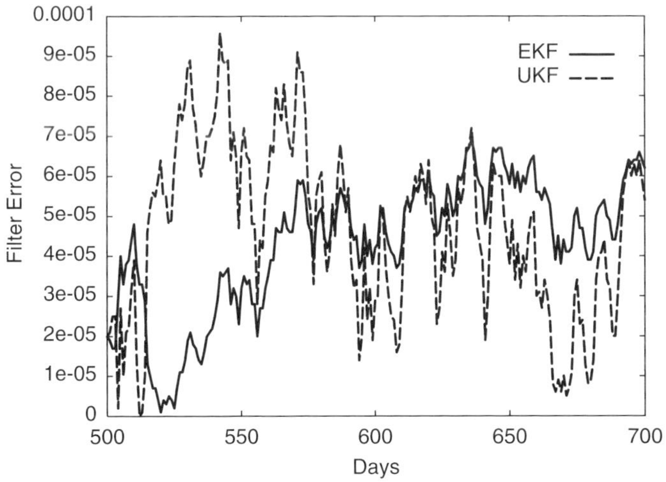

FIGURE 2.17 EKF and UKF Absolute Filtering-Errors for the Same Time-Series. As we can see, there is no clear superiority of one algorithm over the other.

However, the estimated parameter set $\Psi = (\omega, \theta, \xi, \rho)$ can have a different set of values depending on which filter is actually used.[20]

This leads us to the question, how sensitive are these filters to Ψ? In order to answer, we can run an estimation for EKF and use the estimated parameters in UKF and observe how good a fit we obtain. The results show that this sensitivity is fairly low. Again, this might be due to the relative insensitivity of the filters to the parameter set Ψ or the *non-uniqueness* of the optimal parameter set. As we will see, the answer to this question also depends on the sample size.

Optimization Constraints for the Square Root Model In terms of the optimization *constraints*, in addition to the usual

$$
\begin{aligned}
\omega &\geq 0 \\
\theta &\geq 0 \\
\xi &\geq 0 \\
-1 \leq \rho &\leq 1
\end{aligned}
\tag{2.12}
$$

[20]Note, however, that the values of the resulting long-term volatilities $\sqrt{\frac{\omega}{\theta}}$ are rather close.

we need to make sure that the value of the variance remains positive; that is,

$$v_k + (\omega - \theta v_k)\Delta t + \xi\sqrt{v_k}\sqrt{\Delta t}Z_k \geq 0$$

for any $v_k \geq 0$ and any Gaussian random value Z_k. For a Gaussian random variable Z_k and any positive real number Z^*, we can write $Z_k \geq -Z^*$ with a probability P^*. For instance if $Z^* = 4$ then $P^* = 0.999968$. Therefore, *fixing* a choice of Z^*, it is almost always enough for us to have

$$v_k + (\omega - \theta v_k)\Delta t - \xi\sqrt{v_k}\sqrt{\Delta t}Z^* \geq 0$$

for any $v_k \geq 0$.

Considering the function $f(x) = x + (\omega - \theta x)\Delta t - \xi\sqrt{x}\sqrt{\Delta t}Z^*$, it is fairly easy to see that $f(0) = \omega\Delta t \geq 0$ by assumption, and for x very large $f(x) \approx (1 - \theta\Delta t)x$, which is positive if

$$\theta \leq \frac{1}{\Delta t} \tag{2.13}$$

This is most of the time realized for a small Δt such as ours.

Now $f(x)$ being a continuous function and having positive values at zero and infinity, it would be sufficient to make sure that its one minimum on $[0, +\infty]$ is also positive. A simple derivative computation shows that $x_{min} = \frac{\xi^2\Delta t(Z^*)^2}{4(1-\theta\Delta t)^2}$ and therefore the positivity is realized if[21]

$$\xi \leq \frac{2}{Z^*}\sqrt{\omega(1 - \theta\Delta t)} \tag{2.14}$$

which completes our set of constraints.

An Alternative Implementation We could also perform the same estimation, but based on our previous third example. Again we have

$$\ln S_k = \ln S_{k-1} + \left(\mu_S - \frac{1}{2}v_k\right)\Delta t + \sqrt{v_k}\sqrt{\Delta t}B_k$$
$$v_k = v_{k-1} + (\omega - \theta v_{k-1})\Delta t + \xi\sqrt{v_{k-1}}\sqrt{\Delta t}Z_k$$

with B_k and Z_k two normal random sequences with a mean of zero, a variance of one, and a correlation equal to ρ. However, since for a Kalman filter the process noise and the measurement noise must be *uncorrelated*, we introduce

$$y_k = \sqrt{v_k}Z_k$$

[21]Naturally we suppose that $\Delta t > 0$.

and performing the usual Cholesky factorization $B_k = \rho Z_k + \sqrt{1-\rho^2}X_k$, where Z_k and X_k are uncorrelated, we can write

$$\mathbf{x}_k = \begin{pmatrix} v_k \\ y_k \end{pmatrix}$$

and $\mathbf{x}_k = \mathbf{f}(\mathbf{x}_{k-1}, Z_k)$ with

$$\mathbf{f}(x_{k-1}, Z_k) = \begin{pmatrix} v_{k-1} + (\omega - \theta v_{k-1})\Delta t + \xi\sqrt{v_{k-1}}\sqrt{\Delta t}Z_k \\ (v_{k-1} + (\omega - \theta v_{k-1})\Delta t + \xi\sqrt{v_{k-1}}\sqrt{\Delta t}Z_k)^{\frac{1}{2}}Z_k \end{pmatrix}$$

which provides us with the Jacobian

$$\mathbf{A}_k = \begin{pmatrix} 1 - \theta\Delta t & 0 \\ 0 & 0 \end{pmatrix}$$

and

$$\mathbf{W}_k = \begin{pmatrix} \xi\sqrt{v_{k-1}}\sqrt{\Delta t} \\ (v_{k-1} + (\omega - \theta v_{k-1})\Delta t)^{\frac{1}{2}} \end{pmatrix}$$

The measurement equation is

$$z_k = \ln S_k = \ln S_{k-1} + \left(\mu_S - \frac{1}{2}v_k\right)\Delta t + \rho\sqrt{\Delta t}y_k + \sqrt{1-\rho^2}\sqrt{v_k}\sqrt{\Delta t}X_k$$

and therefore

$$\mathbf{H}_k = \begin{pmatrix} -\frac{1}{2}\Delta t & \rho\sqrt{\Delta t} \end{pmatrix}$$

with $u_k = X_k$ and $U_k = \sqrt{1-\rho^2}\sqrt{v_k}\sqrt{\Delta t}$ which completes our set of equations. Note that the observation matrix is

$$\mathbf{O}_k = \begin{pmatrix} -\frac{1}{2}\Delta t & \rho\sqrt{\Delta t} \\ -\frac{1}{2}\Delta t(1 - \theta\Delta t) & 0 \end{pmatrix}$$

which is of full rank. Our system is therefore observable.

The One-Dimensional State Finally, a simpler way of writing the state-space system, *which will be our method of choice hereafter*, would be to subtract from both sides of the state equation $x_k = f(x_{k-1}, w_{k-1})$ a multiple of the quantity $h(x_{k-1}, u_{k-1}) - z_{k-1}$, which is equal to zero. This would allow us to eliminate the correlation between the system and the measurement noises.

In fact, if the system equation is

$$\ln S_k = \ln S_{k-1} + \left(\mu_S - \frac{1}{2}v_{k-1}\right)\Delta t + \sqrt{v_{k-1}}\sqrt{\Delta t}B_{k-1}$$

$$v_k = v_{k-1} + (\omega - \theta v_{k-1})\Delta t + \xi\sqrt{v_{k-1}}\sqrt{\Delta t}Z_{k-1}$$

writing

$$v_k = v_{k-1} + (\omega - \theta v_{k-1})\Delta t + \xi\sqrt{v_{k-1}}\sqrt{\Delta t}Z_{k-1}$$
$$- \rho\xi\left[\ln S_{k-1} + \left(\mu_S - \frac{1}{2}v_{k-1}\right)\Delta t + \sqrt{v_{k-1}}\sqrt{\Delta t}B_{k-1} - \ln S_k\right]$$

posing for every k

$$\tilde{Z}_k = \frac{1}{\sqrt{1-\rho^2}}(Z_k - \rho B_k)$$

we will have as expected $\tilde{Z}_k$ *uncorrelated* with B_k and

$$x_k = v_k = v_{k-1} + \left[(\omega - \rho\xi\mu_S) - \left(\theta - \frac{1}{2}\rho\xi\right)v_{k-1}\right]\Delta t$$
$$+ \rho\xi\ln\left(\frac{S_k}{S_{k-1}}\right) + \xi\sqrt{1-\rho^2}\sqrt{v_{k-1}}\sqrt{\Delta t}\tilde{Z}_{k-1} \quad (2.15)$$

and the measurement equation would be

$$z_k = \ln S_{k+1} = \ln S_k + \left(\mu_S - \frac{1}{2}v_k\right)\Delta t + \sqrt{v_k}\sqrt{\Delta t}B_k \quad (2.16)$$

With this system everything becomes one-dimensional and the computations become much faster both for the EKF and UKF.

For the EKF we will have

$$A_k = 1 - \left(\theta - \frac{1}{2}\rho\xi\right)\Delta t$$

and

$$W_k = \xi\sqrt{1-\rho^2}\sqrt{v_{k-1}}\sqrt{\Delta t}$$

as well as

$$H_k = -\frac{1}{2}\Delta t$$

and

$$U_k = \sqrt{v_k}\sqrt{\Delta t}$$

Again, for the MLE we will try to minimize

$$\phi(\omega, \theta, \xi, \rho) = \sum_{k=1}^{N}\left[\ln(F_k) + \frac{\tilde{z}_k^2}{F_k}\right]$$

with residuals

$$\tilde{\mathbf{z}}_k = \mathbf{z}_k - \mathbf{h}(\hat{\mathbf{x}}_k^-, 0)$$

and

$$\mathbf{F}_k = \mathbf{H}_k \mathbf{P}_k^- \mathbf{H}_k^t + \mathbf{U}_k \mathbf{U}_k^t$$

The same time update and measurement update will be used with the UKF. The ML estimator can be used as usual.

The following is a C++ routine for the implementation of the EKF applied to the Heston model:

```
// log_stock_prices  are the log of stock prices
// muS is the real-world stock drift
// n_stock_prices is the number of the above stock prices
// (omega, theta, xi, rho) are the Heston parameters
// u[] is the set of means of observation errors
// v[] is the set of variances of observation errors
// estimates[] are the estimated observations from the filter

void estimate_extended_kalman_parameters_1_dim(
double *log_stock_prices,
double muS,
int n_stock_prices,
double omega,
double theta,
double xi,
double rho,
double *u,
double *v,
double *estimates)
{
  int i1;
  double  x, x1, W, H, A;
  double  P, P1, z, U, K;
  double delt=1.0/252.0;
  double eps=0.00001;

  x = 0.04;
  P=0.01;
  u[0]=u[n_stock_prices-1]=0.0;
  v[0]=v[n_stock_prices-1]=1.0;
  estimates[0]=estimates[1]=log_stock_prices[0]+eps;

  for (i1=1;i1<n_stock_prices-1;i1++)
  {
    if (x<0) x=0.00001;
```

```
      x1 = x + ( omega-rho*xi*muS - (theta-0.5*rho*xi) * x) * delt +
        rho*xi* (log_stock_prices[i1]-log_stock_prices[i1-1]);
      A  = 1.0-(theta-0.5*rho*xi)*delt;
      W  = xi*sqrt((1-rho*rho) * x * delt);
      P1 = W*W + A*P*A;

      if (x1<0) x1=0.00001;

      H = -0.5*delt;
      U = sqrt(x1*delt);
      K = P1*H/( H*P1*H + U*U);
      z = log_stock_prices[i1+1];
      x = x1 + K * (z - (log_stock_prices[i1] + (muS-0.5*x1)*delt));

      u[i1] = z - (log_stock_prices[i1] + (muS-0.5*x1)*delt);
      v[i1] = H*P1*H + U*U;
      estimates[i1+1] = log_stock_prices[i1] + (muS-0.5*x1)*delt;

      P=(1.0-K*H)*P1;
    }
}

// Having u[] and v[] we can evaluate the (minus log) Likelihood  as
// the sum of      log(v[i1])+u[i1]*u[i1]/v[i1]
// and minimize the sum in order to obtain the optimal parameters
// the minimization could be done for instance via the direction set
routine
// available in the Numerical Recipes in C
```

And what follows next is the same routine for the unscented filter.

```
void estimate_unscented_kalman_parameters_1_dim(
double *log_stock_prices,
double muS,
int n_stock_prices,
double omega,
double theta, double xi,
double rho,
double *u,
double *v,
double *estimates)
```

```
{
  int     i1,i2, i3, t1;
  int     ret;
  int     na=3;
  double  x, xa[3];
  double  X[7], Xa[3][7];
  double  Wm[7], Wc[7], Z[7];
  double  x1;
  double  prod, prod1;
  double  P, P1;
  double **Pa, **proda;
  double  z, U, Pzz, K;
  double  delt=1.0/252.0;
  double  a=0.001 , b=0.0, k=0.0, lambda;
  double eps=0.00001;

  lambda = a*a*(na +k)-na;

  proda= new double * [na];
  Pa =   new double * [na];
  for (i1=0;i1<na;i1++)
  {
    Pa[i1]= new double [na];
    proda[i1]= new double [na];
  }

  xa[1]=xa[2]=0.0;
  x= 0.04;
  u[0]=u[n_stock_prices-1]=0.0;
  v[0]=v[n_stock_prices-1]=1.0;
  estimates[0]=estimates[1]=log_stock_prices[0]+eps;
  xa[0]=x;

  Pa[0][0]= Pa[1][1]= Pa[2][2] = 1.0;
  Pa[1][0]= Pa[0][1]= Pa[1][2]=Pa[2][1]= Pa[0][2]=Pa[2][0]=0;

  for (i1=0;i1<na;i1++)
  {
    for (i2=0;i2<na;i2++)
    {
      proda[i1][i2]=0.0;
    }
  }

  Wm[0]=lambda/(na+lambda);
```

```
Wc[0]=lambda/(na+lambda) + (1-a*a+b);
for (i3=1;i3<(2*na+1);i3++)
{
  Wm[i3]=Wc[i3]=1/(2*(na+lambda));
}

for (t1=1;t1<n_stock_prices-1;t1++)
{

  for (i1=0;i1<na;i1++)
  {
    Xa[i1][0]= xa[i1];
  }

  for (i1=0;i1<na;i1++)
  {
    for (i2=0;i2<na;i2++)
    {
  if (i1==i2)
  {
    if (Pa[i1][i2] < 1.0e-10)
      Pa[i1][i2]= 1.0e-10;
  }
  else
  {
    if (Pa[i1][i2] < 1.0e-10)
      Pa[i1][i2]= 0.0;
  }
      }
    }

  ret = sqrt_matrix(Pa,proda,na);

  for (i3=1;i3<(1+na);i3++)
  {
    for (i1=0;i1<na;i1++)
    {
    Xa[i1][i3]= xa[i1] + sqrt(na+lambda) * proda[i1][i3-1];
    }
  }
  for (i3=(1+na);i3<(2*na+1);i3++)
  {
    for (i1=0;i1<na;i1++)
    {
    Xa[i1][i3]= xa[i1] - sqrt(na+lambda) * proda[i1][i3-na-1];
```

```
    }
  }

  for (i3=0;i3<(2*na+1);i3++)
  {
    if (Xa[0][i3]<0) Xa[0][i3]=0.0001;
    X[i3]= Xa[0][i3] + (omega-muS*rho*xi   -
      (theta-0.5*rho*xi) *Xa[0][i3])*delt +
  rho*xi* (log_stock_prices[t1]-log_stock_prices[t1-1]) +
  xi*sqrt((1-rho*rho)*delt*Xa[0][i3])*Xa[1][i3];
  }


  x1 = 0;
  for (i3=0;i3<(2*na+1);i3++)
  {
    x1 += Wm[i3]*X[i3];
  }

  P1=0.0;
  for (i3=0;i3<(2*na+1);i3++)
  {
    P1 += Wc[i3]*(X[i3]-x1)*(X[i3]-x1);
  }

  z=0;
  for (i3=0;i3<(2*na+1);i3++)
  {
    if (X[i3]<0) X[i3]=0.00001;
    Z[i3] = log_stock_prices[t1] + (muS-0.5*X[i3])*delt +
           sqrt(X[i3]*delt)*Xa[2][i3];
    z += Wm[i3]*Z[i3];
  }

  Pzz=0;
  for (i3=0;i3<(2*na+1);i3++)
  {
    Pzz +=  Wc[i3]*(Z[i3]-z)*(Z[i3]-z);
  }

  prod=0.0;
  for (i3=0;i3<(2*na+1);i3++)
  {
    prod += Wc[i3]*(X[i3]-x1)* (Z[i3]-z);
  }
```

```
    K= prod/Pzz;

     u[t1] = log_stock_prices[t1+1] - z;
     v[t1] - Pzz;
     estimates[t1+1] = z;


    x = x1 + K*(log_stock_prices[t1+1] - z);
    P = P1 - K*K * Pzz;

    xa[0]=x;
    Pa[0][0] = P;

    if (x<0) x=0.0001;

    Pa[1][0]= Pa[0][1]= Pa[1][2]=Pa[2][1]= Pa[0][2]=Pa[2][0]=0;
  }


  for (i1=0;i1<na;i1++)
  {
    delete [] Pa[i1];
    delete [] proda[i1];
  }
  delete [] Pa;
  delete [] proda;


}

// the routine sqrt_matrix() can be constructed via the Cholesly
decomposition
// also available as choldc() in the Numerical Recipes in C
```

Other stochastic volatility models It is easy to generalize the above state-space model to other stochastic volatility approaches. Indeed we could replace the Heston equation with

$$v_k = v_{k-1} + (\omega - \theta v_{k-1})\Delta t + \xi v_{k-1}^{p}\sqrt{\Delta t}Z_k$$

where $p = 1/2$ would naturally correspond to the Heston model, $p = 1$ to the GARCH diffusion-limit model, and $p = 3/2$ to the $\frac{3}{2}$ model described in [177]. This idea will be developed further in the chapter.

Diagnostics

After having estimated the parameter set Ψ, we should test for *model misspecification*. Two important questions are

1. Do the normalized residuals $(\mathbf{z}_k - \hat{\mathbf{z}}_k^-)/\mathbf{F}_k$ follow a standard normal $\mathcal{N}(0, 1)$ law?
2. Do these residuals have zero auto correlation?

Chi-Square Test The first question could be answered by performing a chi-square test. We take a number N_B of intervals or "bins" bounded by the points $x_0, x_1, ..., x_J$. We then count the number of observations N_j within each bin $[x_j, x_{j+1}]$ for j between zero and $N_B - 1$. We then compare these numbers with the theoretical numbers implied by the normal distribution $n_j = [\Phi(x_{j+1}) - \Phi(x_j)]N$ with Φ the cumulative normal function and N the total number of observations. The sum

$$\sum_{j=0}^{N_B-1} \frac{(N_j - n_j)^2}{n_j}$$

asymptotically follows a χ^2_ν law with degrees of freedom ν equal to $N_B - 1$.

Box-Ljung Test The second question could be answered with a Box-Ljung test. We should first calculate a number of autocorrelations

$$r_k = \frac{\sum_{i=1}^{N-k}(\tilde{z}_i - \bar{\tilde{z}})(\tilde{z}_{i+k} - \bar{\tilde{z}})}{\sum_{i=1}^{N}(\tilde{z}_i - \bar{\tilde{z}})^2}$$

for k between one and a prespecified integer K. Once again, $\tilde{z}_i = z_i - \hat{z}_i^-$ and $\bar{\tilde{z}}$ corresponds to their mean. We then consider the sum

$$N(N+2)\sum_{k=1}^{K} \frac{r_k^2}{N-k}$$

which asymptotically follows a χ^2_ν law with degrees of freedom ν equal to $K - p$ where $p = 4$ is the numbers of parameters we estimated.

Test Results In the previously studied SPX examples, we had $N = 1256$. For the normality test, we choose $N_B = 21$ and for the Box-Ljung test we take $K = 24$; in both cases, we will have to compare the outputs to the critical threshold χ^2_{20}, which for a confidence of 0.95 is around 31.5. For the

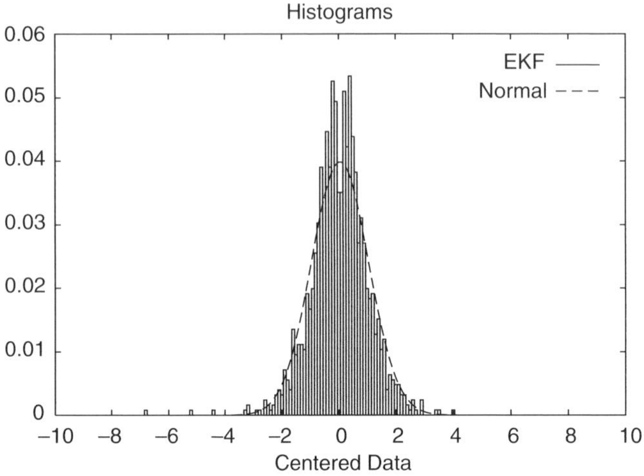

FIGURE 2.18 Histogram for Filtered Data via EKF versus the Normal Distribution. The residuals are fairly normal.

(one-dimensional) EKF, we obtain 27.738862 for the normality test and 0.007889 for the Box-Ljung test. For the (one-dimensional) UKF, we obtain 22.657545 for the normality test and again 0.016053 for the Box-Ljung test. This means that there is very little autocorrelation in our system noise. Also, it seems reasonable to model the noise as approximately normally distributed. The chi-square test proves that the normality assumption is plausible and the Kalman filter can be used. A visual confirmation of this could be achieved by plotting the corresponding histograms. As we can see in Figure 2.18, there are no excessively "fat tails"; however, the central value at zero is higher than the normal distribution.

Variogram Similarly to Fouque et al. [104], we can use a variogram to visualize the volatility behavior of the model. As Galli [110] mentions, the main reasons to use variograms instead of covariance or correlograms are that variograms do not need to estimate the mean, and they are interpretable under wider conditions than are covariances or correlograms.

The expression for the variogram of a process I_t is

$$\gamma_I(h) = \frac{1}{2}\mathbf{E}[(I(t+h) - I(t))^2] \approx \frac{1}{2N_{h_i}} \sum_{t=0}^{N_{h_i}} (I(t+h_i) - I(t))^2$$

where N_{h_i} is the total number of points such that $I(t+h_i)$ exists.

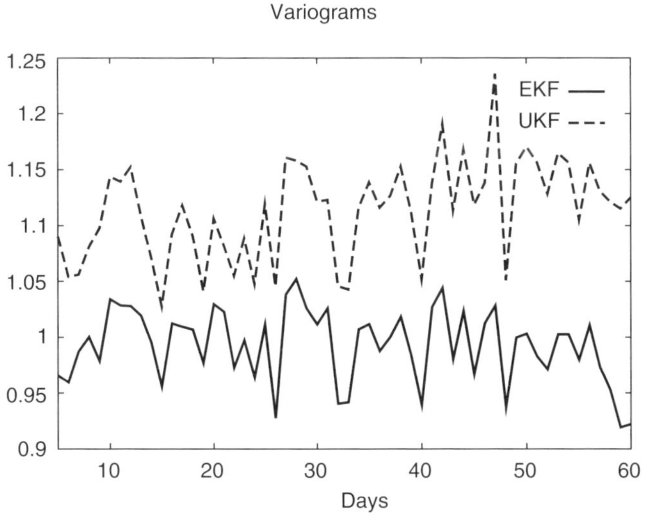

FIGURE 2.19 Variograms for Filtered Data via EKF and UKF. The input corresponds to a sequence of independent Gaussian random variables. As we can see, the variograms are close to one.

For instance, for a sequence of independent Gaussian random variables, we should have

$$\gamma_I(h) = \frac{1}{2}\mathbf{E}[I^2(t+h)] + \frac{1}{2}\mathbf{E}[I^2(t)] - \mathbf{E}[I(t)I(t+h)] = \frac{1}{2} + \frac{1}{2} - 0 = 1$$

In our case, the process I_t could be defined, for instance, as

$$I_t = \frac{z_t - \hat{z}_t^-}{\sqrt{F_t}}$$

which should correspond to a sequence of independent Gaussian random variables.

As we can see in Figure 2.19, the variogram is consistent with the Gaussian assumption, which reconfirms what we observed from the histograms. Another way of expressing the same idea is to build a Brownian motion from the foregoing sequence. Calling the independent Gaussian random variables (B_k), we can write

$$I_n = \sqrt{\Delta t}\sum_{k=0}^{n} B_k$$

and plot the variogram for the Brownian Motion I_n.

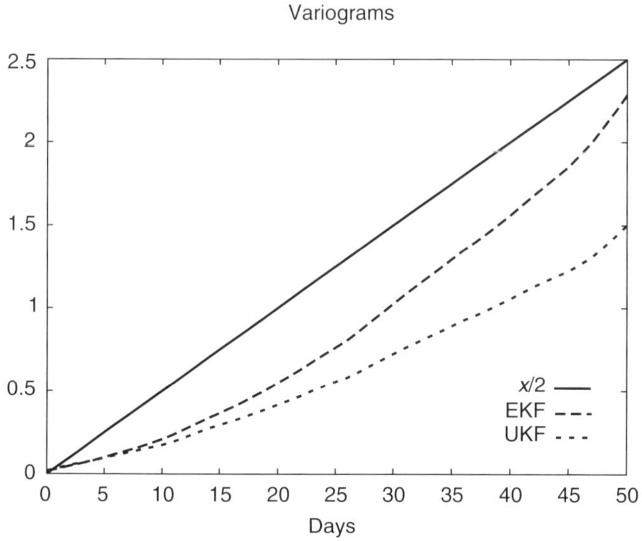

FIGURE 2.20 Variograms for Filtered Data via EKF and UKF. The input corresponds to a Brownian motion. As we can see, the variograms are close to $x/2$.

For a Brownian motion, it is easy to see that the variogram should be linear

$$\gamma_I(h) = \frac{1}{2}(t+h) + \frac{1}{2}t - t = \frac{1}{2}h$$

This could indeed be seen in Figure 2.20.

Particle Filtering

A different approach to filtering and parameter estimation has recently become popular [79], [122], [171]. In this approach, we use Monte Carlo *simulations* instead of Gaussian approximations for $(x_k|z_k)$, as the Kalman or Kushner filters do. This will precisely allow us to deal with fundamentally non-Gaussian situations.[22]

[22]An existing (but less effective) alternative to the particle filtering method is the *grid-based approximation*, such as the one suggested by Kitagawa [170], [108]. The main advantage of the particle filter is that it will make the grid focus adaptively on the state-space regions with higher relevance.

Underlying Theory The idea is based on the *Importance Sampling* technique: We can calculate an expected value

$$\mathbf{E}[f(x_{0:k})] = \int f(x_{0:k})p(x_{0:k}|z_{1:k})dx_{0:k} \tag{2.17}$$

by using a known and simple *proposal* distribution $q()$.

More precisely, it is possible to write

$$\mathbf{E}[f(x_{0:k})] = \int f(x_{0:k})\frac{p(x_{0:k}|z_{1:k})}{q(x_{0:k}|z_{1:k})}q(x_{0:k}|z_{1:k})dx_{0:k}$$

which could be also written as

$$\mathbf{E}[f(x_{0:k})] = \int f(x_{0:k})\frac{w_k(x_{0:k})}{p(z_{1:k})}q(x_{0:k}|z_{1:k})dx_{0:k} \tag{2.18}$$

with

$$w_k(x_{0:k}) = \frac{p(z_{1:k}|x_{0:k})p(x_{0:k})}{q(x_{0:k}|z_{1:k})}$$

defined as the filtering *non-normalized weight* as step k.

Proof:

$$\begin{aligned}\frac{p(x_{0:k}|z_{1:k})}{q(x_{0:k}|z_{1:k})} &= \frac{p(z_{1:k}|x_{0:k})p(x_{0:k})}{p(z_{1:k})q(x_{0:k}|z_{1:k})}\\ &= \frac{w_k(x_{0:k})}{p(z_{1:k})}\end{aligned}$$

(QED)

We therefore have

$$\mathbf{E}[f(x_{0:k})] = \frac{\mathbf{E}_q[w_k(x_{0:k})f(x_{0:k})]}{\mathbf{E}_q[w_k(x_{0:k})]} = \mathbf{E}_q[\tilde{w}_k(x_{0:k})f(x_{0:k})] \tag{2.19}$$

with

$$\tilde{w}_k(x_{0:k}) = \frac{w_k(x_{0:k})}{\mathbf{E}_q[w_k(x_{0:k})]}$$

defined as the filtering *normalized weight* as step k.

Proof: We write

$$\begin{aligned}\mathbf{E}[f(x_{0:k})] &= \frac{1}{p(z_{1:k})}\int f(x_{0:k})w_k(x_{0:k})q(x_{0:k}|z_{1:k})dx_{0:k}\\ &= \frac{\int f(x_{0:k})w_k(x_{0:k})q(x_{0:k}|z_{1:k})dx_{0:k}}{\int p(z_{1:k}|x_{0:k})p(x_{0:k})\frac{q(x_{0:k}|z_{1:k})}{q(x_{0:k}|z_{1:k})}dx_{0:k}}\end{aligned}$$

$$= \frac{\int f(x_{0:k}) w_k(x_{0:k}) q(x_{0:k}|z_{1:k}) dx_{0:k}}{\int w_k(x_{0:k}) q(x_{0:k}|z_{1:k}) dx_{0:k}}$$

which is the ratio of the expectations, as earlier stated. *(QED)*

Using Monte-Carlo sampling from the distribution $q(x_{0:k}|z_{1:k})$ we can write in the discrete framework:

$$\mathbf{E}[f(x_{0:k})] \approx \sum_{i=1}^{N_{sims}} \tilde{w}_k \left(x_{0:k}^{(i)}\right) f\left(x_{0:k}^{(i)}\right) \tag{2.20}$$

with again

$$\tilde{w}_k(x_{0:k}^{(i)}) = \frac{w_k\left(x_{0:k}^{(i)}\right)}{\sum_{j=1}^{N_{sims}} w_k\left(x_{0:k}^{(j)}\right)}$$

Now supposing that our proposal distribution $q()$ satisfies the Markov property, it can be shown that w_k verifies the recursive identity

$$w_k^{(i)} = w_{k-1}^{(i)} \frac{p\left(z_k|x_k^{(i)}\right) p\left(x_k^{(i)}|x_{k-1}^{(i)}\right)}{q\left(x_k^{(i)}|x_{0:k-1}^{(i)}, z_{1:k}\right)} \tag{2.21}$$

which completes the *sequential importance sampling* algorithm.

Proof: The Markov property just mentioned could be written as

$$q(x_{0:k}|z_{1:k}) = q(x_k|x_{0:k-1}, z_{1:k}) q(x_{0:k-1}|z_{1:k-1}) \tag{2.22}$$

We also assume that the state (x_k) is a Markov process, meaning

$$p(x_k|x_{0:k-1}) = p(x_k|x_{k-1})$$

and the observations (z_k) are conditionally independent given the states, so that

$$p(z_k|x_{0:k}) = p(z_k|x_k)$$

Finally we use the fact that at time-step k, all previous observations are perfectly known, and

$$p(z_k|x_k, z_{1:k-1}) = p(z_k|x_k)$$

Therefore

$$w_k(x_k) = \frac{p(z_{1:k}|x_{0:k}) p(x_{0:k})}{q(x_{0:k}|z_{1:k})}$$

$$= \frac{p(z_k|x_k)p(z_{1:k-1}|x_{0:k-1})p(x_k|x_{k-1})p(x_{0:k-1})}{q(x_k|x_{0:k-1}, z_{1:k})q(x_{0:k-1}|z_{1:k-1})}$$

(QED)

It is important to note that what the foregoing means is that the state x_k cannot depend on future observations; that is, *we are dealing with filtering and not smoothing.*

Resampling One major problem with this algorithm is that the variance of the weights increases randomly over time. In order to solve this, we need to use a *resampling* algorithm, which would map our unequally weighted x_k's to a new set of equally weighted sample points. Various methods have been suggested for this. See, for instance, Arulampalam [14], [171]. The basic idea is to compare the cumulative distribution function (CDF) created from the normalized weights with a CDF constructed from a uniformly simulated number $\mathcal{U}[0, 1]$. We would then eliminate the indices having too small a weight and repeat those having a sufficiently large weight.

More accurately, at a given time step k, for $1 \leq j \leq N_{sims}$, if

$$\frac{1}{N_{sims}}(\mathcal{U}[0, 1] + j - 1) \geq \sum_{l=1}^{i} \tilde{w}_k^{(l)}$$

then increment and "skip" i; otherwise, take $x_k^{(i)}$ and set its weight to $\frac{1}{N_{sims}}$.

Note that the resampling algorithm could create a situation where the resulting sample has many repeated points. This is known as *sample impoverishment* and could lead to an extreme case in which all points collapse to a unique particle after a few iterations. This phenomenon is more likely if the process noise is small. One possible solution to this problem is to add a Markov chain Monte Carlo (MCMC) step after the resampling. As will be described further, a *Metropolis-Hastings* (MH) sampling algorithm would be suitable.

Needless to say, the choice of the proposal distribution is crucial. Many suggest using

$$q(x_k|x_{0:k-1}, z_{1:k}) = p(x_k|x_{k-1})$$

since it will give us a simple weight identity

$$w_k^{(i)} = w_{k-1}^{(i)} p(z_k|x_k^{(i)})$$

Based on this type of choice, hereafter we shall simplify and write

$$q(x_k|x_{0:k-1}, z_{1:k}) = q(x_k|x_{k-1}, z_{1:k})$$

without any change to our arguments. However, this choice of the proposal distribution does *not* take into account our most recent observation z_k at all and therefore could become inefficient. Hence aries the idea of using a

Gaussian approximation for the proposal and, in particular, an approximation based on the Kalman filter, in order to incorporate the observations. We therefore will have

$$q(x_k|x_{k-1}, z_{1:k}) = \mathcal{N}(\hat{x}_k, P_k) \tag{2.23}$$

using the same notations as in the section on the Kalman filter. Such filters are sometimes referred to as the *extended particle filter* (EPF) or the *unscented particle filter* (UPF). This is similar to the *iterative gentering algorithm* in Kushner's NLF.

From here, in order to estimate the parameter set Ψ we can either use dual/Joint filter, or use an ML estimator. Note that since the particle filter does not necessarily assume Gaussian noise, the likelihood function to be maximized has a more general form than the one used in previous sections. Given the likelihood at step k

$$l_k = p(z_k|z_{1:k-1}) = \int p(z_k|x_k)p(x_k|z_{1:k-1})dx_k$$

the total likelihood is the product of the l_k's and therefore the log likelihood to be maximized is

$$\ln(L_{1:N}) = \sum_{k=1}^{N} \ln(l_k) \tag{2.24}$$

Now l_k could be written as

$$l_k = \int p(z_k|x_k)\frac{p(x_k|z_{1:k-1})}{q(x_k|x_{k-1}, z_{1:k})}q(x_k|x_{k-1}, z_{1:k})dx_k$$

and given that by construction the $x_k^{(i)}$'s are distributed according to $q()$, we can write the Monte Carlo approximation

$$l_k \approx \sum_{i=1}^{N_{sims}} \frac{p\left(z_k|x_k^{(i)}\right)p\left(x_k^{(i)}|x_{k-1}^{(i)}\right)}{q\left(x_k^{(i)}|x_{k-1}^{(i)}, z_{1:k}\right)} \tag{2.25}$$

which we already computed for the sequential importance sampling weight update.

As we shall see in the next paragraph, it is also possible to interpret the step k likelihood, as a quantity related to the total weight

$$\sum_{i=1}^{N_{sims}} w_k^{(i)}$$

Finally, we could interpret the particle filter as follows. We are using a Monte Carlo simulation (via an importance sampling technique) to calculate the integral $\int f(x_k)p(x_k|z_{1:k})dx_k$. This is exactly what other filtering techniques try to do. The Kushner nonlinear filter (NLF) tries to calculate the integral via a Gaussian quadrature. Indeed, NLF uses Hermite polynomials because it treats the distributions as normal.[23]

Implementation Given the above theory, the algorithm for an extended or unscented particle filter could be implemented in the following way:

1. For time step $k = 0$, choose x_0 and $P_0 > 0$.
   For i such that $1 \leq i \leq N_{sims}$, take
$$x_0^{(i)} = x_0 + \sqrt{P_0} Z^{(i)}$$
   where $Z^{(i)}$ is a standard Gaussian simulated number. Also take $P_0^{(i)} = P_0$ and
$$w_0^{(i)} = \frac{1}{N_{sims}}$$
   While $1 \leq k \leq N$
2. For each simulation index i
$$\hat{x}_k^{(i)} = \mathbf{KF}(x_{k-1}^{(i)})$$
   with $P_k^{(i)}$ the associated a posteriori error covariance matrix. (**KF** could be either the EKF or the UKF.)
3. For each i between 1 and N_{sims}
$$\tilde{x}_k^{(i)} = \hat{x}_k^{(i)} + \sqrt{P_k^{(i)}} Z^{(i)}$$
   where again $Z^{(i)}$ is a standard Gaussian simulated number.
4. Calculate the associated weights for each i
$$w_k^{(i)} = w_{k-1}^{(i)} \frac{p(z_k|\tilde{x}_k^{(i)}) p(\tilde{x}_k^{(i)}|x_{k-1}^{(i)})}{q(\tilde{x}_k^{(i)}|x_{k-1}^{(i)}, z_{1:k})}$$
   with $q()$ the normal density with mean $\hat{x}_k^{(i)}$ and variance $P_k^{(i)}$.
5. Normalize the weights
$$\tilde{w}_k^{(i)} = \frac{w_k^{(i)}}{\sum_{i=1}^{N_{sims}} w_k^{(i)}}$$
6. Resample the points $\tilde{x}_k^{(i)}$ and get $x_k^{(i)}$ and reset $w_k^{(i)} = \tilde{w}_k^{(i)} = \frac{1}{N_{sims}}$.
7. **Increment** k; go back to Step 2 and **Stop** at the end of the **While** loop.

[23]Other filters cited, for instance, in [79] use the more general Legendre polynomials.

From Step 4 we have

$$\bar{l}_k = \sum_{i=1}^{N_{sims}} \frac{p\left(z_k|\tilde{x}_k^{(i)}\right) p\left(\tilde{x}_k^{(i)}|x_{k-1}^{(i)}\right)}{q\left(\tilde{x}_k^{(i)}|x_{k-1}^{(i)}, z_{1:k}\right)}$$

where $\bar{l}_k$ is a Monte Carlo proxy for the likelihood l_k at the step k. As we saw in the previous section, by *minimizing*

$$-\sum_{k=1}^{N} \ln(\bar{l}_k)$$

using, for instance, the direction set algorithm, we will be maximizing the likelihood function and hence we will be obtaining the optimal parameter set $\hat{\Psi}$.

Given the resetting of $w_k^{(i)}$ to a constant $\frac{1}{N_{sims}}$ during the resampling step, we can also replace $\bar{l}_k$ with

$$\tilde{l}_k = \sum_{i=1}^{N_{sims}} w_k^{(i)}$$

which will provide us with an interpretation of the likelihood as the *total weight*.

An Illustration Let us consider once again the case of the previous illustration

$$\xi_k = \xi_{k-1} + \pi + 0.10 w_k$$

and

$$z_k = \xi_k + 0.10 u_k$$

where $\pi \approx 3.14159$ and w_k, u_k are independent Gaussian random variables. We apply the same Kalman filter and then apply the previous algorithm to the system. Calling

$$\mathbf{n}(x, \mathbf{m}, \mathbf{s}) = \frac{1}{\sqrt{2\pi}\mathbf{s}} \exp\left(-\frac{(x - \mathbf{m})^2}{2\mathbf{s}^2}\right)$$

the normal density with mean $\mathbf{m}$ and standard deviation $\mathbf{s}$, we will have

$$q\left(\tilde{x}_k^{(i)}|x_{k-1}^{(i)}, z_{1:k}\right) = \mathbf{n}\left(\tilde{x}_k^{(i)}, \mathbf{m} = \hat{x}_k^{(i)}, \mathbf{s} = \sqrt{P_k^{(i)}}\right)$$

as well as

$$p\left(z_k|\tilde{x}_k^{(i)}\right) = \mathbf{n}\left(z_k, \mathbf{m} = \tilde{x}_k^{(i)}, \mathbf{s} = 0.10\right)$$

and

$$p\left(\tilde{x}_k^{(i)}|x_{k-1}^{(i)}\right) = \mathbf{n}\left(\tilde{x}_k^{(i)}, \mathbf{m} = x_{k-1}^{(i)} + \pi, \mathrm{s} = 0.10\right)$$

Taking 100 particles and 500 observation points, the EPF converges very quickly to $\hat{\pi} = 3.148200$. Alternatively, the simple PF (with no Kalman component) would converge to $\hat{\pi} = 3.140266$.

Note that this example is Gaussian and linear, and therefore the particle filtering is *not* an improvement over the Kalman filter! Indeed the Kalman filter is optimal for Gaussian linear cases.

Application to the Heston Model We could now apply the above particle filtering algorithm to our one-dimensional state, where $x_k = v_k$ and $z_k = \ln S_{k+1}$ as before. Calling

$$\mathbf{n}(x, \mathbf{m}, \mathrm{s}) = \frac{1}{\sqrt{2\pi}\mathrm{s}} \exp\left(-\frac{(x - \mathbf{m})^2}{2\mathrm{s}^2}\right)$$

the normal density with mean $\mathbf{m}$ and standard deviation s, we will have

$$q\left(\tilde{x}_k^{(i)}|x_{k-1}^{(i)}, z_{1:k}\right) = \mathbf{n}\left(\tilde{x}_k^{(i)}, \mathbf{m} = \hat{x}_k^{(i)}, \mathrm{s} = \sqrt{P_k^{(i)}}\right)$$

as well as

$$p\left(z_k|\tilde{x}_k^{(i)}\right) = \mathbf{n}\left(z_k, \mathbf{m} = z_{k-1} + \left(\mu_S - \frac{1}{2}\tilde{x}_k^{(i)}\right)\Delta t, \mathrm{s} = \sqrt{\tilde{x}_k^{(i)}}\sqrt{\Delta t}\right)$$

and

$$p\left(\tilde{x}_k^{(i)}|x_{k-1}^{(i)}\right) =$$

$$\mathbf{n}\left(\tilde{x}_k^{(i)}, \mathbf{m} = x_{k-1}^{(i)} + \left[(\omega - \rho\xi\mu_S) - \left(\theta - \frac{1}{2}\rho\xi\right)x_{k-1}^{(i)}\right]\Delta t + \rho\xi(z_{k-1} - z_{k-2}), \mathrm{s}\right)$$

with

$$\mathrm{s} = \xi\sqrt{1-\rho^2}\sqrt{x_{k-1}^{(i)}}\sqrt{\Delta t}$$

which provides us with the densities we need for the filter implementation.

The estimation of the observable state z_k is

$$\hat{z}_k^- = \frac{1}{N_{sims}}\sum_{i=1}^{N_{sims}} \hat{z}_k^{(i)}$$

with $\hat{z}_k^{(i)}$ the estimation of z_k from $\mathbf{KF}(x_{k-1}^{(i)})$.

Following is a C++ routine for the EPF applied to the Heston model; 1000 particles are being used.

```
// log_stock_prices  are the log of stock prices
// muS is the real-world stock drift
// n_stock_prices is the number of the above stock
prices
// (omega, theta, xi, rho) are the Heston parameters
// ll is the value of (negative log) Likelihood
function
// estimates[] are the estimated observations from the
filter

// The function ran2() is from Numerical Recipes in C
// and generates uniform random variables
// The function Normal_inverse() can be found from
many sources
// and is the inverse of the Normal CDF
// Normal_inverse(ran2(.)) generates a set of Normal
random variables

void estimate_particle_extended_kalman_parameters_1_dim(
double *log_stock_prices,
double muS,
int n_stock_prices,
double omega,
double theta,
double xi,
double rho,
double *ll,
double *estimates)
{
  int     i1, i2, i3;
  double  H, A, x0, P0, z;
  int     M=1000;
  double  x[1000], xx[1000], x1[1000], x2[1000];
  double  P[1000], P1[1000], U[1000], K[1000], W[1000];
  double  w[1000],  u[1000], c[1000];
  double  q, pz, px, s, m, l;
  double  delt=1.0/252.0, x1_sum;
  long    idum=-1;

  A = 1.0-(theta-0.5*rho*xi)*delt;
  H = -0.5*delt;

  x0 = 0.04;
  P0 = 0.000001;
  for (i2=0; i2<M; i2++)
```

```
{
 x[i2] = x0 + sqrt(P0)* Normal_inverse(ran2(&idum));
 P[i2] = P0;
}

*ll=0.0;
for (i1=1;i1<n_stock_prices-1;i1++)
{
  l = 0.0;
  x1_sum=0.0;
  for (i2=0; i2<M; i2++)
  {
    /* EKF for the proposal distribution */
    if (x[i2]<0) x[i2]=0.00001;
    x1[i2] = x[i2] + ( omega-rho*xi*muS - (theta-
      0.5*rho*xi) * x[i2]) * delt + rho*xi*
      (log_stock_prices[i1]-log_stock_prices[i1-1]);
    W[i2]  = xi*sqrt((1-rho*rho) * x[i2] * delt);
    P1[i2] = W[i2]*W[i2] + A*P[i2]*A;
    if (x1[i2]<0) x1[i2]=0.00001;
    U[i2] = sqrt(x1[i2]*delt);
    K[i2] = P1[i2]*H/( H*P1[i2]*H + U[i2]*U[i2]);
    z = log_stock_prices[i1+1];
    x2[i2] = x1[i2] + K[i2] * (z - (log_stock_prices[i1]
    + (muS-0.5*x1[i2])*delt));
    x1_sum+= x1[i2];
    P[i2]=(1.0-K[i2]*H)*P1[i2];
    /* sample */
    xx[i2] = x2[i2]+sqrt(P[i2])*Normal_inverse(ran2(&idum));
    if (xx[i2]<0) xx[i2]=0.00001;
    /* calculate weights */
    m = x2[i2];
    s = sqrt(P[i2]);
    q = 0.39894228/s * exp( - 0.5* (xx[i2] - m)*
        (xx[i2] - m)/(s*s) );
    m = log_stock_prices[i1] + (muS-0.5*xx[i2])*delt;
    s = sqrt(xx[i2]*delt);
    pz = 0.39894228/s * exp( - 0.5* (z - m)*(z - m)/(s*s) );
    m = x[i2] + ( omega-rho*xi*muS - (theta-0.5*
         rho*xi) * x[i2]) * delt + rho*xi*
        (log_stock_prices[i1]-log_stock_prices[i1-1]);
    s = xi*sqrt((1-rho*rho) * x[i2] * delt);
    px = 0.39894228/s * exp( - 0.5* (xx[i2] - m)*
        (xx[i2] - m)/(s*s) );
```

```
      w[i2] = pz * px / MAX(q, 1.0e-10);
      l += w[i2];
    }
    *ll += log(l);
    estimates[i1+1]= log_stock_prices[i1] +
                     (muS-0.5*x1_sum/M)*delt;
    /* normalize weights */
    for (i2=0; i2<M; i2++)
      w[i2] /= l;
    /* resample and reset weights */
    c[0]=0;
    for (i2=1; i2<M; i2++)
      c[i2] = c[i2-1] + w[i2];
    i2=0;
    u[0] = 1.0/M * ran2(&idum);
    for (i3=0; i3<M; i3++)
    {
      u[i3] = u[0] + 1.0/M *i3;
      while (u[i3] > c[i2])
    i2++;
      x[i3] = xx[i2];
      w[i3] = 1.0/M;
    }
  }

  *ll *= -1.0;

}

// *ll is the value of (negative log) Likelihood
function
// we can minimize it to obtain the optimal
parameter-set
```

Next is the same routine for the unscented filter.

```
void estimate_particle_unscented_kalman_parameters_1_dim(
double *log_stock_prices,
double muS,
int n_stock_prices,
double omega,
double theta,
double xi,
```

```
double rho,

double *ll,
double *estimates)
{
  int       i1, i2, i3, i4;
  int       na=3;
  double    x0, P0;
  double    Wm[7], Wc[7];
  int       M=1000;
  double    x[1000], xx[1000], x1[1000], x2[1000],
            zz[1000], Z[1000][7];
  double    X[1000][7], Xa[1000][3][7];
  double    xa[1000][3], prod[1000];
  double    P[1000], P1[1000], U[1000], K[1000],
            W[1000], Pzz[1000];
  double    w[1000],  u[1000], c[1000];
  double    ***Pa, ***proda;
  double    q, pz, px, s, m, l, z;
  double    delt=1.0/252.0;
  long      idum=-1;
  int       ret;
  double    a=0.001 , b=0.0, k=0.0, lambda;

  proda= new double ** [M];
  Pa =   new double ** [M];
  for (i2=0;i2<M;i2++)
  {
    Pa[i2]= new double * [na];
    proda[i2]= new double * [na];
    for (i1=0;i1<na;i1++)
    {
      Pa[i2][i1]= new double [na];
      proda[i2][i1]= new double [na];
    }
  }

  for (i2=0;i2<M;i2++)
  {
    for (i1=0;i1<na;i1++)
    {
      for (i3=0;i3<na;i3++)
      {
    proda[i2][i1][i3]=0.0;
```

```
        }
      }
    }

    lambda = a*a*(na +k)-na;
    Wm[0]=lambda/(na+lambda);
    Wc[0]=lambda/(na+lambda) + (1-a*a+b);
    for (i3=1;i3<(2*na+1);i3++)
    {
      Wm[i3]=Wc[i3]=1/(2*(na+lambda));
    }

    x0 = 0.04;
    P0 = 0.000001;
    for (i2=0; i2<M; i2++)
    {
     x[i2] = x0 + sqrt(P0)* Normal_inverse(ran2(&idum));
     P[i2] = P0;

      xa[i2][0]=x[i2];
      xa[i2][1]=xa[i2][2]=0.0;

      Pa[i2][0][0]= P[i2];
      Pa[i2][1][1]= Pa[i2][2][2] = 1.0;
      Pa[i2][1][0]= Pa[i2][0][1]= Pa[i2][1][2] =
      Pa[i2][2][1] =
    Pa[i2][0][2] = Pa[i2][2][0] = 0.0;
    }


    *ll=0.0;
    for (i1=1;i1<n_stock_prices-1;i1++)
    {
      l = 0.0;
      estimates[i1+1]=0.0;
      for (i2=0; i2<M; i2++)
      {
        /* UKF for the proposal distribution */
        for (i3=0;i3<na;i3++)
        {
      Xa[i2][i3][0]= xa[i2][i3];
        }
```

```
      for (i3=0;i3<na;i3++)
      {
    for (i4=0;i4<na;i4++)
      {
      if (i3==i4)
      {
        if (Pa[i2][i3][i4] < 1.0e-10)
          Pa[i2][i3][i4]= 1.0e-10;
      }
      else
      {
        if (Pa[i2][i3][i4] < 1.0e-10)
          Pa[i2][i3][i4] = 0.0;
      }
    }
          }

      ret = sqrt_matrix(Pa[i2],proda[i2],na);

      for (i3=1;i3<(1+na);i3++)
      {
    for (i4=0;i4<na;i4++)
        {
      Xa[i2][i4][i3]= xa[i2][i4] + sqrt(na+lambda) *
                      proda[i2][i4][i3-1];
    }
      }
      for (i3=(1+na);i3<(2*na+1);i3++)
      {
    for (i4=0;i4<na;i4++)
      {
      Xa[i2][i4][i3]= xa[i2][i4] - sqrt(na+lambda) *
                      proda[i2][i4][i3-na-1];
    }
      }

      for (i3=0;i3<(2*na+1);i3++)
      {
    if (Xa[i2][0][i3]<0) Xa[i2][0][i3]=0.0001;
    X[i2][i3]= Xa[i2][0][i3] + (omega-muS*rho*xi    -
(theta-0.5*rho*xi) *Xa[i2][0][i3])*delt +
    rho*xi* (log_stock_prices[i1]-
```

```
    log_stock_prices[i1-1]) +
    xi*sqrt((1-rho*rho)*delt*Xa[i2][0][i3])*
    Xa[i2][1][i3];
      }

      x1[i2] = 0;
      for (i3=0;i3<(2*na+1);i3++)
      {
      x1[i2] += Wm[i3]*X[i2][i3];
      }

      P1[i2]=0.0;
      for (i3=0;i3<(2*na+1);i3++)
      {
      P1[i2] += Wc[i3]*(X[i2][i3]-x1[i2])*(X[i2][i3]-
      x1[i2]);
      }

      zz[i2]=0;
      for (i3=0;i3<(2*na+1);i3++)
      {
    if (X[i2][i3]<0) X[i2][i3]=0.00001;
    Z[i2][i3] = log_stock_prices[i1] +
(muS-0.5*X[i2][i3])*delt + sqrt(X[i2][i3]*delt)*Xa[i2][2][i3];
      zz[i2] += Wm[i3]*Z[i2][i3];
      }

    Pzz[i2]=0;
    for (i3=0;i3<(2*na+1);i3++)
      {
      Pzz[i2] +=  Wc[i3]*(Z[i2][i3]-zz[i2])*(Z[i2][i3]-
      zz[i2]);
      }

      prod[i2]=0.0;
      for (i3=0;i3<(2*na+1);i3++)
      {
      prod[i2] += Wc[i3]*(X[i2][i3]-x1[i2])* (Z[i2][i3]-
      zz[i2]);
      }


      K[i2]= prod[i2]/Pzz[i2];
```

```
        z = log_stock_prices[i1+1];
        estimates[i1+1] += zz[i2]/M;


        x2[i2] = x1[i2] + K[i2]*(z - zz[i2]);
        P[i2] = P1[i2] - K[i2]*K[i2] * Pzz[i2];


        xa[i2][0]=x2[i2];
        Pa[i2][0][0] = P[i2];


        if (x2[i2]<0) x2[i2]=0.0001;

        Pa[i2][1][0]= Pa[i2][0][1]= Pa[i2][1][2]
        =Pa[i2][2][1]= Pa[i2][0][2]=Pa[i2][2][0]=[0];
        /* sample */
        xx[i2] = x2[i2] + sqrt(P[i2])*
        Normal_inverse(ran2(&idum));
        if (xx[i2]<0) xx[i2]=0.00001;
        /* calculate weights */
        m = x2[i2];
        s = sqrt(P[i2]);
        q = 0.39894228/s * exp( - 0.5* (xx[i2] - m)*
        (xx[i2] - m)/(s*s) );
        m= log_stock_prices[i1] + (muS-0.5*xx[i2])*delt;
        s= sqrt(xx[i2]*delt);
        pz= 0.39894228/s * exp( - 0.5* (z - m)*
        (z - m)/(s*s) );
        m= x[i2] + ( omega-rho*xi*muS -
        (theta-0.5*rho*xi) * x[i2]) * delt +
              rho*xi* (log_stock_prices[i1]-
              log_stock_prices[i1-1]);
        s= xi*sqrt((1-rho*rho) * x[i2] * delt);
        px= 0.39894228/s * exp( - 0.5* (xx[i2] - m)*
        (xx[i2] - m)/(s*s) );

        w[i2]= MAX(pz, 1.0e-10) *
MAX(px, 1.0e-10) / MAX(q, 1.0e-10);
l += w[i2];
     }
     *ll += log(l);
     /* normalize weights */
```

```
    for (i2=0; i2<M; i2++)
      w[i2] /= l;
    /* resample and reset weights */
    c[0]=0;
    for (i2=1; i2<M; i2++)
      c[i2] = c[i2-1] + w[i2];
      i2=0;
      u[0] = 1.0/M * ran2(&idum);
    for (i3=0; i3<M; i3++)
    {
      u[i3] = u[0] + 1.0/M *i3;
      while (u[i3] > c[i2])
    i2++;
      x[i3]= xx[i2];
      w[i3]=1.0/M;
    }
  }

  *ll *= -1.0;

  for (i2=0;i2<M;i2++)
  {
    for (i1=0;i1<na;i1++)
    {
      delete [] Pa[i2][i1];
      delete [] proda[i2][i1];
    }
  }
  for (i2=0;i2<M;i2++)
  {
    delete [] Pa[i2];
    delete [] proda[i2];
  }
  delete [] Pa;
  delete [] proda;


}
```

Test Results The results from an extended particle filter (EPF) are shown in Figure 2.21. The filter was constructed with the one-dimensional Heston

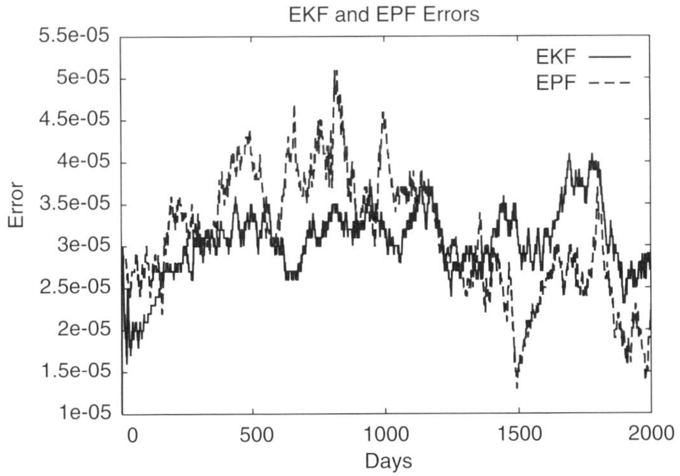

FIGURE 2.21 Filtering Errors: Extended Kalman Filter and Extended Particle Filter Are Applied to the One-Dimensional Heston Model. The PF has better performance.

model and was applied to a simulated time series of 5000 points with

$$\Psi^* = (0.40, 10.0, 0.01, -0.50)$$

As we can see in the figure, no clear superiority of the EPF is detected. The optimal parameters found via EPF are

$$\hat{\Psi}_{EPF} = (0.020331, 0.499987, 0.040000, 0.050026)$$

which could not be considered as an improvement over

$$\hat{\Psi}_{EKF} = (0.065886, 1.711686, 0.180884, 0.147660)$$

Again the long-term-variances $\frac{\omega}{\theta}$ are close to 0.04 for all cases, which is consistent with what we had observed.

The next natural step would be to implement and test the unscented particle filter (UPF), in which everything is done similarly to the EPF except for the choice of the proposal distribution. The use of the UPF has been strongly recommended by Wan and Van der Merwe in [231] and [133]. The authors claim that the filtering error from the UPF is considerably smaller than that from EKF, UKF, or EPF. As we can see in Figure 2.22, it is true that the filtering error resulting from UPF is considerably lower than the error generated from the other filters. However, the optimal parameter set

$$\hat{\Psi}_{UPF} = (0.020132, 0.500031, 0.040000, 0.050004)$$

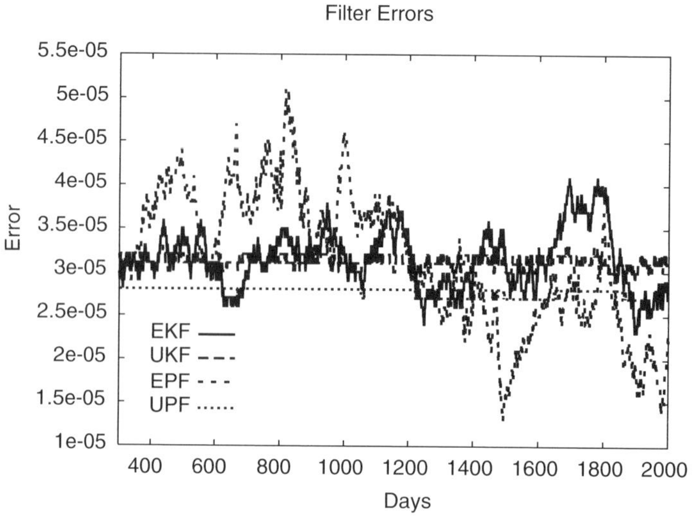

FIGURE 2.22 Filtering Errors: All Filters Are Applied to the One-Dimensional Heston Model. The PF's have better performance.

obtained via UPF is again very different from the original parameter set Ψ^* used in the data generation. We shall analyze the reasons behind this poor inference result more closely in the following sections.

Error Size One possibility is that our time series has too small an error for the filters to make a significant difference. We thus study another case, where $\Delta t = 1$ year. Let us take 200 points generated with the parameter set

$$\Psi^* = (0.02, 0.5, 0.05, -0.5)$$

We obtain

$$\hat{\Psi}_{EKF} = (0.036, 0.093, 0.036, -1.00)$$

and

$$\hat{\Psi}_{UKF} = (0.033, 0.086, 0.033, -0.98)$$

which shows that UKF results are very close to EKF ones. Using the particle filters, we get

$$\hat{\Psi}_{EPF} = (0.019, 0.5, 0.03, -0.58)$$

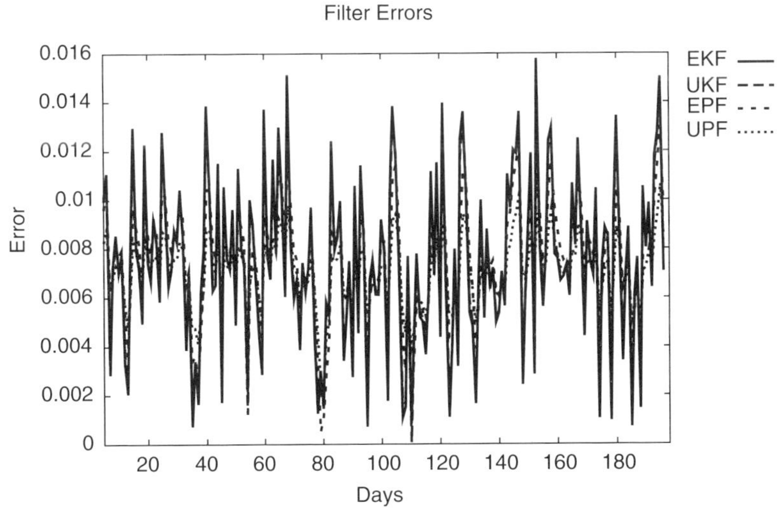

FIGURE 2.23 Filters Are Applied to the One-Dimensional Heston Model. The time series has a larger time-step $\Delta t = 1.0$. Naturally, the errors are larger than the case where $\Delta t = 1/252$.

which is considerably closer to the original set Ψ^*. Therefore EPF did bring an improvement over the traditional nonlinear filters and seems to be simpler and more robust[24] than its competitors.

As for the filtering errors, it can be seen in Figure 2.23 that the EPF errors are smaller than (although comparable to) those produced by EKF and UKF, which is consistent with the particle filtering theory.

As for UPF, we obtain

$$\hat{\Psi}_{UPF} = (0.019480, 0.489375, 0.047030, -0.229242)$$

which is very close to the EPF result. As we can see, the UPF errors are even smaller than those generated by EPF. In addition to the filters just discussed, it would be interesting to test a Gauss-Hermite filter (GHF) [151]. We obtain

$$\hat{\Psi}_{GHF} = (0.020398, 0.524215, 0.069661, -1.000000)$$

which is closer to the real parameter set Ψ^* compared with EKF or UKF results. However, the filtering error is more variable than that of its competitors, as can be seen in Figure 2.24. Note, however, that this would mean that

[24]This is because for a larger time step the nonlinearity and non-Gaussianity have a stronger impact.

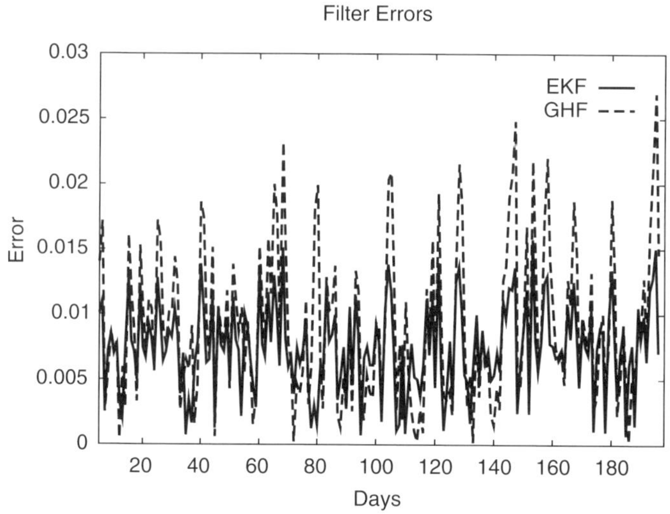

FIGURE 2.24 The EKF and GHF Are Applied to the One-Dimensional Heston Model. The time series has a larger time step $\Delta t = 1.0$. Naturally, the errors are larger than the case where $\Delta t = 1/252$.

we would have access to 200 years of historic data, which is clearly unrealistic.[25] This issue will be revisited in the following sections. Also, here we generated the data via a discrete equation with $\Delta t = 1$. Thus there was no discretization error from a continuous equation. We cannot apply the same method to data coming from a continuous process.

As a measure of performance, we can compute the mean price error (MPE) as well as the root mean square error (RMSE) for each filter. These correspond respectively to the mean and the standard deviation of the plotted errors. For the MPEs, we obtain

	MPE	RMSE
EKF	0.007484269	0.003422215
UKF	0.007660269	0.003733748
GKF	0.009129157	0.005816919
EPF	0.007620208	0.002269224
UPF	0.007076066	0.001359393

[25] What is more, the Girsanov theorem would *not* be valid and (ξ, ρ) would have no reason to be the same under the risk-neutral and real measures.

This shows us again that the particle filters outperform the other ones. Again, let us remember that given 200 points with $\Delta t = 1$ and a true parameter set

$$\Psi^* = (0.02, 0.5, 0.05, -0.5)$$

we obtained

	$\hat{\omega}$	$\hat{\theta}$	$\hat{\xi}$	$\hat{\rho}$
EKF	0.036	0.093	0.036	−1.00
UKF	0.033	0.086	0.033	−0.98
GKF	0.020	0.524	0.070	−1.00
EPF	0.019	0.500	0.033	−0.58
UPF	0.019	0.489	0.047	−0.22

The MH Enhancement As mentioned earlier, the resampling algorithm helps with the issue of *degeneracy*, which means that it will reduce the variance of the weights. However, it might introduce a *sample impoverishment* phenomenon, in which all particles will have a tendency to collapse to one. The Metropolis-Hastings (MH) algorithm could be a solution to this problem and is implemented as follows. After resampling, Step 6, we obtain a set $\tilde{\tilde{x}}_{1:k}^{(i)}$.

6-a. Reapply the Kalman filter (extended or unscented) to this set in order to obtain

$$x_k^{*(i)} = KF\left(\tilde{\tilde{x}}_{k-1}^{(i)}\right)$$

6-b. Choose between $x_k^{*(i)}$ and $\tilde{\tilde{x}}_k^{(i)}$ as follows. Define

$$\alpha = min\left(1, \frac{p(z_k|x_k^{*(i)})p(x_k^{*(i)}|x_{k-1}^{(i)})q(\tilde{\tilde{x}}_k^{(i)}|x_{k-1}^{(i)}, z_{1:k})}{p(z_k|\tilde{\tilde{x}}_k^{(i)})p(\tilde{\tilde{x}}_k^{(i)}|x_{k-1}^{(i)})q(x_k^{*(i)}|x_{k-1}^{(i)}, z_{1:k})}\right)$$

then sample v from $\mathcal{U}[0, 1]$ and choose $x_k^{*(i)}$ if $\alpha > v$ and choose $\tilde{\tilde{x}}_k^{(i)}$ if $\alpha \leq v$.

The result is then $x_k^{(i)}$, and we go to Step 7 as before.

Note that α could be interpreted as the ratio of the non-normalized weights for the two particles we are choosing from. Indeed

$$\alpha = \alpha_k^{(i)} = min\left(1, \frac{w(x_k^{*(i)})}{w(\tilde{\tilde{x}}_k^{(i)})}\right)$$

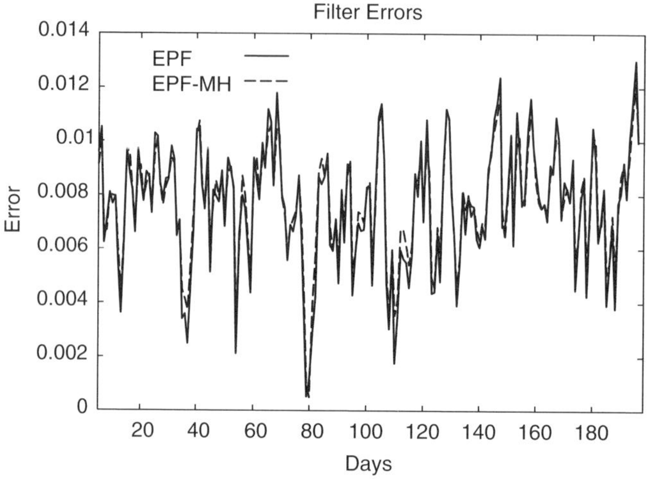

FIGURE 2.25 The EPF Without and with the Metropolis-Hastings Step is Applied to the One-Dimensional Heston Model. The time series has a time step $\Delta t = 1.0$. The improvement is hardly visible.

Applied to the same time series as in the previous paragraphs, the EPF with the MH modification will provide

$$\hat{\Psi}_{EPF-MH} = (0.019, 0.499, 0.040, -0.358)$$

and

$$MPE_{EPF-MH} = 0.007753$$
$$RMSE_{EPF-MH} = 0.001927$$

compared with the previous EPF

$$MPE_{EPF} = 0.00762$$
$$RMSE_{EPF} = 0.002269$$

As we can see from these results and Figure 2.25, there is only a marginal improvement from the introduction of the MH step in the filtering process. This is in line with the findings in the literature, such as in [231].

Comparing Heston with other Models

We can now apply our inference tools to real market data in order to see which model matches the true dynamics of the assets more closely, and therefore perform *model identification*.

The Models It is easy to generalize the Heston state-space model to other stochastic volatility approaches. Indeed we could replace the Heston state equation with

$$v_k = v_{k-1} + (\omega - \theta v_{k-1})\Delta t + \xi v_{k-1}^p \sqrt{\Delta t} Z_{k-1} \tag{2.26}$$

where $p = 1/2$ would naturally correspond to the Heston (square root) model, $p = 1$ to the GARCH diffusion-limit model, and $p = 3/2$ to the 3/2 model. These models have all been described and analyzed in [177]. The new state transition equation would therefore become

$$\begin{aligned} v_k = v_{k-1} &+ \left[\omega - \rho\xi\mu_S v_{k-1}^{p-\frac{1}{2}} - \left(\theta - \frac{1}{2}\rho\xi v_{k-1}^{p-\frac{1}{2}}\right) v_{k-1}\right]\Delta t \\ &+ \rho\xi v_{k-1}^{p-\frac{1}{2}} \ln\left(\frac{S_k}{S_{k-1}}\right) + \xi\sqrt{1-\rho^2} v_{k-1}^p \sqrt{\Delta t} \tilde{Z}_{k-1} \end{aligned} \tag{2.27}$$

where the same choice of state space $x_k = v_k$ is made.

For the EKF, we will have

$$\begin{aligned} A_k = 1 &- \left[\rho\xi\mu_S \left(p - \frac{1}{2}\right) v_{k-1}^{p-\frac{3}{2}} + \theta - \frac{1}{2}\rho\xi\left(p + \frac{1}{2}\right) v_{k-1}^{p-\frac{1}{2}}\right]\Delta t \\ &+ \left(p - \frac{1}{2}\right)\rho\xi v_{k-1}^{p-\frac{3}{2}} \ln\left(\frac{S_k}{S_{k-1}}\right) \end{aligned}$$

and

$$W_k = \xi\sqrt{1-\rho^2} v_{k-1}^p \sqrt{\Delta t}$$

as well as

$$H_k = -\frac{1}{2}\Delta t$$

and

$$U_k = \sqrt{v_k}\sqrt{\Delta t}$$

The same time update and measurement update equations could be used with the UKF or Kushner's NLF.

We could also apply the particle filtering algorithm to our problem. Using the same notations as before and calling

$$\mathbf{n}(x, \mathbf{m}, \mathbf{s}) = \frac{1}{\sqrt{2\pi}\mathbf{s}} \exp\left(-\frac{(x-\mathbf{m})^2}{2\mathbf{s}^2}\right)$$

the normal density with mean $\mathbf{m}$ and standard deviation $\mathbf{s}$, we will have

$$q(\tilde{x}_k^{(i)} | x_{k-1}^{(i)}, z_{1:k}) = \mathbf{n}\left(\tilde{x}_k^{(i)}, \mathbf{m} = \hat{x}_k^{(i)}, \mathbf{s} = \sqrt{P_k^{(i)}}\right)$$

as well as

$$p(z_k|\tilde{x}_k^{(i)}) = \mathbf{n}\left(z_k, \mathbf{m} = z_{k-1} + \left(\mu_S - \frac{1}{2}\tilde{x}_k^{(i)}\right)\Delta t, \mathbf{s} = \sqrt{\tilde{x}_k^{(i)}}\sqrt{\Delta t}\right)$$

and

$$p\left(\tilde{x}_k^{(i)}|x_{k-1}^{(i)}\right) = \mathbf{n}\left(\tilde{x}_k^{(i)}, \mathbf{m}_\mathbf{x}, \mathbf{s} = \xi\sqrt{1-\rho^2}\left(x_{k-1}^{(i)}\right)^p\sqrt{\Delta t}\right)$$

with

$$\mathbf{m}_\mathbf{x} = x_{k-1}^{(i)} + \left[\omega - \rho\xi\mu_S\left(x_{k-1}^{(i)}\right)^{p-\frac{1}{2}} - \left(\theta - \frac{1}{2}\rho\xi\left(x_{k-1}^{(i)}\right)^{p-\frac{1}{2}}\right)x_{k-1}^{(i)}\right]\Delta t$$
$$+ \rho\xi\left(x_{k-1}^{(i)}\right)^{p-\frac{1}{2}}(z_{k-1} - z_{k-2})$$

and as before we have

$$w_k^{(i)} = w_{k-1}^{(i)}\frac{p\left(z_k|\tilde{x}_k^{(i)}\right)p\left(\tilde{x}_k^{(i)}|x_{k-1}^{(i)}\right)}{q\left(\tilde{x}_k^{(i)}|x_{k-1}^{(i)}, z_{1:k}\right)}$$

which provides us with what we need for the filter implementation.

The Results The preceding filters were applied to five years of S&P 500 time series (1996 to 2001), and the filtering errors were considered for the Heston, the GARCH, and the 3/2 models. Daily index closing prices were used for this purpose, and the time interval was set to $\Delta t = 1/252$ (see the following table; Figures 2.26 through 2.32).

Filter and Model	MPE	RMSE
EKF-Heston	3.58207e-05	1.83223e-05
EKF-GARCH	2.78438e-05	1.42428e-05
EKF-3/2	2.63227e-05	1.74760e-05
UKF-Heston	3.00000e-05	1.91280e-05
UKF-GARCH	2.99275e-05	2.58131e-05
UKF-3/2	2.82279e-05	1.55777e-05
EPF-Heston	2.70104e-05	1.34534e-05
EPF-GARCH	2.48733e-05	4.99337e-06
EPF-3/2	2.26462e-05	2.58645e-06
UPF-Heston	2.04000e-05	2.74818e-06
UPF-GARCH	2.63036e-05	8.44030e-07
UPF -3/2	1.73857e-05	4.09918e-06

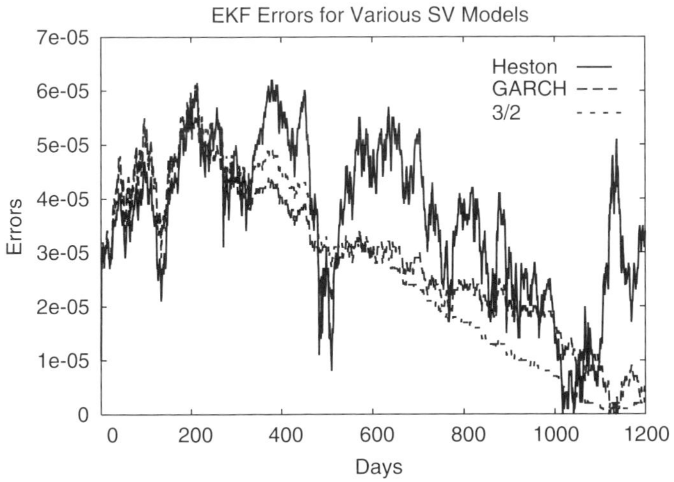

FIGURE 2.26 Comparison of EKF Filtering Errors for Heston, GARCH, and 3/2 Models. The latter seems to perform better.

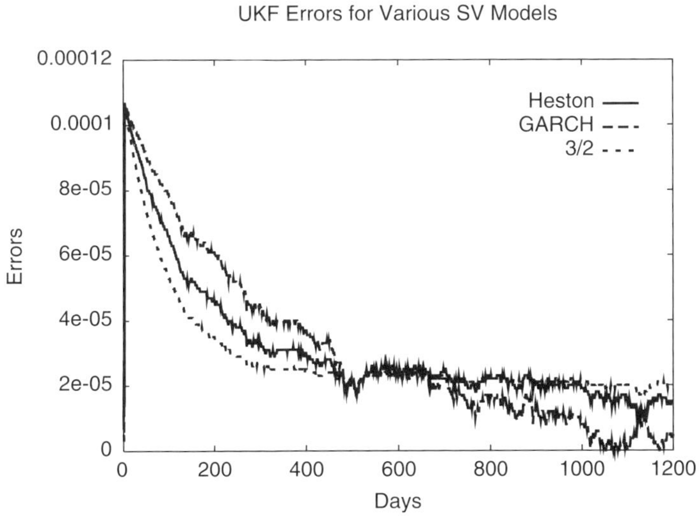

FIGURE 2.27 Comparison of UKF Filtering Errors for Heston, GARCH, and 3/2 Models. The latter seems to perform better.

Two immediate observations can be made: On one hand, particle filters have a better performance than do the Gaussian, which reconfirms what one would anticipate. On the other hand, for most of the filters, the 3/2 model seems to outperform the Heston model, which is in line with the findings of Engle & Ishida [95]. Again, this shows that the filtering process could be

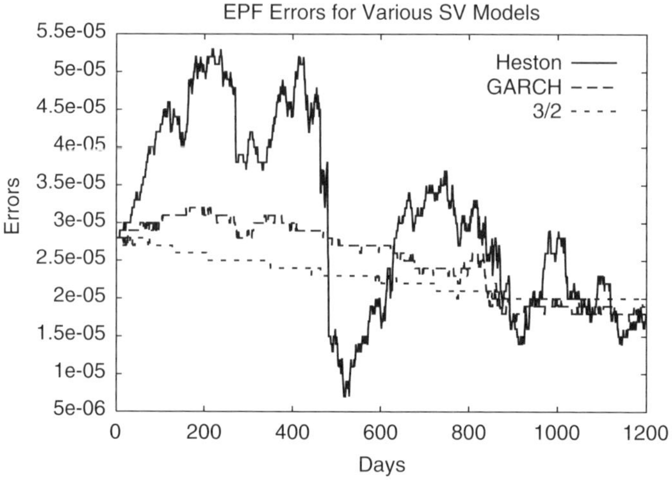

FIGURE 2.28 Comparison of EPF Filtering Errors for Heston, GARCH, and 3/2 Models. The latter seems to perform better.

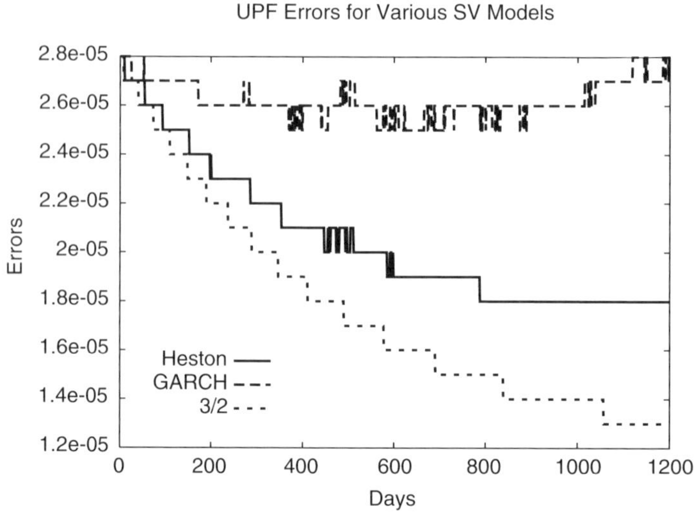

FIGURE 2.29 Comparison of UPF Filtering Errors for Heston, GARCH, and 3/2 Models. The latter seems to perform better.

used not only for parameter estimation but also for model identification. This suggests further filtering on other existing models, such as jump diffusion [190]. Clearly, because of the non-Gaussianity of jump-based models, the particle filtering technique will need to be applied to them.

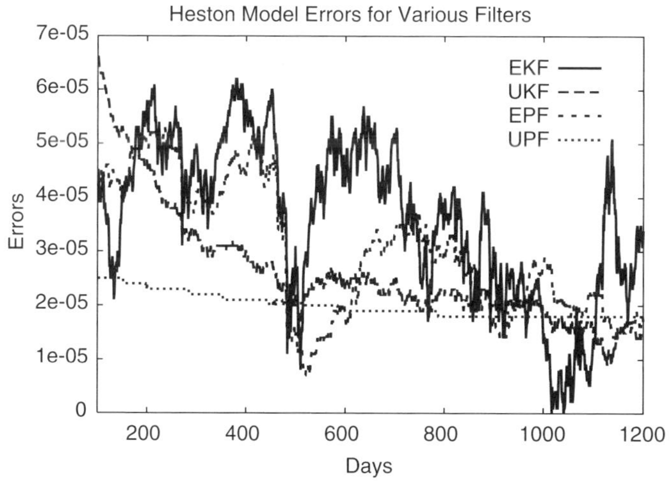

FIGURE 2.30 Comparison of Filtering Errors for the Heston Model. PFs seem to perform better.

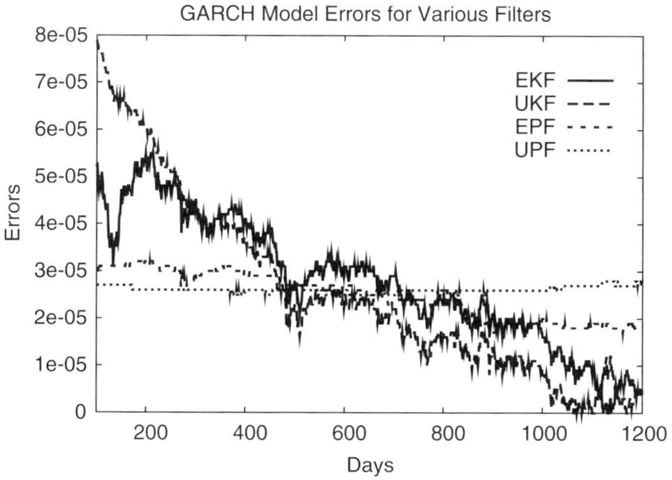

FIGURE 2.31 Comparison of Filtering Errors for the GARCH Model. PFs seem to perform better.

Parameter Learning Revisited We tried a joint filter (JF) via the Kalman filter where the parameters were given a prior distribution. We can now apply the particle filtering techniques to this framework as in [176] and [224]: We simulate $x_k^{(i)}$ at time step k from the prior $p(x_k|x_{k-1}^{(i)})$, and we also simulate

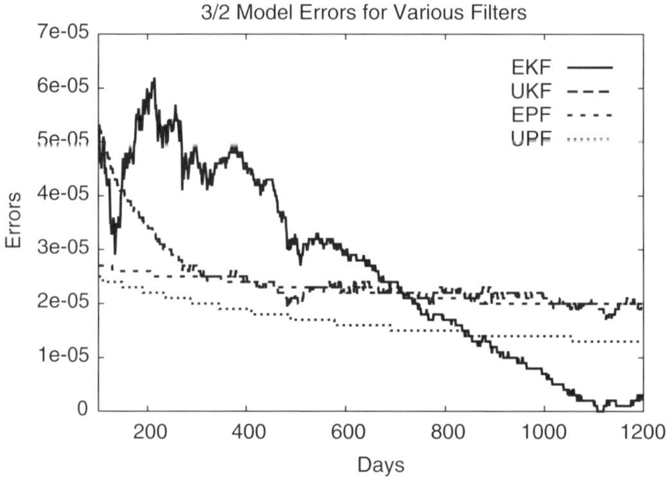

FIGURE 2.32 Comparison of Filtering Errors for the 3/2 Model. PFs seem to perform better.

each parameter $\psi^{(i)}$ from its prior $q(\psi) = \mathcal{N}(m_\psi, s_\psi)$ where these mean and standard deviations are to be determined.

We then update the priors by incorporating the observation z_k

$$p\left(x_k^{(i)}|z_k\right) \propto p\left(z_k|x_k^{(i)}, \psi^{(i)}\right) p\left(x_k^{(i)}|x_{k-1}^{(i)}\right)$$

and similarly

$$p(\psi^{(i)}|z_k) \propto p(z_k|x_k^{(i)}, \psi^{(i)})p(\psi^{(i)}|x_{k-1}^{(i)})$$

and we obtain the posterior distributions. Calling

$$w_k^{(i)} = \frac{p\left(z_k|x_k^{(i)}, \psi^{(i)}\right) w_{k-1}^{(i)}}{\sum_{i=1}^{N_{sims}} p\left(z_k|x_k^{(i)}, \psi^{(i)}\right) w_{k-1}^{(i)}}$$

We now have the posteriors of x_k and ψ, and we can simulate them for the following step via a Metropolis-Hastings (MH) accept/reject technique with the proposal distribution $q(\psi, m_\psi, s_\psi)$ with

$$m_\psi = \sum_{i=1}^{N_{sims}} w_k^{(i)} \psi^{(i)}$$

and

$$s_\psi = \sum_{i=1}^{N_{sims}} w_k^{(i)} \left(\psi^{(i)} - m_\psi\right)^2$$

TABLE 2.2 The True Parameter Set Ψ^* Used for Data Simulation

Ψ^*	$\omega^* = 0.10$	$\theta^* = 10.0$	$\xi^* = 0.03$	$\rho^* = -0.50$

TABLE 2.3 The Initial Parameter Set Ψ_0 Used for the Optimization Process

Ψ_0	$\omega_0 = 0.15$	$\theta_0 = 15.0$	$\xi_0 = 0.02$	$\rho_0 = -0.50$

The MH step will consist of the following. We accept the simulation point $\tilde{\psi}^{(i)}$ from $q()$ with a probability $\alpha(\psi^{(i)}, \tilde{\psi}^{(i)})$, where $\forall i$ between 1 and N_{sims} we have

$$\alpha\left(\psi^{(i)}, \tilde{\psi}^{(i)}\right) = min\left(1.0, \frac{p\left(\tilde{\psi}^{(i)}|z_k\right)/q\left(\tilde{\psi}^{(i)}\right)}{p\left(\psi^{(i)}|z_k\right)/q\left(\psi^{(i)}\right)}\right)$$

In practice, we simulate a uniform random variable u and accept the simulated point $\tilde{\psi}^{(i)}$ if $\alpha > u$, and reject it (and keep $\psi^{(i)}$) otherwise. We keep simulating alternatively the state variable and each parameter by incorporating the observations at each step and wait for the parameters to converge to their ideal mean.

It is important to note that this joint filtering differs from the usual MCMC techniques, such as in [156] and [92], where we update the particles by incorporating *all* observations at each simulation step.

The Performance of the Inference Tools

We have applied various Gaussian and particle-based filters to daily historic data. None of the methodologies performed very well at that frequency.[26] We now try to analyze the reasons.

A known weakness of optimization algorithms is the following. The higher the number of parameters, the worse the performance of the algorithm. This means that a one-parameter optimization should perform best. To test this, we simulate 5000 points[27] via the Heston model with a parameter set Ψ^* as shown in the following (also see Figure 2.33).

---

[26]Note that in this section we are not checking the validity of the assumption that the real stock market follows a Heston (or another) process. We *assume* we know the process exactly and try to recover the embedded parameters.

[27]We made the 5000 daily simulations directly from the discretized SDE with a $\Delta t = 1/252$. We also tried simulating $5,000,000$ points with $\Delta t = 1/252,000$ and sampling 5000 daily points from there. Although the second method is more

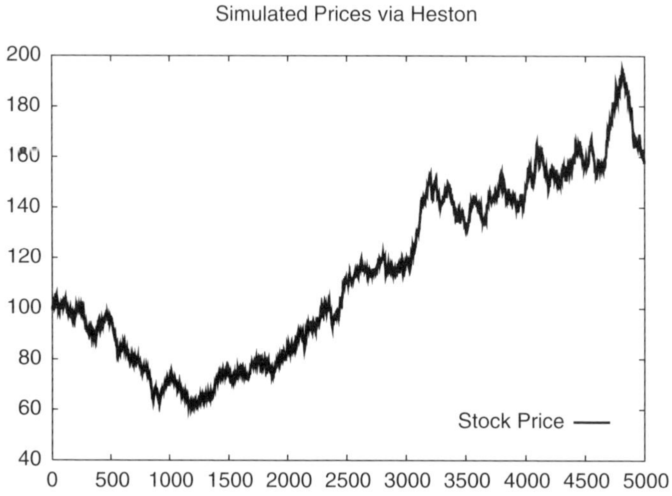

FIGURE 2.33 Simulated Stock-Price Path via Heston Using Ψ^*. This is an artificial time series following the Heston model.

We use a drift of $\mu_S = 0.025$ and a time step $\Delta t = 1/252$ as before. In order to get the best performance, we fix all parameters except one. For instance, to obtain $\hat{\omega}$ we fix $\theta = 10.0, \xi = 0.03, \rho = -0.50, \mu_S = 0.025$; we choose a reasonable initial point ω_0 and then optimize upon ω only. We choose an initial parameter set Ψ_0 as will be shown. The results are displayed in Table 2.4.

TABLE 2.4 The Optimal Parameter Set $\hat{\Psi}$. The estimation is performed individually for each parameter on the artificially generated time series. Particle filters use 1000 simulations.

Filter	$\hat{\omega}$	$\hat{\theta}$	$\hat{\xi}$	$\hat{\rho}$
EKF	0.098212	10.188843	0.052324	−0.873571
UKF	0.107281	10.089381	0.000001	+0.598434
EPF	0.098287	10.130531	0.044437	−0.827729
UPF	0.100581	10.221816	0.051902	−0.487695

correct, the difference in results was small, which means that the Euler discretization is sufficiently accurate at the daily level. This is in agreement with results found by Elerian [92].

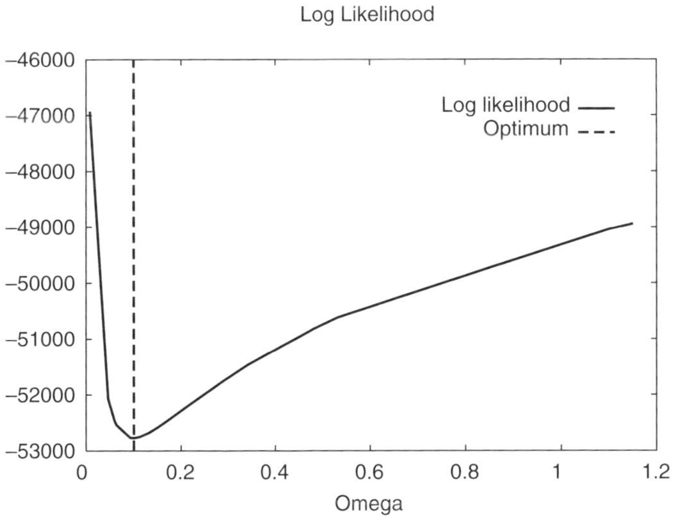

FIGURE 2.34 $f(\omega) = L(\omega, \hat{\theta}, \hat{\xi}, \hat{\rho})$ Has a Good Slope Around $\hat{\omega} = 0.10$.

It is interesting to note that the estimation of the volatility-drift parameters (ω, θ) could be done fairly well via EKF.[28] This makes sense because the dependence on these parameters is linear.

The estimation of volatility and correlation parameters (ξ, ρ) is not as straightforward. This could be seen by plotting the likelihood $L(\Psi)$ as a function of ω, θ, ξ, and ρ separately. We fix three parameters to their optimal values and plot $L(\Psi)$ as a function of the last one. We observe in Figures 2.34 through 2.37 that the likelihood function is fairly easy to optimize for (ω, θ). However, the function is very *flat* around the optimal ξ and ρ. Therein lies the difficulty of finding the optimums!

Sample Size It seems therefore that the estimation is inefficient for the parameter ξ no matter which filter we use. The issue is that of inefficiency (large error variance) for this given sample size. This is indeed one of the shortcomings of maximum likelihood estimators (MLE). For a given sample size, they can very well be inefficient and even have a bias.[29] The choice of the filter will not solve this problem. However, under minimal regularity

---

[28] A joint estimation of (ω, θ) based on the same data set with known (ξ, ρ) provides $(\hat{\omega} = 0.117889, \hat{\theta} = 11.996760)$.

[29] A known and simple example for the bias of MLEs is that of estimating the variance of a Gaussian sequence of a finite size $(x_1, ..., x_N)$. The ML estimate for the mean is $\hat{\mu}_N = \frac{1}{N}\sum_{k=1}^{N} x_k$, and the ML estimate for the variance is

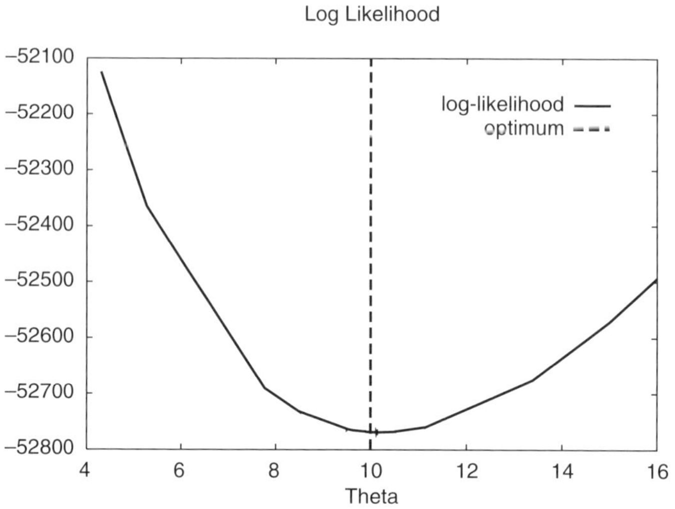

FIGURE 2.35 $f(\theta) = L(\hat{\omega}, \theta, \hat{\xi}, \hat{\rho})$ Has a Good Slope Around $\hat{\theta} = 10.0$.

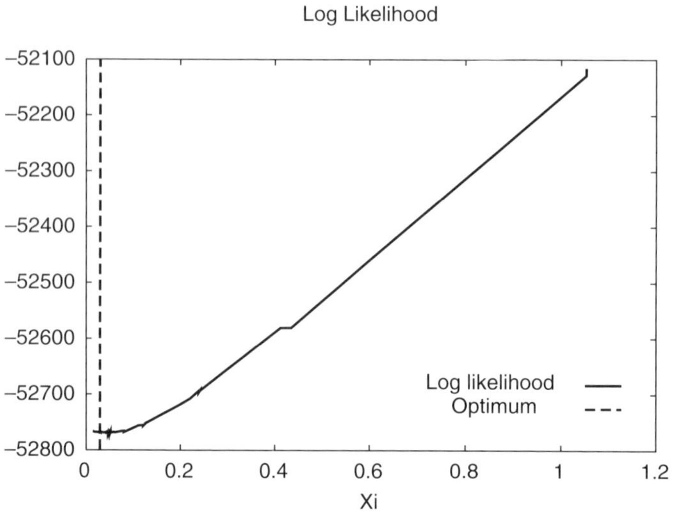

FIGURE 2.36 $f(\xi) = L(\hat{\omega}, \hat{\theta}, \xi, \hat{\rho})$ Is Flat Around $\hat{\xi} = 0.03$.

$\hat{v}_N = \frac{1}{N}\sum_{k=1}^{N}(x_k - \hat{\mu}_N)^2$. The latter ML estimation is biased, and the correct estimation would be $\hat{\hat{v}}_N = \frac{1}{N-1}\sum_{k=1}^{N}(x_k - \hat{\mu}_N)^2$. However, it is clear that as $N \to +\infty$ we have $\hat{v}_N \approx \hat{\hat{v}}_N$ and the bias gradually disappears.

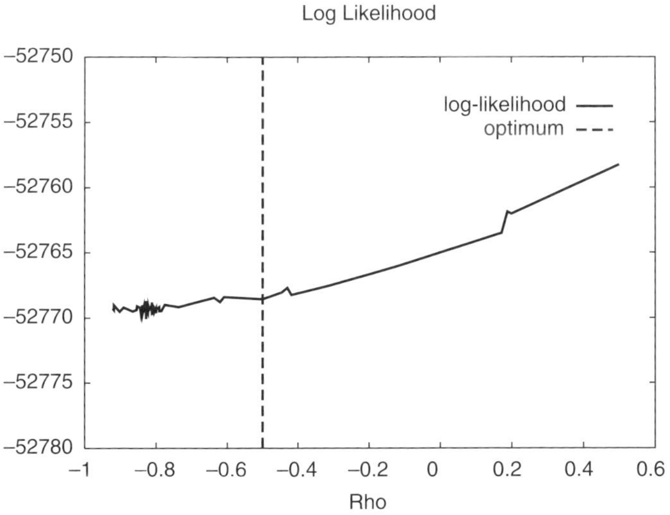

FIGURE 2.37 $f(\rho) = L(\hat{\omega}, \hat{\theta}, \hat{\xi}, \rho)$ Is Flat and Irregular Around $\hat{\rho} = -0.50$.

conditions, MLEs are consistent and therefore asymptotically converge to the correct optimum. This means that the sample size is key. To test this, we can choose larger samples of $N = 50,000$, $N = 100,000$, and $N = 500,000$ points and rerun the simplest filter, namely, the EKF. As expected, the optimum of the likelihood function becomes closer and closer to ξ^*. This can be seen in Figures 2.38 to 2.41 as well as in Table 2.5. The same exact observations could be made for the correlation parameter ρ, and the results are also displayed in Table 2.5. The likelihood graphs are omitted in the interest of brevity.

As for the drift parameters ω and θ, the convergence was good even for $N = 5000$, as previously observed. Unfortunately, in reality we have limited historic data. Even at a daily frequency, 50, 000 points would correspond to 200 years!

One possibility would be to use intra-day data; however, that assumes that the behavior of the stock price is the same intra-day (which is reasonable considering we started with a *continuous* SDE). Moreover, clean intra-day data is usually not readily available and needs preprocessing. Therefore, having p parameters in the optimal parameter set $\hat{\Psi}_N = \left(\hat{\Psi}_N[j]\right)_{1 \le j \le p}$ for a sample size N, we have for each parameter $\Psi[j]$

$$\lim_{N \to +\infty} \hat{\Psi}_N[j] \quad | \quad \left\{\Psi[k] = \Psi^*[k];\ 1 \le k \le p;\ k \ne j\right\} = \Psi^*[j] \quad (2.28)$$

What is more, this is true for any valid initial value $\Psi_0[j]$, which means the MLE is robust.

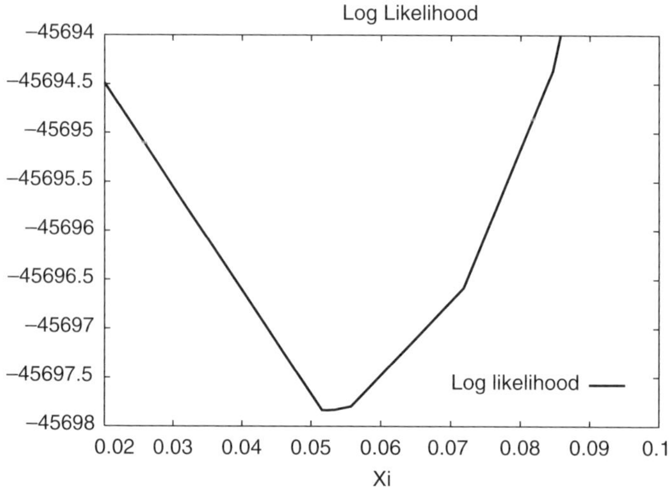

FIGURE 2.38 $f(\xi) = L(\hat{\omega}, \hat{\theta}, \xi, \hat{\rho})$ via EKF for $N = 5000$ Points. The true value is $\xi^* = 0.03$.

TABLE 2.5 The Optimal EKF Parameters $\hat{\xi}$ and $\hat{\rho}$ Given a Sample Size N. The true parameters are $\xi^* = 0.03$ and $\rho^* = -0.50$. The initial values were $\xi_0 = 0.02$ and $\rho_0 = -0.40$.

N	$\hat{\xi}$	$\hat{\rho}$
5000	0.052324	−0.873571
50,000	0.036463	−0.608088
100,000	0.033400	−0.556868
500,000	0.031922	−0.532142

Joint Estimation of the Parameters Let us now assume that we do not know any of the parameters; we choose an initial set Ψ_0 and test the consistency of the MLE. We shall apply the EKF to the data and take the same true parameter set Ψ^* as in the previous section. We assume that $\mu_S = 0.025$ is known; otherwise, it could be estimated together with the model parameters.

As previously mentioned, the likelihood function becomes flat and therefore harder to maximize under a higher number of parameters. The convergence of the estimator will therefore be slower. Despite this, we can observe in Table 2.8 the asymptotic convergence of the estimator even under the joint estimation of all parameters. We have now

$$\lim_{N \to +\infty} \hat{\Psi}_N = \Psi^* \tag{2.29}$$

TABLE 2.6 The True Parameter Set Ψ^* Used for Data Generation

Ψ^*	$\omega^* = 0.10$	$\theta^* = 10.0$	$\xi^* = 0.03$	$\rho^* = -0.50$

TABLE 2.7 The Initial Parameter Set Ψ_0 Used for the Optimization Process

Ψ_0	$\omega_0 = 0.15$	$\theta_0 = 15.0$	$\xi_0 = 0.02$	$\rho_0 = -0.40$

TABLE 2.8 The Optimal EKF Parameter Set $\hat{\Psi}$ Given a Sample Size N. The four parameters are estimated jointly.

N	$\hat{\omega}$	$\hat{\theta}$	$\hat{\xi}$	$\hat{\rho}$
5000	0.150854	15.294576	0.266175	−0.128835
50,000	0.126387	12.748852	0.020521	−1.000000
100,000	0.136023	13.700906	0.044353	−0.439961
500,000	0.100097	10.030336	0.061688	−0.257305
1,000,000	0.105264	10.548642	0.043818	−0.356234
2,000,000	0.103183	10.334876	0.039767	−0.374677
4,000,000	0.105292	10.538019	0.043288	−0.347562
5,000,000	0.101097	10.118951	0.028588	−0.514346

which corresponds to the generalization of (2.28) in the previous section.

We ran other filters (UKF, EPF, UPF) on the same data set and observed only marginal improvement. The results are omitted in the interest of brevity. It therefore seems that the fundamental issue is related to the slow convergence of the MLEs *regardless of the filtering method.*

A related issue previously mentioned is the size of the observation error $U_k \propto \sqrt{\Delta t}$, which is large compared with the observation function $H_k \propto \Delta t$ for daily observations.

Error Size Revisited As previously mentioned, this underlines the more fundamental problem for the SV estimation: By definition, volatility represents the noise of the stock process. Indeed if we had taken the spot price S_k as the observation and the variance v_k as the state, we would have

$$S_{k+1} = S_k + S_k \mu_S \Delta t + S_k \sqrt{v_k} \sqrt{\Delta t} B_k$$

we would then have an observation function gradient $H = 0$ and the system would be *unobservable*! It is precisely because we use a Taylor second-order

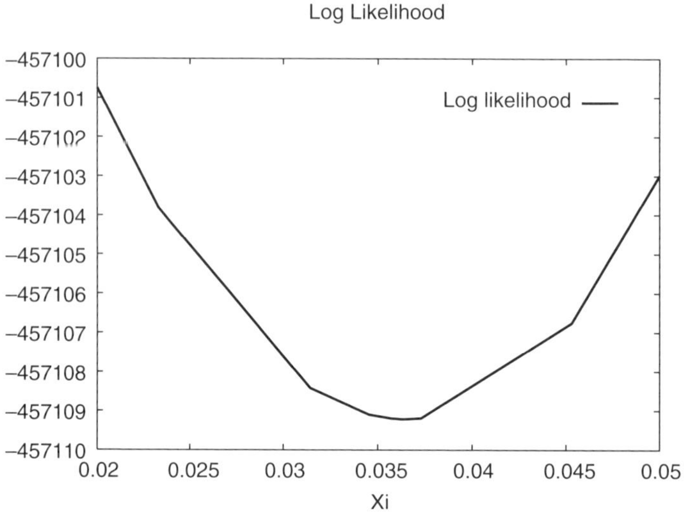

FIGURE 2.39 $f(\xi) = L(\hat{\omega}, \hat{\theta}, \xi, \hat{\rho})$ via EKF for $N = 50,000$ Points. The true value is $\xi^* = 0.03$.

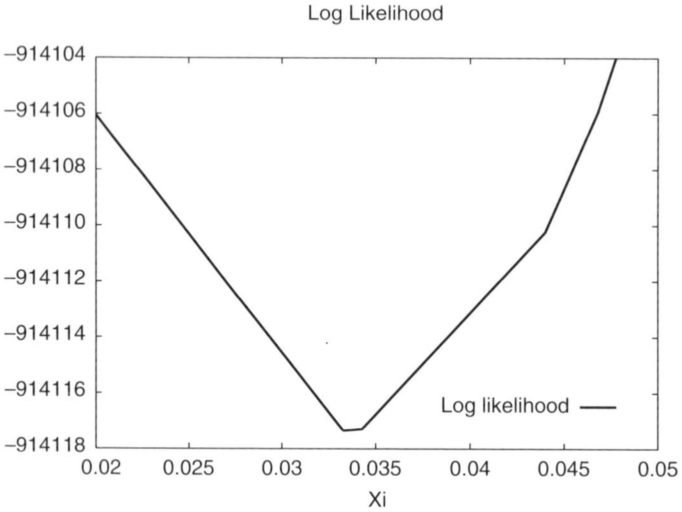

FIGURE 2.40 $f(\xi) = L(\hat{\omega}, \hat{\theta}, \xi, \hat{\rho})$ via EKF for $N = 100,000$ Points. The true value is $\xi^* = 0.03$.

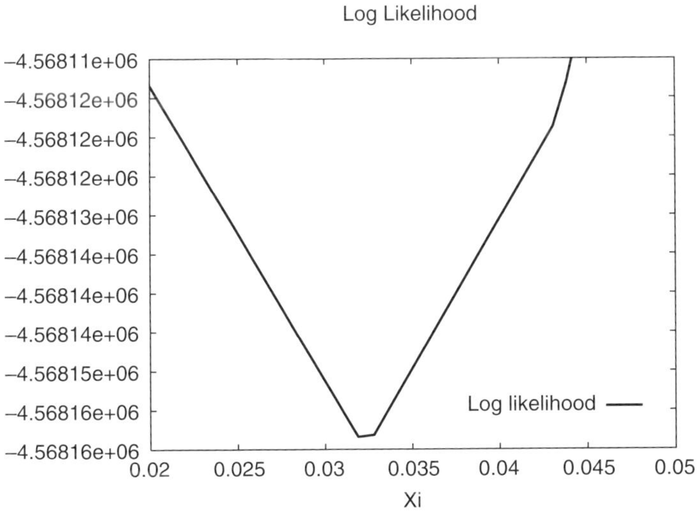

FIGURE 2.41 $f(\xi) = L(\hat{\omega}, \hat{\theta}, \xi, \hat{\rho})$ via EKF for $N = 500,000$ Points. The true value is $\xi^* = 0.03$.

expansion

$$\ln(1 + x) \approx x - \frac{1}{2}x^2$$

that we obtain access to v_k through the observation function. However, in

$$\ln\left(\frac{S_{k+1}}{S_k}\right) = \left(\mu_S - \frac{1}{2}v_k\right)\Delta t + \sqrt{v_k}\sqrt{\Delta t}B_k$$

the error remains *dominant* as the first order of the expansion.[30] Harvey, Ruiz, and Shephard [130] use the approximation $\Delta t = o(\sqrt{\Delta t})$ and take

$$z_k = \ln\left(\ln^2\left(\frac{S_{k+1}}{S_k}\right)\right) \approx \ln(v_k) + \ln(\Delta t) + \ln\left(B_k^2\right)$$

Note that under this form EKF would blow up because $z_k^- = h(v_k, 0) = -\infty$. They therefore use the fact that $\mathbf{E}[\ln(B_k^2)] = -1.27$ and $stdev[\ln(B_k^2)] =$

[30]Note that this is different from a variance Swap where we work with the *expected values*. The approximation is perfectly valid if for the return $R = \Delta S/S$ we write

$$\mathbf{E}[\ln(1 + R) - R] \approx -\frac{1}{2}v$$

but again, the approximation breaks if we work for one sample path.

TABLE 2.9 The Optimal EKF Parameter Set $\hat{\Psi}$ via the HRS Approximation Given a Sample Size N. The four parameters are estimated jointly.

N	$\hat{\omega}$	$\hat{\theta}$	$\hat{\xi}$	$\hat{\rho}$
5000	0.722746	71.753861	0.044602	−1.000000
50,000	0.234110	23.575193	0.028056	−1.000000
100,000	0.150512	15.186113	0.017748	−1.000000
500,000	0.109738	11.020391	0.027140	−0.531481

$\pi/\sqrt{2}$ and consider the Gaussian approximation

$$\ln\left(B_k^2\right) \sim -1.27 + \frac{\pi}{\sqrt{2}}\mathcal{N}(0,1)$$

which may or may not be valid. We call this approximation Harvey-Ruiz-Shephard (HRS) and apply it to the same case as in the previous paragraphs. As can be seen in Table 2.9, the approximation seems to be valid for our example. Note that UKF would not have this problem because we would work with the real nonlinear function $z = h(x, u)$. However, we would still deal with logs of very small quantities, which could be numerically unstable.

Another way of tackling the same equation would be via a particle filter, where

$$z_k = \ln\left(\left|\ln\left(\frac{S_{k+1}}{S_k}\right)\right|\right) \approx \frac{1}{2}\ln(v_k) + \frac{1}{2}\ln(\Delta t) + \ln(|B_k|)$$

and as stated in [10] the density of $\ln(|B_k|)$ is

$$f(x) = 2e^x n(e^x)$$

with $n()$ the normal density.[31]

Testing the same data set provides Table 2.10, which does not seem to improve upon the KF.

It is important to note that even if we took the example of the Heston model, the same issues are true for any stochastic volatility model of type

$$v_k = v_{k-1} + (\omega - \theta v_{k-1})\,\Delta t + \xi v_{k-1}^p \sqrt{\Delta t} Z_{k-1}$$

[31]It is easy to see that if X is a standard normal variable, then the CDF of $\ln(|X|)$ is

$$F(x) = P(\ln(|X|) \le x) = P\left(|X| \le e^x\right) = P\left(-e^x \le X \le e^x\right)$$

therefore

$$F(x) = N\left(e^x\right) - N\left(-e^x\right) = 2N(e^x) - 1$$

and the density is determined by taking the derivative with respect to x as usual.

TABLE 2.10 The Optimal PF Parameter Set $\hat{\Psi}$ Given a Sample Size N. The four parameters are estimated jointly.

N	$\hat{\omega}$	$\hat{\theta}$	$\hat{\xi}$	$\hat{\rho}$
5000	0.147212	14.999999	0.070407	-0.555263

including the GARCH diffusion and the 3/2 models. As previously mentioned, even if the transition equation is different here, the observation equation remains the same. Applying the EKF, we have the transition matrix and noise

$$A_k = 1 - \left[\rho\xi\mu_S\left(p - \frac{1}{2}\right)v_{k-1}^{p-\frac{3}{2}} + \theta - \frac{1}{2}\rho\xi\left(p + \frac{1}{2}\right)v_{k-1}^{p-\frac{1}{2}}\right]\Delta t + \left(p - \frac{1}{2}\right)\rho\xi v_{k-1}^{p-\frac{3}{2}}\ln\left(\frac{S_k}{S_{k-1}}\right)$$

$$W_k = \xi\sqrt{1-\rho^2}v_{k-1}^p\sqrt{\Delta t}$$

However, we still have the observation matrix and noise

$$H_k = -\frac{1}{2}\Delta t$$

and

$$U_k = \sqrt{v_k}\sqrt{\Delta t}$$

and the same problem of $\Delta t = o\left(\sqrt{\Delta t}\right)$ still exists at observation level for any value of p.

Another point that should be mentioned is that even if ξ and ρ are separately harder to estimate than ω and θ, the product $\rho\xi$ appears in the equations at the same level. Indeed, as we just saw, in A_k only the product $\rho\xi$ is available. However, at the noise level W_k, we can distinguish the two parameters ρ and ξ. For instance, in our previous EKF joint estimation table, we had for $50,000$ points $\hat{\xi} \approx 0.020521$, $\hat{\rho} \approx -1.0000$ and again, the individual estimations of ξ and ρ remained far from their true values. However, we have $\hat{\xi}\hat{\rho} \approx -0.020521$, which is much closer to $\xi^*\rho^* = -0.015$. Interestingly, the product $\rho\xi$ is what we need to determine the skewness of the distribution.[32] However, we do need to determine ξ alone to obtain the distribution kurtosis.

It is also worth noting that in a GARCH framework, we do not have this problem of poor observability for the discrete case. In fact, at each

[32] This remark will be addressed in the following chapter.

TABLE 2.11 Real and Optimal Parameter Sets Obtained via NGARCH MLE. The 5000 points were generated via the one-factor NGARCH with daily parameters.

	ω	α	β	c
Ψ^*	0.00000176	0.0626	0.89760	0.00
$\hat{\Psi}$	0.00000200	0.0530	0.89437	0.05

point in time, v_k is known exactly as a function of previous observations. Only later, we go to the two-factor diffusion limit, as Nelson [194] does. However, we have to bear in mind that this GARCH diffusion limit is a very special case of the stochastic volatility problem, since it misses the second source of randomness in the discrete case. As Corradi [61] explains, a discrete GARCH model may very well converge toward a one-factor diffusion process *without stochastic volatility*. Interestingly, when discretizing the one-factor continuous process, we can recover GARCH, whereas when discretizing the two-factor continuous process we will *not* obtain GARCH but the two-factor discrete process we have been working with.

This explains why GARCH MLE (without filtering) can recover parameters used in a simulated time series of length 5000 created via a one-factor GARCH process, whereas it cannot recover the diffusion-limit parameters from a time series created via a two-factor stochastic volatility process as accurately.[33] One can see this in Tables 2.11 and 2.12.

This also explains why estimating ω and θ alone works so much better with 5000 points. After all, if we had $\xi = 0$ and therefore a deterministic

[33]Needless to say, whether the equations are written via yearly (stochastic volatility convention) or daily (GARCH convention) parameters will not change the nature of the problem. It would be tempting to try to get around the $\Delta t = o(\sqrt{\Delta t})$ problem by rewriting the equations via daily parameters $\mu_S^d = \mu_S \Delta t$ and $v_k^d = \Delta t v_k$ as well as $\omega^d = \Delta t^2 \omega$, $\theta^d = \Delta t \theta$ and $\xi^d = \Delta t \xi$ with ρ remaining unchanged. Dropping the superscript d for simplifying the notations, we shall have

$$\ln S_{k+1} = \ln S_k + \mu_S - \frac{1}{2} v_k + \sqrt{v_k} B_k$$

$$v_{k+1} = v_k + \omega - \theta v_k + \xi \sqrt{v_k} Z_k$$

which seems to have eliminated the difficulty. However, now we have

$$v_k = o(\sqrt{v_k})$$

which was not the case with yearly variances, and the same poor observability problem arises again! We therefore see that the heart of the difficulty is a low signal-to-noise ratio (SNR) for the problem at hand.

TABLE 2.12 Real and Optimal Parameter Sets Obtained via NGARCH MLE as well as EKF. The 5000 points were generated via the two-factor GARCH diffusion limit with annual parameters.

	ω	θ	$\xi\rho$
Ψ^*	0.100000	10.00	−0.015
$\hat{\Psi}_{GARCH}$	0.063504	6.84	−0.019
$\hat{\Psi}_{EKF}$	0.148000	14.48	−0.023

instantaneous variance, we would have no observability problem to talk about. Indeed, v_t would be exactly known at each time step, as is the case in a GARCH framework.

Finally, we can now see better why the estimation worked fairly well even with 200 points if $\Delta t = 1$ year—simply because we do *not* have $\Delta t = o(\sqrt{\Delta t})$ and the observability is much more accurate. Nevertheless, with such a large Δt, other problems, such as strong nonlinearity and the nonapplicability of the Grisanov theorem arise. Not to mention the fact that 200 points would correspond to 200 years of data!

High-Frequency Data Given that the results seem to converge for a large number of data points, one idea would be to use a higher sampling frequency. If instead of using daily data we sample every five seconds, then with a ten-year range we will have $10 \times 252 \times 6.5 \times 60 \times 60 \div 5 = 11,793,600$ data points, which is very sufficient for our MLEs. For testing the use of high-frequency data, we can generate via Monte Carlo $5,000,000$ points with a $\Delta t = 1/252,000$, which corresponds to 20 years. We obtain the results in Table 2.13. Both rows have reasonable results. It is, however, notable that the EKF/HRS method seems to perform better than the plain EKF.

It may seem a little surprising that for the same time period $[0, T]$ dividing Δt by 1000 and multiplying N by 1000 helps us. Why don't the

TABLE 2.13 The Optimal Parameter Set $\hat{\Psi}$ for $5,000,000$ Data Points. The sampling is performed 1000 times a day and therefore the data set corresponds to 5000 business days. The four parameters are estimated jointly.

	$\hat{\omega}$	$\hat{\theta}$	$\hat{\xi}$	$\hat{\rho}$
EKF	0.090280	9.019962	0.042984	−0.283236
EKF/HRS	0.092372	9.224421	0.030951	−0.507763

two operations cancel one another? Observing the negative of log-likelihood function in an EKF framework

$$\phi(\omega, \theta, \xi, \rho) = \sum_{k=1}^{N}\left[\ln(F_k) + \frac{\tilde{z}_k^2}{F_k}\right]$$

with

$$\tilde{\mathbf{z}}_k = \mathbf{z}_k - \mathbf{h}(\hat{\mathbf{x}}_k^-, 0)$$

and

$$\mathbf{F}_k = \mathbf{H}_k\mathbf{P}_k^-\mathbf{H}_k^t + \mathbf{U}_k\mathbf{U}_k^t$$

We can see that *considering first-order terms*, dividing Δt by 1000, or equivalently multiplying it by $\epsilon = 1/1000$, will cause the transition matrix A_k to be unchanged, the transition noise W_k to be multiplied by $\sqrt{\epsilon}$, the observation matrix $\boldsymbol{H}_k$ to be multiplied by ϵ, and the observation noise U_k to be multiplied by $\sqrt{\epsilon}$. Furthermore, A_k being unchanged will cause $\boldsymbol{P}_k^-$ and $\boldsymbol{P}_k$ to remain unchanged as well. Therefore, $\tilde{\mathbf{z}}_k$ will be multiplied by $\sqrt{\epsilon}$, the term $\boldsymbol{F}_k$ will be multiplied by ϵ, and the fraction used in the log-likelihood sum will remain the same. This causes the sum $\phi(\omega, \theta, \xi, \rho)$ to be higher by a factor $1/\epsilon$, which shows that higher frequency does allow us to obtain a higher likelihood function and therefore better convergence. This is in agreement with what we observed in the above test.

The Frequency of the Observations Note that the ideal stochastic differential equations are supposed to be continuous; however, we only have discrete observations obtained via an Euler scheme. This introduces a discretization error that may become important as the time interval Δt becomes larger. As mentioned in [92], [164], and [201], the solution would be to *fill the missing data* via additional simulations in time: For the observation time step $1 \le k \le N$, the simulation $1 \le i \le N_{sims}$, and the additional time step $1 \le j \le M$, we would have the particles

$$\tilde{x}^{(i)}_{k+\frac{j}{M}} = \tilde{x}^{(i)}_{k+\frac{j-1}{M}} + \left(\omega - \theta\tilde{x}^{(i)}_{k+\frac{j-1}{M}}\right)\frac{\Delta t}{M} + \xi\sqrt{\tilde{x}^{(i)}_{k+\frac{j-1}{M}}}\sqrt{\frac{\Delta t}{M}}Z^{(i)}_{k+\frac{j}{M}}$$

and the observation

$$z_{k+1} = z_k + \sum_{j=1}^{M}\left(\mu_S - \frac{1}{2}\tilde{x}_{k+\frac{j}{M}}\right)\frac{\Delta t}{M} + \sqrt{\sum_{j=1}^{M}\tilde{x}_{k+\frac{j}{M}}\frac{\Delta t}{M}}B_k$$

where each $Z^{(i)}_{k+\frac{j}{M}}$ has a correlation ρ with B_k. Naturally, the innovations Z_l are mutually uncorrelated. However, as discussed in [164], the discretization error is small when $\Delta t = 1/252$, which is the case we are dealing with.

TABLE 2.14 Mean and (Standard Deviation) for the Estimation of Each Parameter via EKF Over $P = 500$ Paths of Lengths $N = 5000$ and $N = 50,000$. The true values are $(\omega^* = 0.10, \theta^* = 10, \xi^* = 0.03, \rho^* = -0.50)$.

	$\hat{\omega}$	$\hat{\theta}$	$\hat{\xi}$	$\hat{\rho}$
$N = 5000$	0.11933899	11.92271488	0.056092146	−0.34321724
	(0.098995729)	(9.673829518)	(0.049741887)	(0.297433861)
$N = 50,000$	0.102554592	10.26233092	0.04383931	−0.351998284
	(0.027020734)	(2.706564396)	(0.013004526)	(0.074998408)

Sampling Distribution Even if in practice we deal with *one* historic path, we should determine the distribution of the optimal parameter set as follows. We simulate $P = 500$ paths of length $N = 5000$ and estimate for each path j the optimal set $\hat{\Psi}^{(j)}$. We then can estimate

$$\bar{\hat{\Psi}} = \frac{1}{P}\sum_{j=0}^{P-1} \hat{\Psi}^{(j)}$$

as well as the variance

$$V(\hat{\Psi}) = \frac{1}{P}\sum_{j=0}^{P-1} (\hat{\Psi}^{(j)} - \bar{\hat{\Psi}})^2$$

In this way we will know how the estimator performs on average and how far we could be from this average. The distribution of the parameter set around its mean is referred to as the *sampling distribution* [168]. As we can see in Table 2.14, the average-estimated parameter set is closer to the true set than the one-path-estimated set we were considering in the previous section. However, the corresponding standard deviation is quite high and we could very well get poor results as previously seen.

From Figures 2.42 to 2.45, we can see that for this data length N and this sample size P the parameters ω and θ are determined via EKF in a fairly unbiased way. However, the estimator is not efficient and has a large standard deviation. As for ξ and ρ, we have both bias and inefficiency. This is not surprising given the results of the previous paragraphs. We obtained good results for (ω, θ) when estimated alone, and not so good results for (ξ, ρ). As mentioned, classical filtering theory works well when the parameters affect the drift of the observation and not the noise. This causes a slow convergence problem for all our parameters. But this is doubly true for (ξ, ρ) since they

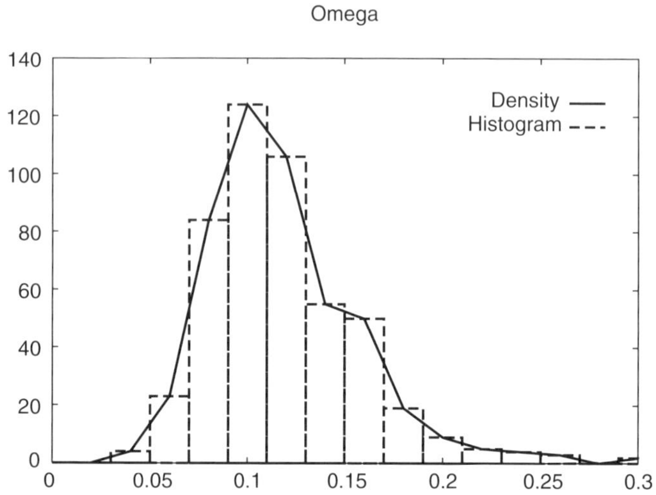

FIGURE 2.42 Density for $\hat{\omega}$ Estimated from 500 Paths of Length 5000 via EKF. The true value is $\omega^* = 0.10$. The sampling distribution is fairly unbiased, but is inefficient.

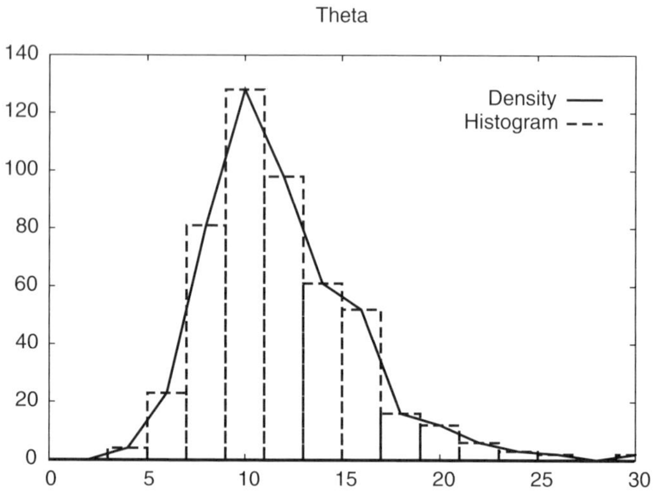

FIGURE 2.43 Density for $\hat{\theta}$ Estimated from 500 Paths of Length 5000 via EKF. The true value is $\theta^* = 10$. The sampling distribution is fairly unbiased, but is inefficient.

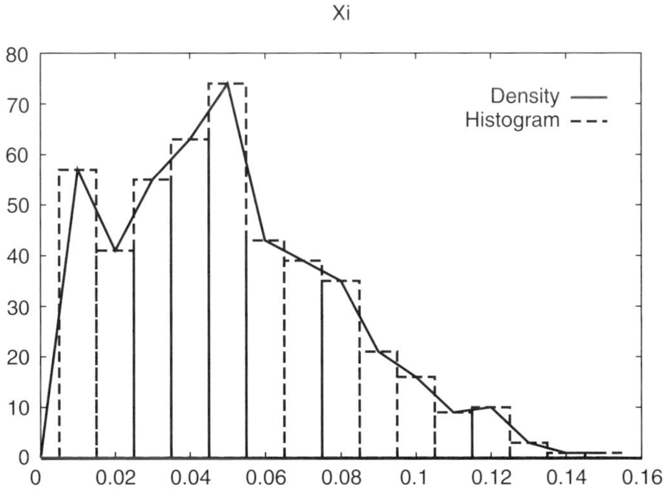

FIGURE 2.44 Density for $\hat{\xi}$ Estimated from 500 Paths of Length 5000 via EKF. The true value is $\xi^* = 0.03$. The sampling distribution is inefficient and even has a bias.

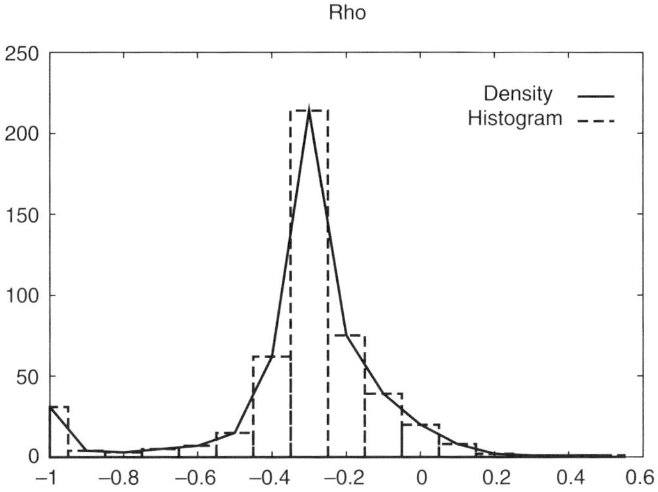

FIGURE 2.45 Density for $\hat{\rho}$ Estimated from 500 Paths of Length 5000 via EKF. The true value is $\rho^* = -0.50$. The sampling distribution is inefficient and even has a bias.

affect the "noise of the noise." As previously observed, the bias and inefficiency will disappear as $N \to +\infty$, as is the case for any MLE estimator. The biases and the standard deviations are smaller for $N = 50,000$ than for $N = 5000$ as we can see in Table 2.14.

The Bayesian Approach

Even if our method of choice is the classical one, it is worth going over the Bayesian philosophy and methodologies, which have some similarities but also some fundamental differences compared with our point of view. The MLE methodology is a classical (frequentist) approach, in which we assume that there is a set of unknown but fixed parameters. Alternatively, in the Bayesian approach the parameters are considered as random variables with a given prior distribution. We then use the observations (the likelihood) to update these distributions and obtain the posterior distributions.

It would seem that in order to be as objective as possible and to use the observations as much as possible, one should use priors that are *noninformative*. However, this sometimes creates degeneracy issues and one should choose a different prior for this reason.

Markov Chain Monte Carlos (MCMC) include the *Gibbs sampler* as well as the *Metropolis-Hastings* (MH) algorithm. The theoretical justification is provided by the *Hammersley-Clifford* theorem and the *ergodic averaging* theorem. Details can for instance, be found in [34] or [163].

Briefly, the Hammersley-Clifford theorem states that having a parameter set Ψ, a state x, and an observation z, we can obtain the joint distribution $p(\Psi, x|z)$ from $p(\Psi|x, z)$ and $p(x|\Psi, z)$, under some mild regularity conditions. Therefore by applying the theorem iteratively, we can break a complicated multidimensional estimation problem into many simple one-dimensional problems. Creating a Markov Chain $\Psi^{(i)}$ via a Monte Carlo process, the ergodic averaging theorem states that the time average of a parameter will converge toward its posterior mean.

The Gibbs Sampler The Gibbs sampler consists of iterative simulations from the posterior distributions. Having a parameter set

$$\Psi = (\Psi_j)_{1 \le j \le J}$$

a hidden state

$$x = (x_k)_{1 \le k \le N}$$

and an observation set

$$z = (z_k)_{1 \le k \le N}$$

We proceed as follows: Initialize the state vector and the parameter set to $x^{(0)}$ and $\Psi^{(0)}$, and choose the prior distribution $p(\psi)$. For each simulation index i between 1 and N_{sims}, do:

1. Simulate $x^{(i)}$ as

$$x^{(i)} \sim p(x|z, \Psi^{(i-1)})$$

2. Simulate each parameter from its posterior conditional on partially updated parameters: For each j between 1 and J

$$\Psi_j^{(i)} \sim p(\psi|z, x, \Psi_0^{(i)}, ..., \Psi_{j-1}^{(i)}, \Psi_{j+1}^{(i-1)}, ..., \Psi_J^{(i-1)})$$

with

$$p(\psi|z, x, ...) \propto p(z|x, \psi, ...)p(x|\psi)p(\psi)$$

3. Go back to Step 1 and stop after i reaches N_{sims}.
4. Calculate the posterior mean for each parameter after allowing a "burn-in" period

$$\hat{\Psi}_j = \frac{1}{N_{sims} - i_0} \sum_{i=i_0+1}^{N_{sims}} \Psi_j^{(i)}$$

with, for instance, $i_0 = N_{sims}/10$.

It is important to note that in some cases, the prior and the posterior distributions are the same and only differ in parameters. In this case the priors are referred to as *conjugate priors*.

The justification is available for instance in [55] and can be summed up as follows: Having two random variables (X, Y), we can write

$$\mathbf{E}[X] = \int xp(x)dx$$

but

$$p(x) = \int p(x|y)p(y)dy = \int p(x|y) \int p(y|\xi)p(\xi)d\xi dy$$

therefore, we have

$$p(x) = \int p(\xi)h(x, \xi)d\xi$$

with

$$h(x, \xi) = \int p(x|y)p(y|\xi)dy$$

which shows that $p(x)$ is a stationary solution for the foregoing integral equation, and $h(x, \xi)$ corresponds to the limit transition density.

Similarly, it is possible to show that for a sequence (x_k) generated from a Gibbs Sampler, we have

$$P(x_k|x_0) = \int P(x_{k-1}|x_0)P(x_k, x_{k-1})dx_{k-1}$$

It is therefore possible to see that as $k \to +\infty$ we have

$$P(x_k|x_0) \to p(x_k)$$

and

$$P(x_k|x_{k-1}) \to h(x_k, x_{k-1})$$

which are the stationary marginal and transition densities.

A Simple Illustration For a simple illustration, consider a sequence of normally distributed data points z with an unknown mean μ and an unknown variance $1/\lambda$. The parameter λ is often referred to as the *precision* of the distribution. One possible way to proceed is to choose uniform (noninformative) priors $p(\mu)$ and $p(\lambda) \propto 1/\lambda$ and use the known results [34]

$$p(\mu|z, \sigma) = N(\bar{Z}, \sigma)$$

with $N(m, s)$ the normal distribution with mean m and standard deviation s and

$$\bar{Z} = \frac{1}{N}\sum_{k=1}^{N} z_k$$

as well as

$$p(\lambda|z, \mu) = G\left(\frac{N}{2}, \frac{S}{2}\right)$$

with $G(a, A)$ the previously described gamma distribution[34] and

$$S = \sum_{k=1}^{N}(z_k - \mu)^2$$

and again

$$\sigma = 1/\sqrt{\lambda}$$

We therefore know both posterior distributions and can simulate from them iteratively and perform Gibbs sampling as described above.

[34]Note that $G(a, A) = P(a, Ax)$ to use our previous notations.

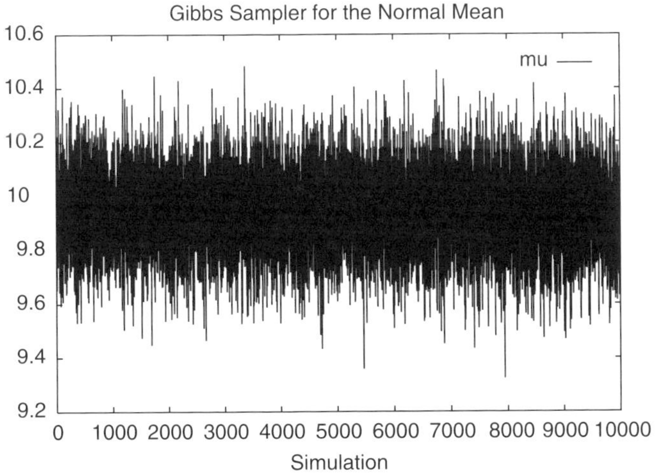

FIGURE 2.46 Gibbs Sampler for μ in $N(\mu, \sigma)$. The true value is $\mu^* = 10.0$.

For testing this, we generated a time series of 1000 Gaussian points with a mean of $\mu^* = 10$ and a standard deviation of $\sigma^* = 5$. We applied the Gibbs sampler via $N_{sims} = 10,000$ simulations and considered the average between the 1000th and $10,000^{th}$ simulations. We chose initial values $\mu_0 = 7.0$ and $\sigma_0 = 3.0$ and obtained

$$\hat{\mu} = 9.943416$$

$$\hat{\sigma} = 4.816300$$

We ploted the simulations from the posteriors in Figures 2.46 and 2.47.

The Metropolis-Hastings Algorithm The Gibbs sampler is fast and simple when the posterior distributions are known and easy to sample from. However, in practice, and in particular for our stochastic volatility problem, this often is not the case. We assume for simplicity that we do know the posteriors for the parameters and therefore can use the Gibbs sampler for them; however, we cannot do the same for the latent state.

In this case, the Metropolis-Hastings (MH) algorithm approach can be used for x as follows: Initialize the state vector and the parameter set to $x^{(0)}$ and $\Psi^{(0)}$ and choose the prior distribution $p(\psi)$. Also choose a proposal distribution $q(x|z, \Psi)$ for the state. For each simulation index between 1 and N_{sims} do:

1-a. Simulate from the proposal distribution

$$x^{(i)} \sim q(x|z, \Psi)$$

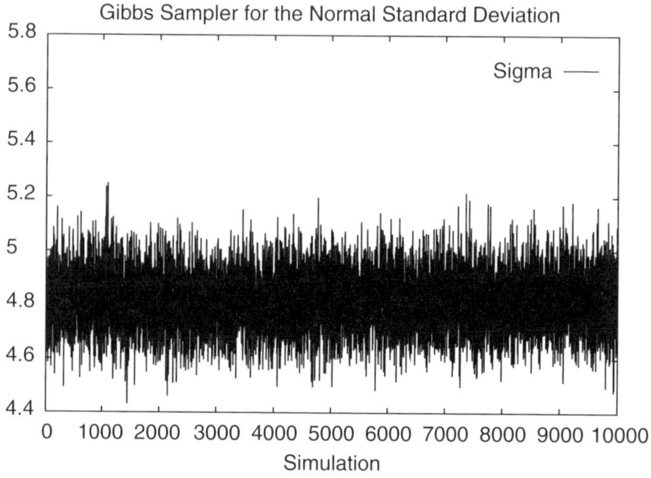

FIGURE 2.47 Gibbs Sampler for σ in $N(\mu, \sigma)$. The true value is $\sigma^* = 5.0$.

1-b. Compare with a randomly generated uniform random variable u the ratio

$$\alpha = min\left(1, \frac{p(x^{(i)}|z, \Psi)/q(x^{(i)}|z, \Psi)}{p(x^{(i-1)}|z, \Psi)/q(x^{(i-1)}|z, \Psi)}\right)$$

and accept $x^{(i)}$ if $\alpha > u$; otherwise, reject it and set $x^{(i)} = x^{(i-1)}$.

2. Simulate $\Psi^{(i)}$ via a Gibbs sampler.
3. Go back to Step 1-a and continue until i reaches N_{sims}.
4. Calculate the posterior mean for each parameter after allowing a "burn-in" period

$$\hat{\Psi}_j = \frac{1}{N_{sims} - i_0} \sum_{i=i_0+1}^{N_{sims}} \Psi_j^{(i)}$$

with, for instance, $i_0 = N_{sims}/10$.

Two special cases are worth being mentioned.

- First, if we simulate from the posterior, the MH ratio becomes 1.0 and every simulation will be accepted. This is therefore a Gibbs sampler.
- Second, if we simulate from the prior, the MH ratio becomes the likelihood ratio, which makes the computation simpler. We shall use this second case extensively in our stochastic volatility inferences.

The justification for the MH algorithm is available, for instance, in [58] or [120]. The idea is to find the transition probability from x to y $P(x, y)$ such that for a given target density π we would have the invariant distribution property

$$\pi(dy) = \int P(x, dy)\pi(x)dx$$

It is possible to express the transition probability $P(x, dy)$ as

$$P(x, dy) = p(x, y)dy + \left(1 - \int p(x, z)dz\right)\delta_x(dy)$$

with $\delta_x()$ the Dirac function. The first term corresponds to the passage probability from x to a point in dy and the second term to the probability of staying at x.

Now, if the function $p(x, y)$ satisfies the *reversibility* condition

$$\pi(x)p(x, y) = \pi(y)p(y, x)$$

then we can see that $\pi()$ is the invariant distribution as described previously. Indeed then calling the *rejection* probability

$$r(x) = 1 - \int p(x, z)dz$$

we have

$$\begin{aligned}
\int P(x, A)\pi(x)dx &= \int \left[\int_A p(x, y)dy + r(x)\delta_x(A)\right]\pi(x)dx \\
&= \int_A \left[\int p(x, y)\pi(x)dx\right]dy + \int_A r(x)\pi(x)dx \\
&= \int_A \left[\int p(y, x)\pi(y)dx\right]dy + \int_A r(x)\pi(x)dx \\
&= \int_A (1 - r(y))\pi(y)dy + \int_A r(x)\pi(x)dx \\
&= \int_A \pi(y)dy
\end{aligned}$$

which proves that $\pi(x)$ is the invariant distribution for the transition probability $P(x, y)$.

However, in practice, the reversibility condition is hardly ever satisfied, and therefore we need to construct an MH density that would indeed be reversible. Taking any proposal density $q(x, y)$, we would simply write

$$p_{MH}(x, y) = q(x, y)min\left(1, \frac{\pi(y)/q(x, y)}{\pi(x)/q(y, x)}\right)$$

Then $p_{MH}(x, y)$ would be reversible and hence admit $\pi(x)$ as its invariant distribution.

Proof: To see why, let us consider the case where $\frac{\pi(y)/q(x,y)}{\pi(x)/q(y,x)} > 1$, which means its inverse is smaller than 1. We would then have

$$p_{MH}(x, y)\pi(x) = q(x, y)\pi(x) = q(y, x)\frac{\pi(x)/q(y, x)}{\pi(y)/q(x, y)}\pi(y) = p_{MH}(y, x)\pi(y)$$

(QED)

One more point we need to explain is the "blocking" technique. Having two random variables X_1, X_2, the *product* of the conditional transition densities, admits the joint distribution $\pi(X1, X2)$ for invariant distribution. This is why we can alternate between parameters and hidden states.

Thus

$$\begin{aligned}
&\int\int P_1(x_1, dy_1|x_2)P_2(x_2, dy_2|y_1)\pi(x_1, x_2)dx_1dx_2 \\
&= \int P_2(x_2, dy_2|y_1)\left[\int P_1(x_1, dy_1|x_2)\pi_{1|2}(x_1|x_2)dx_1\right]\pi_2(x_2)dx_2 \\
&= \int P_2(x_2, dy_2|y_1)\pi_{1|2}(dy_1|x_2)\pi_2(x_2)dx_2 \\
&= \int P_2(x_2, dy_2|y_1)\pi_{2|1}(x_2|y_1)\pi_1(dy_1)dx_2 \\
&= \pi_1(dy_1)\int P_2(x_2, dy_2|y_1)\pi_{2|1}(x_2|y_1)dx_2 \\
&= \pi_1(dy_1)\pi_{2|1}(dy_2|y_1) = \pi(dy_1, dy_2)
\end{aligned}$$

which proves that $\pi(x_1, x_2)$ is the invariant distribution for this product transition probability.

Illustration We use the same example as for the Gibbs sampler, only this time we simulate from the priors and use the likelihood ratio to accept or reject the simulations. We choose the priors

$$\mu \sim N(7.0, 3.0)$$

and

$$\sigma \sim \frac{1}{\sqrt{G(1/9.0, 1.0)}}$$

We obtain after $M = 10,000$ simulations

$$\hat{\mu} = 9.989504$$

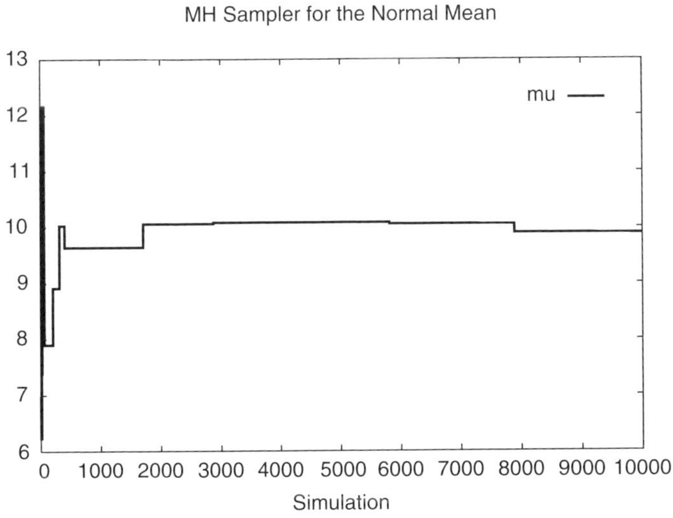

FIGURE 2.48 Metropolis-Hastings Algorithm for μ in $N(\mu, \sigma)$. The true value is $\mu^* = 10.0$.

and

$$\hat{\sigma} = 4.797105$$

Naturally, the evaluation of the Markov Chain is different from that of the Gibbs sampler. This can be seen in Figures 2.48 and 2.49.

A Few Distributions Here are a few distributions commonly used in MCMC algorithms.

The student cumulative distribution function

$$F(x, \nu) = 1 - I\left(\frac{\nu}{\nu + x^2}, \frac{\nu}{2}, \frac{1}{2}\right)$$

with $I(x, a, b)$ the incomplete beta function (IBF)

$$I(x, a, b) = \frac{B(x, a, b)}{B(1, a, b)}$$

where

$$B(x, a, b) = \int_0^x t^{a-1}(1 - t)^{b-1} dt$$

with a, b two strictly positive parameters. A few plots of the IBF are provided in Figure 2.50.

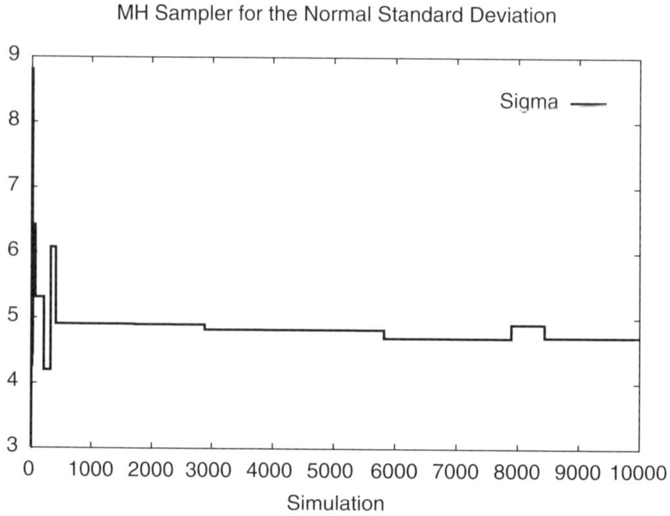

FIGURE 2.49 Metropolis-Hastings Algorithm for σ in $N(\mu, \sigma)$. The true value is $\sigma^* = 5.0$.

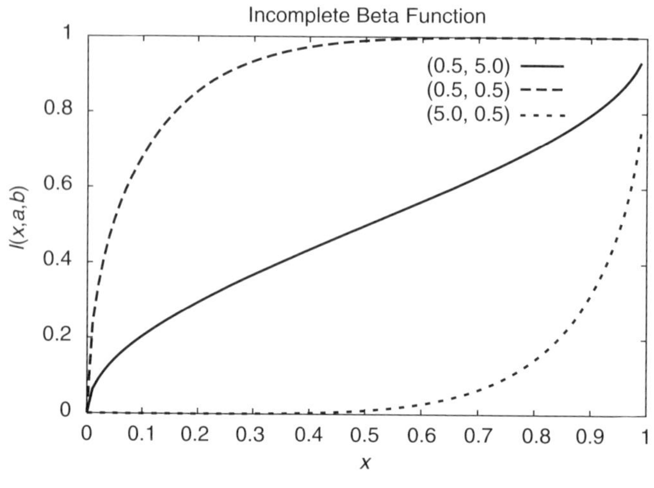

FIGURE 2.50 Plots of the Incomplete Beta Function. Implementation is based on code from *Numerical Recipes in C*.

The inverse-gamma (IG) cumulative distribution function $IG(a, x)$ could be defined from that of the previously defined gamma distribution $P(a, x)$

$$P(a, x) = \frac{1}{\Gamma(a)} \int_0^x e^{-t} t^{a-1} dt$$

By definition, if the random variable X is gamma-distributed, $Y = 1/X$ will be IG-distributed and therefore

$$IG(a,x) = P(Y \leq x) = P\left(X \geq \frac{1}{x}\right) = 1 - P\left(a, \frac{1}{x}\right)$$

As for the densities, they are related by

$$f_{IG}(a,x) = \frac{1}{x^2} f_G\left(a, \frac{1}{x}\right)$$

Regression Analysis We have the following useful results as described in [34] and [163] using some of the previous distributions. Considering a univariate regression

$$Y = \beta X + \epsilon$$

where

$$\epsilon \sim \mathcal{N}\left(0, \sigma^2\right)$$

We suppose we know the priors

$$p(\beta) = N(a, A)$$

where a corresponds to the mean and A to the variance.

$$p\left(\sigma^2\right) = IG(b, B)$$

with the density

$$f_{IG}(x, b, B) = \frac{B^b e^{-\frac{B}{x}}}{\Gamma(b) x^{b+1}}$$

Then we have for the β posterior:

$$p\left(\beta|Y, X, \sigma^2\right) \propto p\left(Y|X, \beta, \sigma^2\right) p(\beta) \propto N(a^*, A^*)$$

with

$$a^* = \left(\frac{1}{A} + \frac{1}{2} X^t X\right)^{-1} \left(\frac{a}{A} + \frac{X^t Y}{\sigma^2}\right)$$

$$A^* = \left(\frac{1}{A} + \frac{X^t X}{\sigma^2}\right)^{-1}$$

As for the σ^2 posterior we have

$$p(\sigma^2|Y, X, \beta) \propto p(Y|X, \beta, \sigma^2) p(\sigma^2) \propto IG(b^*, B^*)$$

with

$$b^* = T + b$$

and

$$B^* = (Y - \beta X)^t (Y - \beta X) + B$$

Application to Gaussian SV Models (Heston) Various MCMC approaches have been suggested for the SV problem. Jacquier, Polson, and Rossi [156] were first to a apply a hybrid of the Gibbs sampler and the MH algorithm to a log-SV model. Kim, Shephard, and Chib [169] used a slightly different approach for the same model.

Here, we describe the method employed by Forbes, Martin, and Wright (FMW) [103]. Using their notations

$$dv_t = \kappa(\theta - v_t)dt + \sigma_v\sqrt{v_t}dZ_t$$

Obviously our $(\omega, \theta, \xi, \rho)$ could easily be obtained as $(\kappa\theta, \kappa, \sigma_v, \rho)$. The algorithm becomes as follows.

Initialize $v^{(0)} = (v_k^{(0)})_{1\leq k\leq N}$ and choose constant and therefore non informative priors for the parameter set[35]

$$\Psi = (\kappa, \theta, \sigma_v, \rho)$$

1. We simulate the state v_t from the Heston prior; we have for any time step k between 1 and N and simulation i

$$v_k^{(i)} = v_{k-1}^{(i)} + \kappa(\theta - v_{k-1}^{(i)})\Delta t + \sigma_v\sqrt{v_{k-1}^{(i)}\Delta t}Z_{k-1}$$

As previously mentioned, the MH ratio is therefore the likelihood ratio:

$$\alpha = min\left(1.0, \frac{p(\ln S|v^{(i)}, \Psi)}{p(\ln S|v^{(i-1)}, \Psi)}\right)$$

where

$$p(\ln S|v, \Psi) \propto \prod_{k=1}^{N} \frac{1}{\sqrt{(1-\rho^2)\Delta t v_{k-1}}} \exp\left\{-\frac{1}{2(1-\rho^2)v_{k-1}\Delta t}(\ln S_k - \mu_k)^2\right\}$$

with

$$\mu_k = \ln S_{k-1} + \left(\mu_S - \frac{1}{2}v_{k-1}\right)\Delta t + \frac{\rho}{\sigma_v}(v_k - [\theta\kappa\Delta t + (1-\kappa\Delta t)v_{k-1}])$$

Any negative variance would be rejected in the MH step.

2. The Heston equation

$$v_k = v_{k-1} + \kappa(\theta - v_{k-1})\Delta t + \sigma_v\sqrt{v_{k-1}\Delta t}Z_{k-1}$$

---

[35] As before, we assume for simplicity that μ_S is known. Adding it to the parameter set would be easy.

could be rewritten

$$\frac{v_k - (1 - \kappa\Delta t)v_{t-1}}{\sqrt{v_{t-1}\Delta t}} = \theta\frac{\kappa\Delta t}{\sqrt{v_{t-1}\Delta t}} + \sigma_v Z_{k-1}$$

which is a linear regression

$$y_k = \theta x_k + e_k$$

with

$$y_k = \frac{v_k - (1 - \kappa\Delta t)v_{t-1}}{\sqrt{v_{t-1}\Delta t}}$$

$$x_k = \frac{\kappa\Delta t}{\sqrt{v_{t-1}\Delta t}}$$

and

$$e_k \sim N(0, \sigma_v)$$

Hence, taking constant priors, we have

$$\theta|\kappa, \sigma_v, v \sim N(\bar{\theta}, \sigma_\theta)$$

with

$$\bar{\theta} = \frac{\sum_{k=1}^{N} x_k y_k}{\sum_{k=1}^{N} x_k^2}$$

and

$$\sigma_\theta = \sigma_v / \sqrt{\sum_{k=1}^{N} x_k^2}$$

What is more

$$\sigma_v^2|\kappa, v \sim IG(N - 1, s_v^2)$$

with

$$s_v^2 = \sum_{k=1}^{N} (y_k - \bar{\theta}x_k)^2$$

It is also possible to show that

$$p(\kappa|v) \propto St(\bar{\kappa}, \sigma_\kappa)\left(\sum_{k=1}^{N} x_k^2\right)^{-\frac{1}{2}}$$

where $St(m, s)$ corresponds to Student's law of mean m and standard deviation s. The expressions for these mean and standard deviations could be found in [103].

We can therefore simulate from the priors, except we have an adjustment factor $\left(\sum_{k=1}^{N} x_k^2\right)^{-\frac{1}{2}}$ to multiply the prior by. The MH ratio will therefore be

$$\alpha = min\left(1.0, \frac{p(\ln S|v, \kappa^{(i)}, \theta^{(i)}, \sigma_v^{(i)}, \rho)\left(\sum_{k=1}^{N}\left(x_k^{(i)}\right)^2\right)^{-\frac{1}{2}}}{p(\ln S|v, \kappa^{(i-1)}, \theta^{(i-1)}, \sigma_v^{(i-1)}, \rho)\left(\sum_{k=1}^{N}\left(x_k^{(i-1)}\right)^2\right)^{-\frac{1}{2}}}\right)$$

3. As for the correlation paramater ρ, we choose a normal proposal distribution and use a constant prior again. Therefore

$$\alpha = min\left(1.0, \frac{p\left(\ln S|v, \kappa, \theta, \sigma_v, \rho^{(i)}\right)/q\left(\rho^{(i)}|v, \kappa, \theta, \sigma_v, S\right)}{p\left(\ln S|v, \kappa, \theta, \sigma_v, \rho^{(i-1)}\right)/q\left(\rho^{(i)}|v, \kappa, \theta, \sigma_v, S\right)}\right)$$

with $q()$ the normal distribution with mean

$$\frac{\sum_{k=1}^{N} x_k y_k}{\sum_{k=1}^{N} x_k^2}$$

and variance

$$\frac{\Delta t}{\sum_{k=1}^{N} x_k^2}$$

with

$$x_k = \frac{v_k - \kappa\theta\Delta t - (1 - \kappa\Delta t)v_{k-1}}{\sigma_v\sqrt{v_{k-1}}}$$

$$y_k = \frac{\ln S_k - \ln S_{k-1} - \left(\mu_S - \frac{1}{2}v_{k-1}\right)\Delta t}{v_{k-1}}$$

Note that for any of the foregoing parameters if we simulate one that does not satisfy the usual constraints $\theta \geq 0$, $\kappa \geq 0$, $\sigma_v \geq 0$, $\sigma_v \leq 2\kappa\theta$, and $-1 \leq \rho \leq 1$, then we simply do not accept them during the MH accept/reject step. Also note that we update $(\kappa, \theta, \sigma_v)$ in a "block" instead of updating them one by one. This technique is used by many since it makes the algorithm faster.

For the actual results, the reader could refer to Forbes et al. [103]. The authors test their Bayesian estimator against simulated data, and observe inefficiency. This is in agreement with our observations when applying MLE techniques to simulated data.

Using the Characteristic Function

In a recent article [31], the use of the *characteristic function* has been suggested for the purpose of filtering. In this approach, however, we have to limit ourselves to the case where $F(U, V, x_t) = \mathbf{E}[\exp(Uz_{t+1} + Vx_{t+1})|x_t]$ has a known form. One natural form would be the affine process, where

$$F(U, V, x_t) = \mathbf{E}[\exp(Uz_{t+1} + Vx_{t+1})|x_t] = \exp\{C(U, V) + D(U, V)x_t\}$$

After choosing the initial conditions, the time update equation

$$p(z_{t+1}, x_{t+1}|t) = \int p(z_{t+1}, x_{t+1}|x_t)p(x_t|t)dx_t$$

becomes in terms of the characteristic function

$$\begin{aligned} F_{zx|t}(U, V) &= \mathbf{E}_t[\mathbf{E}\,(\exp(Uz_{t+1} + Vx_{t+1})|x_t)] \\ &= \mathbf{E}[\exp\{C(U, V) + D(U, V)x_t\}|z_{1:t}] \\ &= \exp[C(U, V)]G_{t|t}[D(U, V)] \end{aligned}$$

where $G_{t|s}(U) = \mathbf{E}[\exp(Ux_t)|z_{1:s}]$ is the moment-generating function of x_t conditional on the observations up to time s.

The Measurement Update equation

$$p(x_{t+1}|t+1) = \frac{p(z_{t+1}, x_{t+1}|t)}{p(z_{t+1}|t)}$$

becomes in terms of the characteristic function

$$G_{t+1|t+1}(V) = \frac{\int_{-\infty}^{+\infty} F_{zx|t}(iU, V)\exp(-iUz_{t+1})dU}{\int_{-\infty}^{+\infty} F_{zx|t}(iU, 0)\exp(-iUz_{t+1})dU}$$

This remarkably gives us a one-step induction expression

$$G_{t+1|t+1}(V) = \frac{\int_{-\infty}^{+\infty} \exp[C(iU, V) - iUz_{t+1}]G_{t|t}[D(iU, V)]dU}{\int_{-\infty}^{+\infty} \exp[C(iU, 0) - iUz_{t+1}]G_{t|t}[D(iU, 0)]dU}$$

which allows us to determine the a posteriori estimate and errors

$$\hat{x}_t = G'_{t|t}(0)$$

and

$$P_t = Var_t(x_t) = G''_{t|t}(0) - \left(G'_{t|t}(0)\right)^2$$

at each iteration.

In this framework, the likelihood function could be written as

$$L_{1:T} = \prod_{t-0}^{T-1} l_t$$

with

$$l_t = \frac{1}{2\pi}\int_{-\infty}^{+\infty} \exp[C(iU,0) - iUz_{t+1}]G_{t|t}[D(iU,0)]dU$$

which is equivalent to

$$l_t = \frac{1}{\pi}\int_{0}^{+\infty} \mathcal{R}\left\{\exp[C(iU,0) - iUz_{t+1}]G_{t|t}[D(iU,0)]\right\}dU \qquad (2.30)$$

where $\mathcal{R}\{\}$ corresponds to the real part of a complex number. In order to be able to calculate the integral, we need to know the value of $G_{t|t}(x)$ at each point. For this, Bates [31] suggests making an assumption on the distribution of the hidden state. For a gamma distribution, we have a moment-generating function of the form

$$G_{t|t}(x) = (1 - \kappa x)^{-\upsilon_t}$$

The integral (2.30) can be evaluated numerically; however, when dealing with "outliers" the density of the observation takes near-zero values, which makes the integration difficult. Bates suggests *scaling* transformations equivalent to the importance sampling technique used in particle filtering.

Independently from this, Dragulescu and Yakovenko, [81] and [219], derived a semianalytic expression for the likelihood under the Heston model, by using Fourier inversion. Note that a particle filter calculates this very integral via Monte Carlo simulations.

It is worth noting that the main advantage of our particle filtering approach is its complete generality. Indeed the Bates method would work only for model classes that have an exponentially affine Fourier transform. It is true that the Heston model falls in this category; however, a VGG (variance gamma with gamma-distributed arrival rate) process would not, and therefore could only be analyzed through a simulation-based methodology.

Introducing Jumps

The Model As in Bates [28], let us introduce a jump process (independent from Brownian motion) with a given intensity λ and a fixed[36] fractional jump

[36]We could make j a Gaussian random variable without changing the methodology.

size $0 \leq j < 1$. The number of jumps between t and $t + dt$ will therefore be dN_t. Needless to say, if either the intensity $\lambda = 0$ or the jump size $j = 0$, then we are back to the pure diffusion case.

The new stochastic differential equation for the stock price in the risk-neutral framework will be

$$dS_t = (\mu_S + \lambda j)S_t dt + \sqrt{v_t} S_t dB_t - S_t j dN_t$$

and applying Ito's lemma for semi-Martingales

$$d \ln S_t = \left(\mu_S - \frac{1}{2}v_t + \lambda j \right) dt + \sqrt{v_t} dB_t + \ln(1 - j) dN_t$$

which we can rewrite in the discrete version as

$$\ln S_{k+1} = \ln S_k + \left(\mu_S - \frac{1}{2}v_k + \lambda j \right) \Delta t + \sqrt{v_t}\sqrt{\Delta t} B_k + \mu_k$$

with $\mu_0 = 0$ and

$$\mu_k = \delta_0(0) e^{-\lambda \Delta t} + \delta_0 \left(\ln(1 - j)\right) \left(1 - e^{-\lambda \Delta t}\right)$$

where $\delta_0()$ corresponds to the Dirac delta function.[37]
Also

$$\begin{aligned} v_k = v_{k-1} &+ (\omega - \theta v_{k-1})\Delta t + \xi \sqrt{v_{k-1}}\sqrt{\Delta t} Z_{k-1} \\ &- \rho\xi \left[\ln S_{k-1} + \left(\mu_S + \lambda j - \frac{1}{2} v_{k-1} \right) \Delta t + \sqrt{v_{k-1}}\sqrt{\Delta t} B_{k-1} + \mu_{k-1} - \ln S_k \right] \end{aligned}$$

which completes our set of equations.

It is important to note that the new parameter set is

$$\Psi = (\omega, \theta, \xi, \rho, \lambda, j)$$

which effectively gives us two additional degrees of freedom.[38]

---

[37]This means that $-\infty < \mu_k \leq 0$ for every k. Note that we are assuming that we can have *at most* one jump within $[t, t + \Delta t]$, which means that Δt is small enough. This is completely different from pure-jump models, such as variance gamma.

[38]A related idea was developed by Hamilton [126] as well as Chourdakis [59] and Deng [72]. Chourdakis uses the characteristic function for the jump-diffusion process. Doucet [80] suggests the use of particle filtering for the jump process. Maheu and McCurdy [184] use a fully integrated GARCH likelihood with Poisson jumps. Aït-Sahalia [3] uses moments to separate the diffusion parameters from the jumps. Johannes, Polson, and Stroud [164] use the particle filtering technique as well, however, in a Bayesian MCMC framework. Finally, Honoré [142] shows that an MLE approach always works for a constant jump size.

The Generic Particle Filter Since μ_k is following a Poisson process, we have to use a non-Gaussian filter. The use of a generic particle filter (GPF) is therefore natural. In a generic particle filter, the proposal distribution $q(x_k)$ is simply set equal to $p(x_k|x_{k-1})$. The state x_k could be chosen as

$$x_k = \begin{pmatrix} \mu_k \\ v_k \end{pmatrix}$$

and the transition equation becomes

$$x_k = \begin{pmatrix} \delta_0(0)e^{-\lambda\Delta t} + \delta_0(\ln(1-j))(1-e^{-\lambda\Delta t}) \\ v_{k-1} + [(\omega - \rho\xi(\mu_S + \lambda j) - (\theta - \frac{1}{2}\rho\xi)v_{k-1}]\Delta t + \rho\xi[\ln(\frac{S_k}{S_{k-1}}) - \mu_{k-1}] + \xi\sqrt{1-\rho^2}\sqrt{v_{k-1}}\sqrt{\Delta t}\tilde{Z}_{k-1} \end{pmatrix}$$

It becomes therefore possible to implement a particle filter as follows.

1. Choose v_0 and $P_0 > 0$ and set $\mu_0 = 0$, so for i in $1, \ldots, N_{sims}$

$$x_0^{(i)} = \begin{pmatrix} 0 \\ v_0 + \sqrt{P_0}Z^{(i)} \end{pmatrix}$$

   Then for each k with $1 \leq k \leq N$ do
2. Write the new $\tilde{x}_k^{(i)} = (\tilde{\mu}_k^{(i)}, \tilde{v}_k^{(i)})^t$ as the result of simulations

$$\tilde{v}_k^{(i)} \sim \mathcal{N}\left(\mathbf{m} = v_{k-1}^{(i)} + \left[\omega - \rho\xi(\mu_S + \lambda j) - \left(\theta - \frac{1}{2}\rho\xi\right)v_{k-1}^{(i)}\right] \times \Delta t + \rho\xi\left[\ln\left(\frac{S_k}{S_{k-1}}\right) - \mu_{k-1}^{(i)}\right], \mathbf{s}\right)$$

   with $\mathbf{s} = \xi\sqrt{1-\rho^2}\sqrt{v_{k-1}^{(i)}}\sqrt{\Delta t}$ and

$$\tilde{\mu}_k^{(i)} = 0$$

   if $\mathcal{U}[0,1] \leq e^{-\lambda\Delta t}$ and

$$\tilde{\mu}_k^{(i)} = \ln(1-j)$$

   otherwise.
3. Define the weights

$$w_k^{(i)} = w_{k-1}^{(i)} p(z_k|\tilde{x}_k^{(i)})$$

   with

$$p(z_k|\tilde{x}_k^{(i)}) = n\left(z_k, z_{k-1} + \left(\mu_S + \lambda j - \frac{1}{2}\tilde{v}_k^{(i)}\right)\Delta t + \tilde{\mu}_k^{(i)}, \sqrt{\tilde{v}_k^{(i)}\Delta t}\right)$$

4. Normalize the weights

$$\tilde{w}_k^{(i)} = \frac{w_k^{(i)}}{\sum_{i=1}^{N_{sims}} w_k^{(i)}}$$

5. Resample the points $\tilde{x}_k^{(i)}$ and get $x_k^{(i)}$ and reset $w_k^{(i)} = \tilde{w}_k^{(i)} = 1/N_{sims}$. This completes the generic particle filtering algorithm.
Note that there is no Kalman filtering here and therefore

$$\hat{z}_k^- = \frac{1}{N_{sims}} \sum_{i=1}^{N_{sims}} \hat{z}_k^{(i)}$$

with $\hat{z}_k^{(i)}$ the estimation of z_k from $x_{k-1}^{(i)}$

$$\hat{z}_k^{(i)} = z_{k-1} + \left(\mu_S + \lambda j - \frac{1}{2} v_{k-1}^{(i)}\right) \Delta t + \mu_{k-1}^{(i)}$$

and the estimation error is $z_k - \hat{z}_k^-$ as before.
The likelihood maximization is not different from the EPF or UPF. We need to maximize

$$\sum_{k=1}^{N} \ln\left(\sum_{i=1}^{N_{sims}} w_k^{(i)}\right)$$

where $w_k^{(i)}$'s are defined at Step 3.

Extended/Unscented Particle Filters Using the same model, we can take advantage of the independence of v_k and μ_k and apply the (nonlinear) Gaussian Kalman filter to the former. In this case, the Steps 2 and 3 should be replaced with:

2-a. Write $\hat{x}_k^{(i)} = \left(\hat{\mu}_k^{(i)}, \hat{v}_k^{(i)}\right)^t$ with

$$\hat{v}_k^{(i)} = \mathbf{KF}(v_{k-1}^{(i)})$$

with $P_k^{(i)}$ the associated a posteriori error covariance matrix, KF the extended or unscented Kalman filter, and

$$\hat{\mu}_k^{(i)} = \mu_{k-1}^{(i)}$$

2-b. Now take the simulations

$$\tilde{v}_k^{(i)} \sim \mathcal{N}\left(\hat{v}_k^{(i)}, P_k^{(i)}\right)$$

and

$$\tilde{\mu}_k^{(i)} = 0$$

if $\mathcal{U}[0,1] \leq e^{-\lambda \Delta t}$ and

$$\tilde{\mu}_k^{(i)} = \ln(1-j)$$

otherwise.

3. Define the weights

$$w_k^{(i)} = w_{k-1}^{(i)} \frac{p(z_k|\tilde{x}_k^{(i)})p(\tilde{x}_k^{(i)}|x_{k-1}^{(i)})}{q(\tilde{x}_k^{(i)}|x_{k-1}^{(i)}, z_{1:k})}$$

with

$$p\left(z_k|\tilde{x}_k^{(i)}\right) = n\left(z_k, z_{k-1} + \left(\mu_S + \lambda j - \frac{1}{2}\tilde{v}_k^{(i)}\right)\Delta t + \tilde{\mu}_k^{(i)}, \sqrt{\tilde{v}_k^{(i)}\Delta t}\right)$$

$$p\left(\tilde{x}_k^{(i)}|x_{k-1}^{(i)}\right) = n\left(\tilde{v}_k^{(i)}, \mathbf{m}, \mathbf{s} = \xi\sqrt{1-\rho^2}\sqrt{v_{k-1}^{(i)}}\sqrt{\Delta t}\right) p\left(\tilde{\mu}_k^{(i)}|\mu_{k-1}^{(i)}\right)$$

with

$$\mathbf{m} = v_{k-1}^{(i)} + \left[\omega - \rho\xi(\mu_S + \lambda j) - \left(\theta - \frac{1}{2}\rho\xi\right)v_{k-1}^{(i)}\right]\Delta t + \rho\xi\ln\left(\frac{S_k}{S_{k-1}}\right) - \rho\xi\mu_{k-1}^{(i)}$$

and

$$q\left(\tilde{x}_k^{(i)}|x_{k-1}^{(i)}, z_{1:k}\right) = n\left(\tilde{v}_k^{(i)}, \hat{v}_k^{(i)}, P_k^{(i)}\right) p\left(\tilde{\mu}_k^{(i)}|\mu_{k-1}^{(i)}\right)$$

Note that as for the GPF, the terms $p\left(\tilde{\mu}_k^{(i)}|\mu_{k-1}^{(i)}\right)$ cancel out and need *not* be evaluated.

The rest of the algorithm remains the same. This way we will not lose the information contained in the Kalman gain for the Gaussian dimension.

The following is the C++ code for the application of EPF to the Bates model.

```
// log_stock_prices  are the log of stock prices
// muS is the real-world stock drift
// n_stock_prices is the number of the above stock prices
// (omega, theta, xi, rho, lambda, j) are the Bates
parameters
// ll is the value of (negative log) Likelihood function
// estimates[] are the estimated observations from the
filter
```

```
// The function ran2() is from Numerical Recipes in C
// and generates uniform random variables
// The function Normal_inverse() can be found from
many sources
// and is the inverse of the Normal CDF
// Normal_inverse(ran2(.)) generates a set of Normal
random variables

void estimate_particle_jump_diffusion_parameters_1_dim(
double *log_stock_prices,
double muS, int n_stock_prices,
double omega,
double theta,
double xi,
double rho,
double lambda,
double j,
double *ll,
double *estimates)
{
 int     i1, i2, i3;
 double  H, A, x0, P0, z;
 int     M=1000;
 double  x[1000], xx[1000], x1[1000], x2[1000];
 double  mu[1000], mm[1000], m1[1000], m2[1000];
 double  P[1000], P1[1000], U[1000], K[1000], W[1000];
 double  w[1000],  u[1000], c[1000];
 double  q, pz, px, s, m, l;
 double  delt=1.0/252.0, x1_sum, m1_sum;
 long    idum=-1;
 int     i1_prev=0;
 double  u_t=0.0;
 int     *jump;

 jump= new int [n_stock_prices];
 for (i1=0; i1<n_stock_prices; i1++)
   jump[i1]=0;

 A = 1.0-(theta-0.5*rho*xi)*delt;
 H = -0.5*delt;

 x0 = 0.04;
 P0 = 0.000001;
 for (i2=0; i2<M; i2++)
 {
```

```
  x[i2] = x0 + sqrt(P0)* Normal_inverse(ran2(&idum));
  mu[i2]=0;
  P[i2] = P0;
 }

 *ll=0.0;
 for (i1=1;i1<n_stock_prices-1;i1++)
 {
   l = 0.0;
   x1_sum=0.0;
   m1_sum=0.0;
   for (i2=0; i2<M; i2++)
   {
     /* EKF for the proposal distribution */
     if (x[i2]<0) x[i2]=0.00001;
     x1[i2] = x[i2] + ( omega-rho*xi*(muS+lambda*j) -
(theta-0.5*rho*xi) * x[i2]) * delt +
   rho*xi* (log_stock_prices[i1]-
     log_stock_prices[i1-1]) - rho*xi*mu[i2];
     m1[i2]=mu[i2];
     W[i2]  = xi*sqrt((1-rho*rho) * x[i2] * delt);
     P1[i2] = W[i2]*W[i2] + A*P[i2]*A;
     if (x1[i2]<0) x1[i2]=0.00001;
     U[i2] = sqrt(x1[i2]*delt);
     K[i2] = P1[i2]*H/( H*P1[i2]*H + U[i2]*U[i2]);
     z = log_stock_prices[i1+1];
     x2[i2] = x1[i2] + K[i2] *
    (z - (log_stock_prices[i1] +
     (muS+lambda*j-0.5*x1[i2])*delt + m1[i2]));
     m2[i2]= m1[i2];
     x1_sum+= x1[i2];
     m1_sum+= m1[i2];
     P[i2]=(1.0-K[i2]*H)*P1[i2];
     /* sample */
     xx[i2] = x2[i2] + sqrt(P[i2])*
     Normal_inverse(ran2(&idum));
     if (xx[i2]<0) xx[i2]=0.00001;

     if (ran2(&idum) < exp(-lambda*delt))
   mm[i2]=0.0;
     else
   mm[i2]=log(1.0-j);

     /* calculate weights */
     m = x2[i2];
```

```
    s = sqrt(P[i2]);
    q = 0.39894228/s * exp( - 0.5* (xx[i2] - m)*
    (xx[i2] - m)/(s*s) );
    m= log_stock_prices[i1] +
    (muS+lambda*j-0.5*xx[i2])*delt + mm[i2];
    s= sqrt(xx[i2]*delt);
    pz= 0.39894228/s *
    exp( - 0.5* (z - m)*(z - m)/(s*s) );
    m= x[i2] + ( omega-rho*xi*(muS+lambda*j) -
    (theta-0.5*rho*xi) * x[i2]) * delt +
  rho*xi* (log_stock_prices[i1]-
    log_stock_prices[i1-1]) -rho*xi*mu[i2];
    s= xi*sqrt((1-rho*rho) * x[i2] * delt);
    px= 0.39894228/s *
    exp( - 0.5* (xx[i2] - m)*(xx[i2] - m)/(s*s) );

    w[i2]= pz * px / MAX(q, 1.0e-10);
    l += w[i2];
  }
  *ll += log(l);
  estimates[i1+1]= log_stock_prices[i1] +
  (muS+lambda*j-0.5*x1_sum/M)*delt+m1_sum/M;
  /* normalize weights */
  for (i2=0; i2<M; i2++)
    w[i2] /= l;
  /* resample and reset weights */
  c[0]=0;
  for (i2=1; i2<M; i2++)
    c[i2] = c[i2-1] + w[i2];
  i2=0;
  u[0] = 1.0/M * ran2(&idum);
  for (i3=0; i3<M; i3++)
  {
    u[i3] = u[0] + 1.0/M *i3;
    while (u[i3] > c[i2])
  i2++;
    x[i3]= xx[i2];
    mu[i3]=mm[i2];
    w[i3]=1.0/M;
  }
}

*ll *= -1.0;

delete [] jump;
```

```
}

// *ll corresponds to the (negative log) Likelihood
// which we will need to minimize to obtain optimal
parameters
```

The Srivastava Approach Srivastava [222] suggests the following approach for simulating the jump component. Instead of allowing a jump at each time interval $[t_k, t_k + \Delta t]$ with a probability $1 - e^{-\lambda \Delta t}$ as we do now, we can flag the time steps such that

$$t_{k-1} < \frac{1}{\lambda} \ln \left(\frac{1}{\mathcal{U}[0,1]} \right) \leq t_k$$

where $\mathcal{U}[0,1]$ is a uniform random variable between zero and one, and then perform a jump of size $|\ln(1-j)|$ on these steps for all paths. We therefore would first initialize $t_p = 0$ and loop through k's between 1 and N, and if

$$e^{-\lambda(t_k - t_p)} \leq \mathcal{U}[0,1] < e^{-\lambda(t_{k-1} - t_p)}$$

we flag this k and set $t_p = t_k$ and resimulate $\mathcal{U}[0,1]$. In the particle filter, we would set for *all* indices i's

$$\tilde{\mu}_k^{(i)} = \ln(1-j)$$

for the flagged k's, and we would set $\tilde{\mu}_k^{(i)} = 0$ for other indices.

It is important to note that in this approach the simulation for the jump component is completely "orthogonal" to the diffusion SIS part. Indeed the index i in the foregoing is irrelevant for the entity $\tilde{\mu}_k^{(i)}$. This means that in the KF step, the weight calculation and the resampling are independent of the Jump component altogether.

Numeric results As a check, we simulate a time series with the parameter set

$$\Psi^* = (\omega^* = 0, \theta^* = 0, \xi^* = 0, \rho^* = 0, \lambda^* = 2.52, j^* = 0.20)$$

which corresponds to a jump frequency of $\lambda \Delta t = 0.01$ and a jump size of 20 percent. We generated $N = 245$ points and used $M = 1000$ particles.

The estimated set via the above EPF is

$$\hat{\Psi} = (\hat{\omega} = 0.23, \hat{\theta} = 1.5, \hat{\xi} = 0.34, \hat{\rho} = 0.21, \hat{\lambda} = 2.65, \hat{j} = 0.20)$$

As we see, the diffusion parameters are not close to the original ones, but this is probably due to the small Δt, as previously discussed. The jump parameters are close to the original ones, which means that the filter is valid for the jump

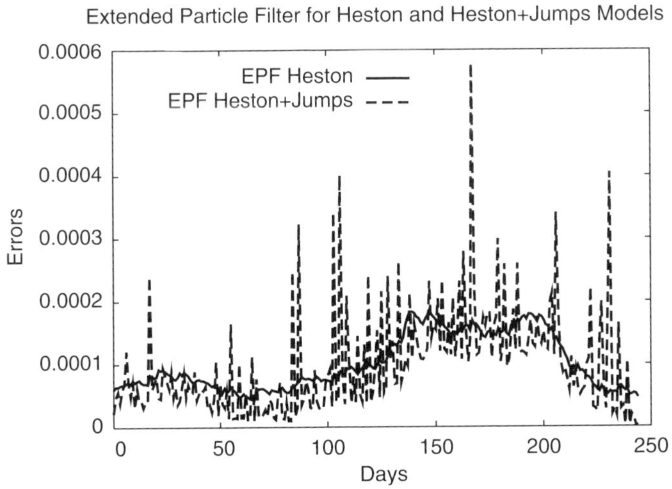

FIGURE 2.51 Comparison of EPF Results for Heston and Heston+Jumps Models. The presence of jumps can be seen in the residuals.

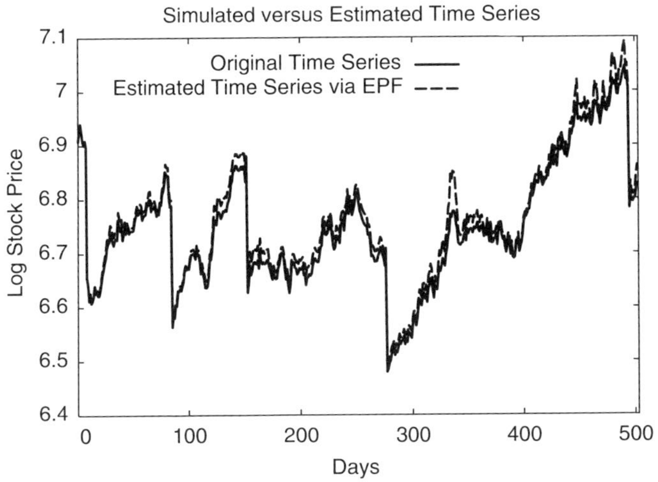

FIGURE 2.52 Comparison of EPF Results for Simulated and Estimated Jump-Diffusion Time Series. The filtered data matches the real data fairly well.

component. Note that despite the difference in the diffusion parameters, the estimated and original time series are rather close for a new simulation, as can be seen in Figures 2.51 and 2.52. This reconfirms our previous remark: When the parameters affect the *drift* of the observation (as opposed to its *noise*), their estimation is far more accurate and requires fewer data points.

The Optimization Algorithm It is important to realize that the likelihood function here (owing to the jumps) is *not differentiable everywhere*, and, therefore, gradient-based maximization methods could not be applied. The optimization could, however, still be carried out via the direction set algorithm as previously described. Note that as mentioned in [164] so far there has been no formal proof on the convergence of the discretized jump diffusion equations toward the continuous ones; however, empirical evidence makes the convergence assumption plausible.

Pure Jump Models

The variance gamma with stochastic arrival (VGSA) and the variance gamma with gamma arrival (VGG) models were defined in Chapter 1. These models are non-Gaussian, and we could apply the particle filtering technique to them. We are *not* dealing with diffusion models, and therefore we do not have the Girsanov theorem. We are estimating the parameter set

$$\Psi = (\mu_S, \theta, \sigma, \nu, \ldots)$$

In order to make the back-testing simpler, we suppose that we know the stock drift and try to estimate the other parameters. However, as mentioned earlier, for a high-frequency data set we have

$$\Delta t = o\left(\sqrt{\Delta t}\right)$$

and the drift term has a negligible impact.

VG The variance gamma model has the advantage of offering an integrated density, which allows us to calculate the exact likelihood. Calling $z = \ln(S_k/S_{k-1})$ and $h = t_k - t_{k-1}$ and posing $x_h = z - \mu_S h - \frac{h}{\nu}\ln(1 - \theta\nu - \sigma^2\nu/2)$, we have

$$p(z|h) = \frac{2\exp\left(\theta x_h/\sigma^2\right)}{\nu^{\frac{h}{\nu}}\sqrt{2\pi}\sigma\Gamma\left(\frac{h}{\nu}\right)}\left(\frac{x_h^2}{2\sigma^2/\nu+\theta^2}\right)^{\frac{h}{2\nu}-\frac{1}{4}} K_{\frac{h}{\nu}-\frac{1}{2}}\left(\frac{1}{\sigma^2}\sqrt{x_h^2\left(2\sigma^2/\nu+\theta^2\right)}\right)$$

and the likelihood is

$$L_{1:N} = \prod_{k=1}^{N} p(z_k|z_{k-1}, h)$$

The implementation of this estimation procedure is straightforward and has already been done in [182].

One could also back-test the estimation procedure in the following way: First choose a parameter set (θ, σ, ν) as well as a drift μ_S and a time-step Δt. Then simulate via Monte Carlo a gamma-distributed random variable as well as a Gaussian one. Deduce an artificial stock-price time series, apply the MLE procedure to it, and try to recover the original parameter set.

Using $\Delta t = 1/252$, $\mu_S^* = 0.05$, and

$$\begin{aligned} \theta^* &= 0.02 \\ \sigma^* &= 0.2 \\ \nu^* &= 0.005 \end{aligned}$$

We simulated 500 data points, applied the MLE, and found an optimal parameter set $\hat{\Psi} = (0.018, 0.22, 0.006)$, which is close to the original set.

VGSA Using the same notations as in the previous chapter, the Euler discretized VGSA process could be written via the auxiliary variable

$$y_k = y_{k-1} + \kappa(\eta - y_{k-1})\Delta t + \lambda\sqrt{y_{k-1}}\sqrt{\Delta t}W_{k-1}$$

and the state

$$x_k = F_\nu^{-1}(y_k \Delta t, \mathcal{U}[0, 1])$$

as well as the observation $z_k = \ln S_{k+1}$

$$z_k = z_{k-1} + (\mu_S + \omega)\Delta t + \theta x_k + \sigma\sqrt{x_k}B_k$$

with $\omega = \frac{1}{\nu}\ln(1 - \theta\nu - \sigma^2\nu/2)$.

The Filtering Algorithm The PF algorithm could therefore be written as follows.

1. **Initialize** the arrival-rate $y_0^{(j)}$, the state $x_0^{(i)}$, and the weight $w_0^{(i)}$ for j between 1 and M_{sims}, and i between 1 and N_{sims}

While $1 \leq k \leq N$

2. **Simulate** the arrival-rate y_k for j between 1 and M_{sims}

$$y_k^{(j)} = y_{k-1}^{(j)} + \kappa\left(\eta - y_{k-1}^{(j)}\right)\Delta t + \lambda\sqrt{y_{k-1}^{(j)}}\sqrt{\Delta t}\mathcal{N}^{-1}\left(\mathcal{U}^{(j)}[0, 1]\right)$$

3-a. **Simulate** the state x_k for each $y_k^{(j)}$ and for i between 1 and N_{sims}

$$\tilde{x}_k^{(i|j)} = F_\nu^{-1}\left(y_k^{(j)}\Delta t, \mathcal{U}^{(i)}[0, 1]\right)$$

3-b. Compute the unconditional **state**

$$\tilde{x}_k^{(i)} = \int \tilde{x}_k^{(i)}(y_k)p(y_k|y_{k-1})dy_k \approx \frac{1}{M_{sims}} \sum_{j=1}^{M_{sims}} \tilde{x}_k^{(i|j)}$$

4. Calculate the associated **weights** for each i

$$w_k^{(i)} = w_{k-1}^{(i)} p\left(z_k|\tilde{x}_k^{(i)}\right)$$

with

$$p\left(z_k|\tilde{x}_k^{(i)}\right) = n(z_k, m, s)$$

the normal density with mean $m = z_{k-1} + (\mu_S + \omega)\Delta t + \theta\tilde{x}_k^{(i)}$ and standard deviation $s = \sigma\sqrt{\tilde{x}_k^{(i)}}$

5. **Normalize** the weights

$$\tilde{w}_k^{(i)} = \frac{w_k^{(i)}}{\sum_{i=1}^{N_{sims}} w_k^{(i)}}$$

6. **Resample** the points $\tilde{x}_k^{(i)}$ and get $x_k^{(i)}$ and reset $w_k^{(i)} = \tilde{w}_k^{(i)} = 1/N_{sims}$.
7. **Increment** k, go back to Step 2, and **Stop** at the end of the **While** loop.

Parameter Estimation As usual, the log likelihood to be maximized is

$$\ln(L_{1:N}) = \sum_{k=1}^{N} \ln\left(\sum_{i=1}^{N_{sims}} w_k^{(i)}\right)$$

The maximization takes place over the parameter set $\Psi = (\kappa, \eta, \lambda, \nu, \theta, \sigma)$. Again, in reality the stock drift μ_S should be estimated together with the other parameters; however, with a view to simplifying, we suppose we know μ_S in our back-testing procedures.

A More Efficient Algorithm We could take advantage of the fact that VG provides an integrated density of stock return. Calling $z = \ln(S_k/S_{k-1})$ and $h = t_k - t_{k-1}$, and posing $x_h = z - \mu_S h - \frac{h}{\nu}\ln(1 - \theta\nu - \sigma^2\nu/2)$, we have

$$p(z|h) = \frac{2\exp(\theta x_h/\sigma^2)}{\nu^{\frac{h}{\nu}}\sqrt{2\pi}\sigma\Gamma(\frac{h}{\nu})} \left(\frac{x_h^2}{2\sigma^2/\nu + \theta^2}\right)^{\frac{h}{2\nu}-\frac{1}{4}} K_{\frac{h}{\nu}-\frac{1}{2}}\left(\frac{1}{\sigma^2}\sqrt{x_h^2(2\sigma^2/\nu + \theta^2)}\right)$$

As we can see, the dependence on the gamma distribution is "integrated out" in the above.

For VGSA, for a given arrival rate $dt^* = y_t dt$, we have a VG distribution and

$$d \ln S_t = (\mu_S + \omega)dt + B(\gamma(dt^*, 1, \nu); \theta, \sigma)$$

and the corresponding integrated density becomes

$$p(z|h, h^*) = \frac{2\exp(\theta x_h/\sigma^2)}{\nu^{\frac{h^*}{\nu}}\sqrt{2\pi}\sigma\Gamma\left(\frac{h^*}{\nu}\right)}\left(\frac{x_h^2}{2\sigma^2/\nu+\theta^2}\right)^{\frac{h^*}{2\nu}-\frac{1}{4}} K_{\frac{h^*}{\nu}-\frac{1}{2}}\left(\frac{1}{\sigma^2}\sqrt{x_h^2(2\sigma^2/\nu+\theta^2)}\right) \tag{2.31}$$

Indeed, as described in [182] for VG, we have

$$p(z|h) = \int_0^{+\infty} p(z|g, h)p(g|h)dg$$

with $p(z|g, h)$ a normal density and $p(g|h)$ a gamma density. More accurately

$$p(z|g, h) = \frac{1}{\sigma\sqrt{2\pi g}} \exp\left(-\frac{1}{2\sigma^2 g}\left(z - \mu_S h - \frac{h}{\nu}\ln\left(1 - \theta\nu - \sigma^2\nu/2\right) - \theta g\right)^2\right)$$

and

$$p(g|h) = \frac{g^{\frac{h}{\nu}-1}\exp(-\frac{g}{\nu})}{\nu^{\frac{h}{\nu}}\Gamma(\frac{h}{\nu})}$$

Now, for VGSA we simply have a different arrival rate h^* for the gamma process and therefore

$$p(z|h, h^*) = \int_0^{+\infty} p(z|g, h)p(g|h^*)dg$$

which demonstrates the point. This gives us the idea of using the arrival rate as the state, and we use the following algorithm.

1. **Initialize** the state $x_0^{(i)}$ and the weight $w_0^{(i)}$ for i between 1 and N_{sims}

While $1 \le k \le N$

2. **Simulate** the state x_k for i between 1 and N_{sims}

$$\tilde{x}_k^{(i)} = x_{k-1}^{(i)} + \kappa(\eta - x_{k-1}^{(i)})\Delta t + \lambda\sqrt{x_{k-1}^{(i)}}\sqrt{\Delta t}\mathcal{N}^{-1}\left(\mathcal{U}^{(i)}[0, 1]\right)$$

3. Calculate the associated **weights** for each i

$$w_k^{(i)} = w_{k-1}^{(i)} p(z_k|\tilde{x}_k^{(i)})$$

with $p(z_k|\tilde{x}_k^{(i)})$ as defined in (2.31), where h will be set to Δt and h^* to the simulated state $\tilde{x}_k^{(i)}$ times Δt

4. **Normalize** the weights

$$\tilde{w}_k^{(i)} = \frac{w_k^{(i)}}{\sum_{i=1}^{N_{sims}} w_k^{(i)}}$$

5. **Resample** the points $\tilde{x}_k^{(i)}$ and get $x_k^{(i)}$ and reset $w_k^{(i)} = \tilde{w}_k^{(i)} = 1/N_{sims}$.
6. **Increment** k, go back to Step 2 and **Stop** at the end of the **While** loop.

The advantage of this method is that there is one simulation process instead of two, and we "skip" the gamma distribution altogether. However, the dependence of the observation z_k on x_k is highly nonlinear, which makes the convergence more difficult.

An Extended/Unscented Particle Filter Finally, a natural idea would be to use a proposal distribution $q(x)$ for the state, *taking into account the observation information*. In order to be able to use a Kalman-based proposal distribution (EPF or UPF), we need a Gaussian approximation. Note that given the strong non-Gaussianity of the equations, we absolutely need the particle filtering aspect. The Gaussian *approximation* for the observation equation would be[39]

$$z_k = z_{k-1} + \left(\mu_S + \omega + \theta x_k\right)\Delta t + \sqrt{\theta^2\nu + \sigma^2}\sqrt{x_k \Delta t}B_k$$

which is of the form $z_k = h(x_k, B_k)$ and allows us to use the Kalman filtering algorithm. We therefore replace Steps 2 and 3 of the previous algorithm with the following.

2-a. Apply an extended/unscented **Kalman filter** for i between 1 and N_{sims} to the state $x_{k-1}^{(i)}$ and obtain

$$\hat{x}_k^{(i)} = \mathbf{KF}\left(x_{k-1}^{(i)}\right)$$

as well as the associated covariance $P_k^{(i)}$.

2-b. **Simulate** the state for i between 1 and N_{sims}

$$\tilde{x}_k^{(i)} = \hat{x}_k^{(i)} + \sqrt{P_k^{(i)}}\mathcal{N}^{-1}\left(\mathcal{U}^{(i)}[0,1]\right)$$

3. Calculate the associated **weights** for each i

$$w_k^{(i)} = w_{k-1}^{(i)} \frac{p\left(z_k|\tilde{x}_k^{(i)}\right) p\left(\tilde{x}_k^{(i)}|x_{k-1}^{(i)}\right)}{q\left(\tilde{x}_k^{(i)}|x_{k-1}^{(i)}, z_{1:k}\right)}$$

[39]We are using the fact that for $X(t) = B\left(\gamma(t,1,\nu);\theta,\sigma\right)$ we have a mean θt and a variance $(\theta^2\nu + \sigma^2)t$ as stated in [182].

with $p\left(z_k|\tilde{x}_k^{(i)}\right)$ as defined in (2.31), where h will be set to Δt and h^* to the simulated state $\tilde{x}_k^{(i)}$ times Δt, where $p\left(\tilde{x}_k^{(i)}|x_{k-1}^{(i)}\right)$ is the normal density with mean $x_{k-1}^{(i)} + \kappa\left(\eta - x_{k-1}^{(i)}\right)\Delta t$ and standard deviation $\lambda\sqrt{x_{k-1}^{(i)}}\sqrt{\Delta t}$, and where $q\left(\tilde{x}_k^{(i)}|x_{k-1}^{(i)}, z_{1:k}\right)$ is the normal density with mean $\hat{x}_k^{(i)}$ and standard deviation $\sqrt{P_k^{(i)}}$.

The rest of the algorithm is exactly the same as the previous one. What follows is a C++ routine for the EPF applied to VGSA.

```
// log_stock_prices  are the log of stock prices
// muS is the real-world stock drift
// n_stock_prices is the number of the above stock prices
// (kappa,eta,lambda,sigma,theta,nu) are the VGSA parameters
// ll is the value of (negative log) Likelihood function
// estimates[] are the estimated observations from the filter
// errors are the observation errors

// The function ran2() is from Numerical Recipes in C
// and generates uniform random variables
// The function Normal_inverse() can be found from
many sources
// and is the inverse of the Normal CDF
// Normal_inverse(ran2(.)) generates a set of Normal
random variables

// The Bessel and Gamma functions bessik() and gammln()
// are also available in Numerical Recipes in C




void estimate_particle_extended_VGSA_parameters_bessel(
double *log_stock_prices,
double mu,
int n_stock_prices,
double kappa,
double eta,
double lambda,
double sigma,
double theta,
double nu,
double *ll,
double *estimates,
```

```
double *errors)
{
  int       i1, i2, i3;
  double    y0, z, omega;
  int       M=1000;
  double    x[1000], xx[1000], X;
  double    w[1000],  u[1000], c[1000];
  double    pz, px, q, s, m, l, x1_sum;
  long      idum=-1;
  double    delt=1.0/252.0;
  double    eps=1.0e-30;
  double    Ka,Ia,Kp,Ip, Kx,Knu;

  double    H, A, x0, P0;
  double    P[1000], P1[1000], U[1000], K[1000], W[1000];
  double    x1[1000], x2[1000];

  /* initialize */
  omega=log(1.0-theta*nu- sigma*sigma*nu/2.0)/nu;
  x0 = 1.0;
  P0 = 0.000001;
  for (i2=0; i2<M; i2++)
  {
    x[i2] = x0 + sqrt(P0)* Normal_Inverse(ran2(&idum));
    P[i2] = P0;
  }
  A = 1.0-kappa*delt;
  H = theta*delt;
  /* time loop */
  *ll=0.0;
  for (i1=1;i1<n_stock_prices-1;i1++)
  {
    z = log_stock_prices[i1+1]-log_stock_prices[i1];
    X= z - mu*delt - delt/nu*log(1.0-theta*nu-
  sigma*sigma*nu/2.0);
    l = 0.0;
    x1_sum=0.0;
    for (i2=0; i2<M; i2++)
    {
      /* EKF for the proposal distribution */
      x1[i2] = x[i2] + kappa*(eta - x[i2])*delt;
      W[i2]  = lambda*sqrt(x[i2] * delt);
      P1[i2] = W[i2]*W[i2] + A*P[i2]*A;
      x1[i2]=MAX(x1[i2],eps);
```

```
      U[i2] = sqrt(theta*theta*nu+sigma*sigma)*
sqrt(x1[i2]*delt);
      K[i2] = P1[i2]*H/( H*P1[i2]*H + U[i2]*U[i2]);
      x2[i2] = x1[i2] + K[i2] *
      (z - (mu+omega+theta*x1[i2])*delt);
      x1_sum+= x1[i2];
      P[i2]=(1.0-K[i2]*H)*P1[i2];
      /* sample */
      xx[i2] = x2[i2] + sqrt(P[i2])*
      Normal_Inverse(ran2(&idum));
      xx[i2]=MAX(xx[i2],eps);
      /* calculate weights */
      m = x2[i2];
      s = sqrt(P[i2]);
      q = 0.39894228/s * exp( - 0.5* (xx[i2] - m)*
      (xx[i2] - m)/(s*s) );
      m = x[i2] + kappa*(eta - x[i2])*delt;
      s = lambda*sqrt(x[i2] * delt);
      px = 0.39894228/s * exp( - 0.5* (xx[i2] - m)*
      (xx[i2] - m)/(s*s) );
      Kx  = MAX(eps, 1.0/(sigma*sigma)*
      sqrt(X*X*(2*sigma*sigma/nu+theta*theta)));
      Knu = MAX(eps, (xx[i2]*delt/nu-0.5));
      bessik(Kx , Knu , &Ia, &Ka, &Kp, &Ip);
      pz=2.0*exp(theta*X/(sigma*sigma)) /
    (pow(nu,xx[i2]*delt/nu)*sigma*
    exp(gammln(xx[i2]*delt/nu))) *0.39894228*
    pow(X*X/(2*sigma*sigma/nu+theta*theta),
    0.5*xx[i2]*delt/nu-0.25) * Ka;

       w[i2]= pz * px / MAX(q, eps);
      l += w[i2];
    }
    *ll += log(l);
    /* estimates[i1+1] for z[i1] => error term */
    estimates[i1+1]= log_stock_prices[i1+1]-
(log_stock_prices[i1] + (mu+omega+theta*x1_sum/M)*
delt);
    errors[i1]    = (theta*theta*nu + sigma*sigma)*
    x1_sum/M*delt;
    /* normalize weights */
    for (i2=0; i2<M; i2++)
      w[i2] /= l;
    /* resample and reset weights */
    c[0]=0;
```

```
    for (i2=1; i2<M; i2++)
      c[i2] = c[i2-1] + w[i2];
    i2=0;
    u[0] = 1.0/M * ran2(&idum);
    for (i3=0; i3<M; i3++)
    {
      u[i3] = u[0] + 1.0/M *i3;
      while (u[i3] > c[i2])
    i2++;
      x[i3]= xx[i2];
      w[i3]=1.0/M;
    }
  }

  *ll *= -1.0;

}

// *ll represents the (negative log) Likelihood
```

Numeric Results We performed the same kind of back-testing procedure as for the VG model, using either of the foregoing particle filters applied to an artificially generated stock-price time series. We chose $\Delta t = 1/252$, $\mu_S^* = 0$, $y_0 = 1$ and

$$\Psi^* = (\kappa^* = 0, \eta^* = 0, \lambda^* = 0, \nu^* = 0.005, \theta^* = 0.02, \sigma^* = 0.2)$$

after applying the importance sampling/resampling PF via the modified Bessel function, we found

$$\hat{\Psi} = (0.13, 0.001, 0.37, 0.0048, 0.018, 0.21)$$

which seems to indicate that the estimation process for (ν, θ, σ) works well, whereas the one for (κ, η, λ) does not. However, if we simulate two sets of spot-price times series with these different parameter sets, we will see that the generated paths are very similar. See Figures 2.53 and 2.54. This also confirms our previous remarks about the estimation of the parameters affecting the noise.

We performed a second test with a more realistic choice of parameters, with once again $\Delta t = 1/252$, $N_{sims} = 100$, and 500 data points corresponding to two years. The real values were

$$\Psi^* = (\kappa^* = 2.10, \eta^* = 5.70, \lambda^* = 2.00, \nu^* = 0.05, \theta^* = -0.40, \sigma^* = 0.20)$$

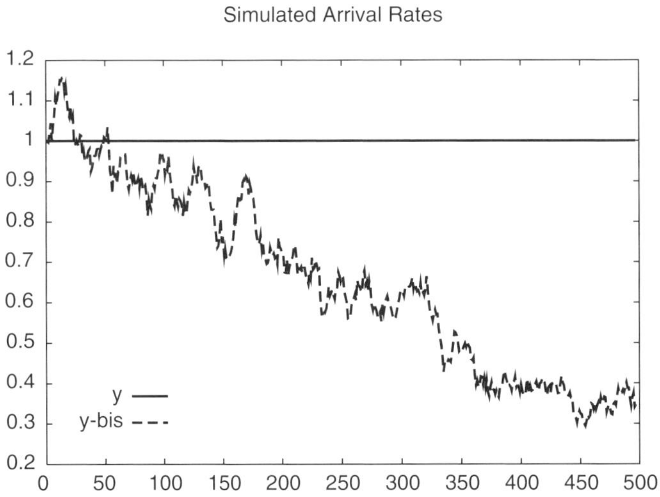

FIGURE 2.53 The Simulated Arrival Rates via $\Psi = (\kappa = 0, \eta = 0, \lambda = 0, \sigma = 0.2, \theta = 0.02, \nu = 0.005)$ and $\Psi = (\kappa = 0.13, \eta = 0, \lambda = 0.40, \sigma = 0.2, \theta = 0.02, \nu = 0.005)$ Are Quite Different; compare with Figure 2.54.

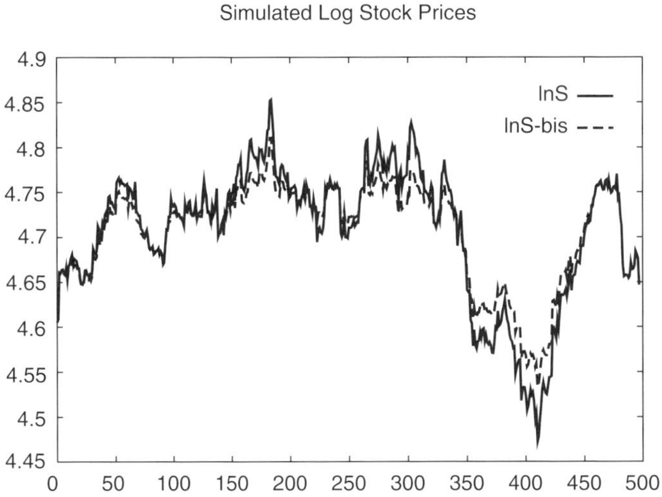

FIGURE 2.54 However, the Simulated Log Stock Prices are Close. (Compare with Figure 2.53.)

Note that θ has a negative value that corresponds to the negative skewness of the distribution. We choose a fairly reasonable initial set

$$\Psi_0 = (\kappa_0 = 2.00, \eta_0 = 6.00, \lambda_0 = 1.50, \nu_0 = 0.03, \theta_0 = -0.30, \sigma_0 = 0.30)$$

and

$$\mu_0 = \mu^* = 0.05$$

We find the optimal parameter set

$$\hat{\Psi} = (\hat{\kappa} = 4.25, \hat{\eta} = 7.89, \hat{\lambda} = 3.25, \hat{\nu} = 0.047, \hat{\theta} = -0.40, \hat{\sigma} = 0.19)$$

and

$$\hat{\mu} = \mu^* = 0.05$$

Again we see that the estimations for the three VG parameters (ν, θ, σ) are much more accurate than those corresponding to the arrival process (κ, η, λ)—and this despite our choosing the initial arrival parameters close to the real ones. As previously stated, the time series of spot prices has little sensitivity to the arrival-rate parameters and a higher degree of sensitivity to the gamma process parameters. Again, this shows that estimation methodologies such as MLE work much better when applied to parameters that affect the drift of an observation, and not its noise.

Diagnostics As for diagnostics, we need to estimate the observation error associated with the algorithm. We define once again

$$\hat{z}_k^{(i)} = z_{k-1} + \left(\mu_S + \omega + \theta \tilde{x}_k^{(i)}\right)\Delta t$$

$$\hat{z}_k^{-} = \frac{1}{N_{sims}} \sum_{i=1}^{N_{sims}} \hat{z}_k^{(i)}$$

or

$$\hat{z}_k^{-} = z_{k-1} + (\mu_S + \omega)\Delta t + \theta \Delta t \frac{1}{N_{sims}} \sum_{i=1}^{N_{sims}} \tilde{x}_k^{(i)}$$

and the error term

$$e_k = z_k - \hat{z}_k^{-}$$

The variance associated with this error is

$$s_k = \left(\theta^2 \nu + \sigma^2\right) \frac{1}{N_{sims}} \sum_{i=1}^{N_{sims}} \tilde{x}_k^{(i)} \Delta t$$

and

$$\tilde{e}_k = e_k / s_k$$

would represent the normalized error.

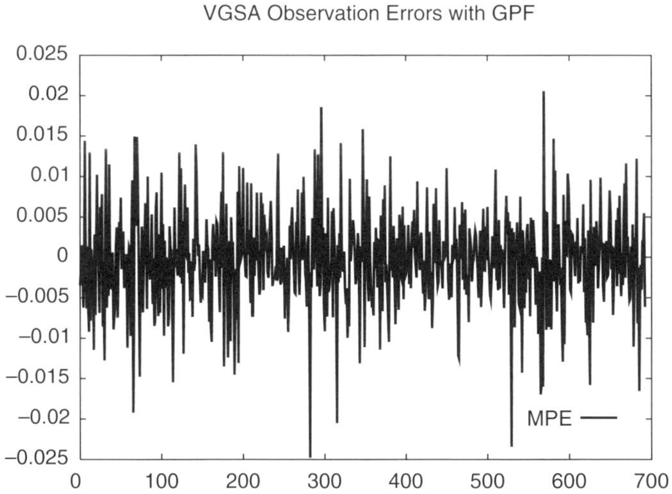

FIGURE 2.55 The Observation Errors for the VGSA Model with a Generic Particle Filter.

TABLE 2.15 MPE and RMSE for the VGSA Model Under a Generic PF as well as the EPF.

	MPE	RMSE
PF	-0.000350241	0.005867065
EPF	-4.74747e-07	0.005869782

MPE/RMSE In order to measure the performance, once again we use the mean price error (MPE) and the root mean-squared error (RMSE). As an example, we use the S&P 500 data between 1992 and 1994 (as used in [182]). For the generic particle filter (GPF) and the extended particle filter (EPF), we find the results in Table 2.15.

As we can see, the use of the extended Kalman filter as the proposal distribution brings some improvement. Also see Figures 2.55 and 2.56.

Chi-Square Test The residuals are normal; a χ^2_{20} test provides us with a value of 10.397699, which is below the threshold value of 31.5 for a confidence of 0.95. This means that the non-Gaussianity was "filtered out" of the time series successfully. This could also be observed in the corresponding histogram in Figure 2.57.

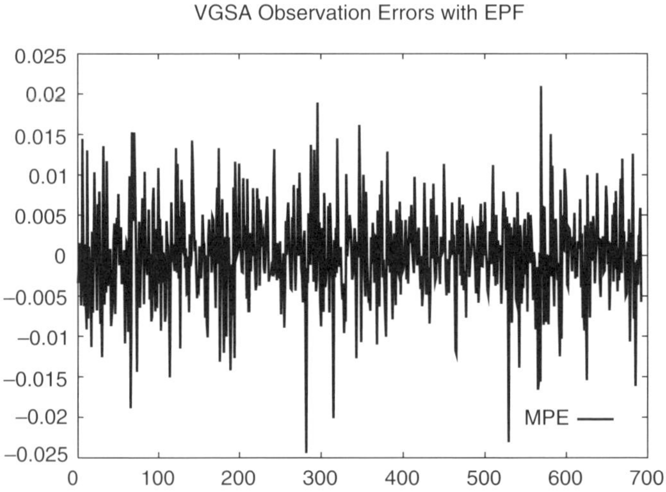

FIGURE 2.56 The Observation Errors for the VGSA Model and an Extended Particle Filter.

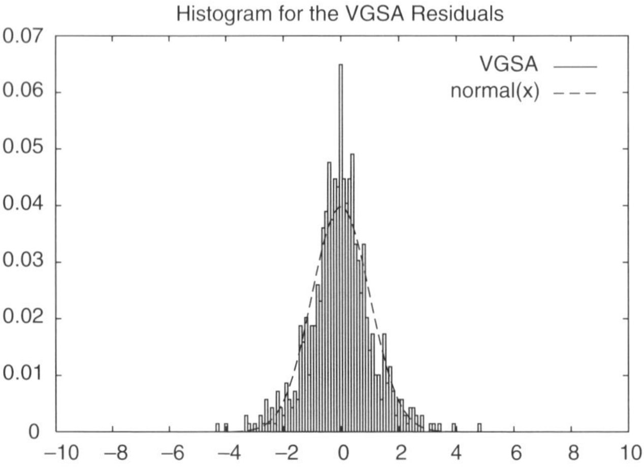

FIGURE 2.57 The VGSA Residuals Histogram. The residuals are fairly normal.

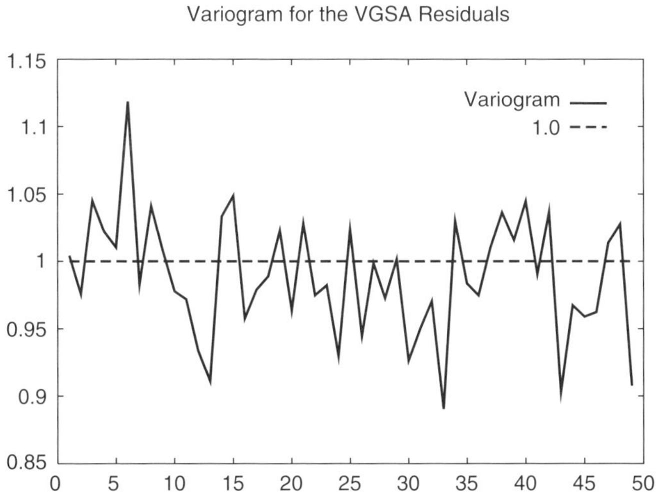

FIGURE 2.58 The VGSA Residuals Variogram. The variogram is close to 1 as expected.

Auto-Correlation Having $p = 7$ parameters and taking $K = 27$, we shall have $K - p = 20$, so we will compare the output of the Box-Ljung test to the χ^2_{20} threshold, which, as previously mentioned, for a confidence of 0.95 is around 31.5. We find a value of 0.001138, which definitely passes the test. This shows that the residuals are indeed uncorrelated.

Variogram The variogram still indicates that we have independent and identically distributed random variables. Calling

$$\gamma_h = \frac{1}{2}\mathbf{E}\left[(\tilde{e}_{k+h} - \tilde{e}_k)^2\right] = \frac{1}{2}\mathbf{E}\left[\tilde{e}^2_{k+h}\right] + \frac{1}{2}\mathbf{E}\left[\tilde{e}^2_k\right] - \mathbf{E}[\tilde{e}_{k+h}\tilde{e}_k]$$

we should obtain $\frac{1}{2}+\frac{1}{2}-0 = 1$, which is indeed the case as seen in Figure 2.58.

VGG The observation is $z_k = \ln S_{k+1}$

$$z_k = z_{k-1} + (\mu_S + \omega)\Delta t + \theta x_k + \sigma\sqrt{x_k}B_k$$

with $\omega = \frac{1}{\nu}\ln(1 - \theta\nu - \sigma^2\nu/2)$, and the hidden state is

$$x_k = Y_k(\Delta t)$$

We could take advantage of the fact that VG provides an integrated density of stock return [182]. Calling $z = \ln(S_k/S_{k-1})$ and $h = t_k - t_{k-1}$ and posing

$$\xi_h = z - \mu_S h - \frac{h}{\nu}\ln(1 - \theta\nu - \sigma^2\nu/2)$$

we have

$$p(z|h) = \frac{2\exp(\theta\xi_h/\sigma^2)}{\nu^{\frac{h}{\nu}}\sqrt{2\pi}\sigma\Gamma\left(\frac{h}{\nu}\right)}\left(\frac{\xi_h^2}{2\sigma^2/\nu+\theta^2}\right)^{\frac{h}{2\nu}-\frac{1}{4}} K_{\frac{h}{\nu}-\frac{1}{2}}\left(\frac{1}{\sigma^2}\sqrt{\xi_h^2(2\sigma^2/\nu+\theta^2)}\right)$$

where $K_\alpha(x)$ corresponds to the modified Bessel function of second kind. As we can see, the dependence on the gamma distribution is "integrated out." For the VGG for a given arrival rate $dt^* = dY_t$ we have a VG distribution and

$$d\ln S_t = (\mu + \omega)dt + B(\gamma(dt^*, 1, \nu); \theta, \sigma)$$

and the corresponding integrated density becomes

$$p(z|h, h^*) = \frac{2\exp(\theta\xi_h/\sigma^2)}{\nu^{\frac{h^*}{\nu}}\sqrt{2\pi}\sigma\Gamma(\frac{h^*}{\nu})}\left(\frac{\xi_h^2}{2\sigma^2/\nu+\theta^2}\right)^{\frac{h^*}{2\nu}-\frac{1}{4}} K_{\frac{h^*}{\nu}-\frac{1}{2}}\left(\frac{1}{\sigma^2}\sqrt{\xi_h^2(2\sigma^2/\nu+\theta^2)}\right) \tag{2.32}$$

hence the idea of using the arrival rate as the state and using the following algorithm.

1. **Initialize** the state $x_0^{(i)}$ and the weight $w_0^{(i)}$ for i between 1 and N_{sims}

   While $1 \le k \le N$

2. **Simulate** the state x_k for i between 1 and N_{sims}

   $$\tilde{x}_k^{(i)} = F^{-1}\left(\mu_a, \nu_a; \Delta t, \mathcal{U}^{(i)}[0, 1]\right)$$

   where as before F represents the gamma CDF.
3. Calculate the associated **weights** for each i

   $$w_k^{(i)} = w_{k-1}^{(i)} p(z_k|\tilde{x}_k^{(i)})$$

   with $p(z_k|\tilde{x}_k^{(i)})$ as defined in (2.32) where h will be set to Δt and h^* to $\tilde{x}_k^{(i)}$
4. **Normalize** the weights

   $$\tilde{w}_k^{(i)} = \frac{w_k^{(i)}}{\sum_{i=1}^{N_{sims}} w_k^{(i)}}$$

5. **Resample** the points $\tilde{x}_k^{(i)}$ and get $x_k^{(i)}$ and reset $w_k^{(i)} = \tilde{w}_k^{(i)} = 1/N_{sims}$.
6. **Increment** k, go back to Step 2 and **Stop** at the end of the **While** loop.

As for VGSA, numeric tests were carried out in the following way. After choosing a time step $\Delta t = 1/252$, $\mu_S = 0$ and a parameter set

$$\Psi = (\mu_a = 10.0, \nu_a = 0.01, \nu = 0.05, \sigma = 0.2, \theta = 0.002)$$

an artificial time series of $N = 500$ spot prices was generated. The preceding filtering algorithm was then applied to this time series and the resulting likelihood was maximized. The optimal parameter set was

$$\hat{\Psi} = (9.17, 0.19, 0.012, 0.21, 0.0019)$$

It therefore seems that the parameters ν and ν_a are not recovered properly. Hence we ask, how sensitive are the observable spot prices to these variables? Simulating two time series with the two different parameter sets, we can see in Figure 2.59 that the results *could* be very close. This once again brings up the issue of inference reliability. Not having enough data points, we can get parameter sets that are quite different from the real ones and that could generate similar time series. This is consistent with what we have seen for diffusion-based processes.

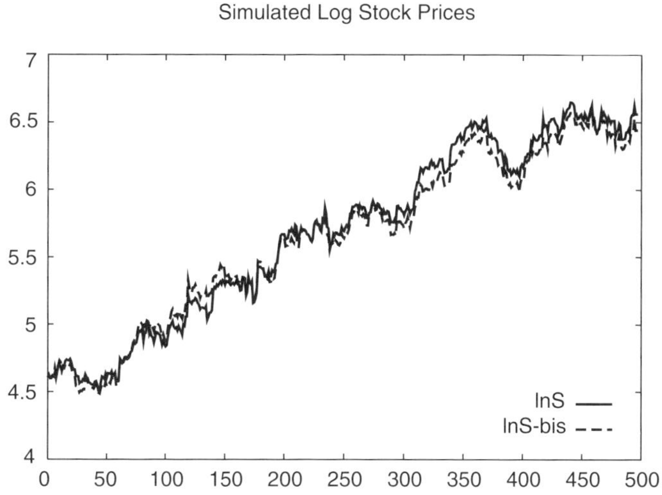

FIGURE 2.59 Simulation of VGG-based Log Stock Prices with Two Different Parameter Sets $\Psi = (\mu_a = 10.0, \nu_a = 0.01, \nu = 0.05, \sigma = 0.2, \theta = 0.002)$ and $\Psi = (9.17, 0.19, 0.012, 0.21, 0.0019)$. The observed time series remain close.

A Bayesian Approach for VGSA An approach similar to the one in the paragraph on the Bayesian approach for Heston could be used here, because the latent state follows the same square-root SDE. The only thing that changes is the likelihood function. Instead of having a conditionally log normal observation, we have a conditionally VG observation. Furthermore, we do know the density of the VG distribution under a closed form as previously mentioned.

Indeed as previously mentioned, we have the state (the arrival rate)

$$dy_t = \kappa(\theta - y_t)dt + \sigma_y\sqrt{y_t}dW_t$$

and the observation

$$d\ln S_t = (\mu_S + \omega)dt + B(\gamma(dt^*, 1, \nu); \theta, \sigma)$$

and the corresponding conditional likelihood becomes

$$p(\ln S_k|y_k, \Psi) = \frac{2\exp(\theta x_h/\sigma^2)}{\nu^{\frac{h^*}{\nu}}\sqrt{2\pi}\sigma\Gamma(\frac{h^*}{\nu})}\left(\frac{x_h^2}{2\sigma^2/\nu + \theta^2}\right)^{\frac{h^*}{2\nu}-\frac{1}{4}} \times K_{\frac{h^*}{\nu}-\frac{1}{2}}\left(\frac{1}{\sigma^2}\sqrt{x_h^2(2\sigma^2/\nu + \theta^2)}\right)$$

with $K_\alpha(x)$ the modified Bessel function and

$$x_h = \ln(S_k/S_{k-1}) - \mu_S h - \frac{h}{\nu}\ln\left(1 - \theta\nu - \sigma^2\nu/2\right)$$
$$h = \Delta t$$

and

$$h^* = y_k\Delta t$$

Finally, integrating over time, we have

$$p(\ln S|y, \Psi) = \prod_{k=1}^{N} p(\ln S_k|y_k, \Psi)$$

Note that in the classical VGSA model there is no correlation between the system noise and the observation noise. This means that the likelihood function will not depend on the parameters κ, θ, σ_y, and therefore the MH update step becomes almost a Gibbs sampler (except for the adjustment factor $\sum_{k=1}^{N} x_k^2$).

RECAPITULATION

We tested three categories of models: the Heston/GARCH category where a pure diffusion assumption was used, the Bates category where Poisson jumps were added to the stock SDE, and the VG category where a gamma distribution was applied to the time dimension.

Model Identification

We saw from the table in Section 2.3.10 that in the pure diffusion category, a power of 3/2 outperformed the Heston model (power of 1/2). As stated, this is in line with the findings of Engle & Ishida [95].

Needless to say, adding Poisson jumps (Bates model) will reduce the MPE/RMSE of the filters; however, it will also cause the number of parameters to increase. A simple comparison between the residual errors is therefore not fair. In other words, given the fundamental differences between the categories, we need to judge their appropriateness not by comparing the residuals, but by using financial arguments such as, *should the stock process contain jumps or not?* Once a category is chosen, then we can compare the performance of models belonging to a given category.

Note that a number of likelihood-based tools exist, such as the Akaike information criterion [100], which will take into the account the number of parameters when assessing the goodness of fit for a model. These tools would therefore allow us to compare models belonging to different categories (e.g, Heston vs. VGSA). However, these criteria remain valid *only asymptotically*. As we saw, this often requires a large number of data points, which may or may not be readily available.

Convergence Issues and Solutions

No matter which category we choose, it seems that the same convergence issues exist. For all the foregoing models, we can see that a parameter affecting the drift of the observation is much easier to estimate than one affecting the noise of the observation. For the pure diffusion category, we saw that all four parameters ω, θ, ξ, and ρ were difficult to estimate (in some cases) and that the two latter parameters, which affect the noise of the noise, were even harder to estimate properly. For the Bates model, we saw that the jump parameters λ, j were much more straightforward to estimate than the aforementioned four diffusion parameters. For the VGSA models, we saw that the VG parameters θ, ν, and σ (which once again, affect the observation drift) are much easier to infer than the arrival-rate parameters κ, η, and λ.

All this was explained via the *poor observability* at a daily frequency level owing to the fact that $\Delta t = o\left(\sqrt{\Delta t}\right)$. We tested the validity of this statement by artificially reducing the observation noise and saw the convergence rate increase dramatically.

As stated, a possible solution would be to employ more observation points via the use of high-frequency data. We saw that the increase in the number of observations and the decrease in Δt (after a certain level) do not cancel, and a higher frequency would indeed cause the likelihood function to have a higher value and provide a better estimation of the parameters. In any case, because we do not know in advance how good the inference results will be and whether we are in the asymptotic area or not, it is always a good idea to perform a simulation test and determine the sampling distribution of each parameter.

In the next chapter, we shall apply these inference tools to a specific question: are the implied distributions from the stock and options markets consistent?

CHAPTER 3

The Consistency Problem

Whether cross-sectional option prices are consistent with the time-series properties of the underlying asset returns is probably the most fundamental of tests.

— David S. Bates

INTRODUCTION

In the previous chapter, we discussed two approaches for stochastic volatility parameter estimation: the cross-sectional one, in which we use a number of options prices for given strike prices (and possibly maturities), and the time-series approach, in which we use the stock prices over a certain period of time. One natural question[1] would therefore be the following: Will the theoretically invariant portion of the parameter sets obtained by the two methods be the same?

More accurately, supposing we are at time $t = 0$ and we use J options with strikes $K_1, ..., K_J$ and with maturity T, we have

$$\hat{\Psi}_{options} = argmin \left\{ \sum_{j=1}^{J} \left[C_{model}(t = 0, S_0, K_j, T, \Psi) - C_{mkt}(t = 0, S_0, K_j, T) \right]^2 \right\} \quad (3.1)$$

These options could include calls or puts. Alternatively, during the period $[0, T]$ we can observe $(S_k)_{0 \leq k \leq N}$ corresponding to the time points $t_0, ..., t_N$

[1]Aït-Sahalia [6], Bakshi et al. [20], and Dumas et al. [88] have already asked a similar question; however, they use a different approach for the time-series treatment.

with $t_0 = 0$ and $t_N = T$, and then apply one of the previously discussed filters and estimate the parameter set via the maximum likelihood method.

$$\hat{\Psi}_{stocks} = argmax\{L(S_0, ..., S_N, \Psi)\} \tag{3.2}$$

Now the question is how different these estimations for (ξ, ρ) are and why.

As we saw in the previous chapter, the size of the time interval Δt and the time-series length are to be questioned: Indeed Δt has to be small enough for us to be able to apply the Girsanov theorem. However, we saw that for a very small Δt, the filtering errors are so little that the MLE will not necessarily converge to the right parameter set. On the other hand, we would need the time series to be as long as possible, which requires a high observation frequency.

This brings up a more fundamental question. The current financial econometrics literature seems to make inference-based conclusions using a limited amount of daily data. As we saw in Chapter 2, the time-series inference results are not necessarily reliable unless the number of observations is sufficiently large. This is the central question of this chapter: Are the implied parameters from the options markets and the assets time series indeed inconsistent?

Many practical issues need to be questioned: How many strikes should we be using in the cross-sectional analysis and which ones? Should we use only OTM puts and calls for liquidity reasons? Many use a penalty function $p()$ in the cross-sectional optimization in order to get reasonable results. Do we need such a function here? In the cross-sectional method, what value for v_0 are we using? Should we estimate this value together with the other four parameters? If so, should *this* estimated $\hat{v}_0$ be used in the time series?

If the results are substantially different for the parameters ξ and ρ (assuming the validity of the Girsanov theorem), can this test be used as an argument *against* the validity of the Heston stochastic volatility model? Or would it mean that the options markets do not predict the stock movements as they should? And if so, does this mean that there is a profitable trading strategy to take? That is, are options systematically mispriced?

If the Heston model is judged to be incorrect, what *is* the correct model—GARCH or 3/2? Is the diffusion assumption itself to be questioned? Do we need to introduce jumps?[2]

---

[2]Note that an alternative method not involving any optimization would be a method of *matching of moments*. Indeed the Heston parameters $\omega, \theta, \xi, \rho$ are analytically related to the first four moments of the time series (mean, variance, skew, kurtosis). The calculation of the moments from the time series is fairly easy. The calculation of the moments from the options would require the use of the Carr-Madan [50] replication strategy using *all* available strike prices. However, because the

Another way to approach the question is to reason in the following manner. If the information contained in the options markets is indeed inconsistent with the one embedded in the assets time series, there should be a regularly and conclusively profitable trade strategy. For instance, a higher volatility-of-volatility and more negative correlation in the options market should indicate the possibility of a profitable *skewness trade* (to be explained later) in absence of crashes. We could therefore use the profit/loss of this trade as an *empirical measure* of the inconsistency of the information.

If (and only if!) there exists a regular and definite profit generated from this strategy, we can conclude that there is inconsistency. It is important to note that this empirical measure is *model free*.

In our empirical analysis, unless stated otherwise, we shall use S&P 500 calls and puts. There are two main reasons for this. First, these are the most liquid european options available on the CBOE. They expire on the third Friday of each contract month at the open. Second, abundant research has already been carried out on these options. Aït-Sahalia [6]; Bakshi, Cao, and Chen [20]; Bates [30]; Dumas, Fleming, and Whaley [88] and many others have all carried out their empirical analysis on S&P 500 options.

The data quality is obviously dependent on the degree of liquidity. Another issue we need to take into account is that of *synchronization* between the spot close price and the option close price. Even if the timing of these two closings is off by a few minutes, the accuracy of the implied volatility can be affected. Bates [32] specifically mentions this issue.

Let us be clear on the fact that this chapter does not constitute a thorough empirical study of the stock versus the options markets. It rather presents a set of examples of application of our inference tools constructed in the previous chapter. There clearly could be many other applications for these tools. As discussed in Chapter 2, model identification is another instance.

THE CONSISTENCY TEST

In this section we shall compare the values of (ξ, ρ) in the results $\hat{\Psi}_{options}$ to $\hat{\Psi}_{stocks}$ obtained via MLE. The time period $[0, T]$ is fixed, and the time interval Δt for the stock is daily, as in Chapter 2.

---

information contained in the first four moments is less complete than the information contained in the density, the optimization method is more accurate. It might seem that by avoiding the numeric optimization involved in our method we would gain precision; however, given that the equations linking the first four moments and the four parameters are *nonlinear*, we would need to solve them *numerically*, which would be similar to an optimization.

The Setting

The test is based on SPX options as of 01/02/2002 expiring in approximately 1 year from the calibration date. The daily time series is taken during a period of 12 years corresponding to approximately 3000 points. The start of the period is 10 years before the calibration date and the end of the period is 1 year after the expiration of the options. Ideally we should *only* use the asset prices between the calibration date and the expiration to see whether the options *predict* the asset movements consistently. However, this would provide us with too few observation points.

In what follows we will be considering one example of comparison between cross-sectional and time-series implied parameters. Many other similar examples were examined. They are not reported here because they do not change the conclusions. The original contribution of our approach is presenting a systematic way to evaluate time-series embedded parameters. We shall do this via the methodologies detailed in Chapter 2.

The Cross-Sectional Results

We consider one-year options as of January 2, 2002, for close-to-the-money options. The calibration is done via LSE Monte Carlo mixing as well as the Fourier inversion applied to the Heston model. We fix the instantaneous variance v_0 at 0.04, and we take the index level at $S_0 = \$1154.67$. As usual we take the appropriate interest-rate r_T and dividend-yield[3] q_T, where T represents the options' maturity. The dividend yield could, for instance, be the one implied from the forward contracts F_T calculated as

$$q_T = r_T - 1/T \ln(F_T/S_0)$$

We use various strike-price sets (K_j) and determine the average optimal one-year parameters. Needless to say, the results are obtained under the risk-neutral measure. We obtain the risk-neutral implied parameter set in Table 3.1. which represents a rather high negative skewness and a high kurtosis.[4] The long-term volatility is $\sqrt{\omega/\theta} \approx 0.17$. Needless to say, these parameter values vary everyday, but usually remain in the same range.

Robustness Issues for the Cross-Sectional Method

1. For the cross-sectional analysis, we have used a mixing Monte Carlo method. The Monte Carlo time steps of this method were spaced *weekly*.

[3] No discrete dividends were considered.

[4] We drop the "hat" notations for optimal parameters in this chapter for simplifiction. For example, instead of $\hat{\omega}$ we simply write ω.

TABLE 3.1 Average Optimal Heston Parameter Set (Under the Risk-Neutral Distribution) Obtained via LSE Applied to One-Year SPX Options in January 2002. Various strike-price sets were used.

ω	θ	ξ	ρ
0.03620	1.1612	0.4202	−0.6735

Therefore, one natural question is how sensitive to this choice the results are. In order to verify this, we reran the simulations with *daily* Monte Carlo time steps and obtained

$$\hat{\Psi}_{options-daily} = (\omega = 0.036846, \theta = 1.169709, \xi = 0.42112, \rho = -0.67458)$$

which is close to the original set. We also checked the results with the volatility-of-volatility series method, as well as the Fourier inversion method, and obtained comparable parameters.

2. For our cross-sectional calibration, we used call bid prices. It is well known that calls and put prices are *not* always consistent. Indeed, as can be seen in Figure 3.1 the Put and Call implied-volatilities are slightly

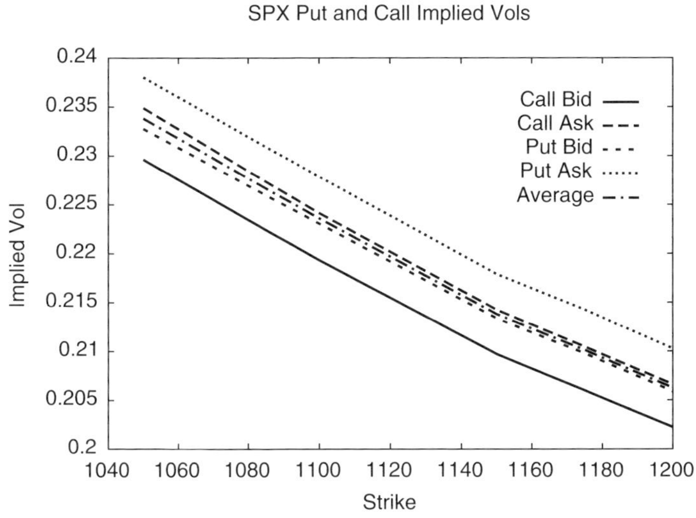

FIGURE 3.1 Implied Volatilities of Close to ATM Puts and Calls as of 01/02/2002. Maturity is 2002/12/21 and index at 1154.67 USD's. The bid–ask spread can clearly be observed.

different, which seems to be a violation of put-call parity.[5] However, this difference is not large enough (the put and call bid–ask spreads actually overlap), and a profitable arbitrage cannot take place simply based upon this difference. This is why we consider the midpoint between puts and calls to be bids and asks.

Our implied volatility is therefore

$$\sigma_{imp} = \frac{1}{4}\left[\sigma_{imp}(Call_{Bid}) + \sigma_{imp}(Call_{Ask}) + \sigma_{imp}(Put_{Bid}) + \sigma_{imp}(Put_{Ask})\right]$$

Using these "mid" implied volatilities as opposed to the original call bids we obtain a parameter set

$$\hat{\Psi}_{options-mid-call-put} = (\omega = 0.043184, \theta = 1.173119, \xi = 0.40258, \rho = -0.64593)$$

3. If we do include v_0 in the set of parameters $\Psi = (\omega, \theta, \xi, \rho, v_0)$, then we obtain

$$\hat{\Psi}_{options-mid-call-put} = (\omega = 0.043224, \theta = 1.144957, \xi = 0.482009, \rho = -0.661427, \sqrt{v_0} = 0.224659)$$

It is possible to see that the optimal $\sqrt{\hat{v}_0}$ is around 0.20, which corresponds to our initial choice.

4. As already mentioned, further-from-the-money options are less reliable in terms of pricing and liquidity. However, disregarding them decreases the cross-sectional sensitivity to the volatility-of-volatility parameter.

   Adding to the previous close-to-the-money strikes, additional further-from-the-money ones, we find

$$\hat{\Psi}_{options} = (\omega = 0.035896, \theta = 1.149324, \xi = 0.386453, \rho = -0.659319, \sqrt{v_0} = 0.221988)$$

   Again, the drift parameters are stable, and so is v_0. The question is, how are the volatility parameters affected? Interestingly, we do not observe a great difference from what we had with the previous sets. We therefore have a good degree of robustness. In any case, we use various sets of strike prices and take an average over the optimal parameter sets.

5. One issue to consider in the cross-sectional method is how the risk-neutral implied distribution or, in our case the parameter set Ψ evolves over time. Needless to say, if the model was perfectly correct these parameters would never change; however, as we know, this is never the case.

[5] This is most probably due to the illiquidity of ITM options, as explained in [192].

The question therefore becomes, how time-homogeneous are these parameters? Considering the same maturity 12/21/2002 but at a date closer to this maturity, we use close-to-the-money strikes. More accurately, we stand at 09/03/2002, take the spot at \$878.02, and use the yield curve as of 09/03/2002.

The strikes are

$$K_{set} = \{775.00, 800.00, 825.00, 850.00, 875.00, 900.00, 925.00, 950.00, 975.00\}$$

The optimization via Monte Carlo mixing provides

$$\hat{\Psi}_{options} = (\omega = 0.0501244, \theta = 1.189817, \xi = 0.547149, \rho = -0.661552, \sqrt{v_0} = 0.265441)$$

which is not too far from the other parameter sets.

Time-Series Results

As mentioned, the first idea is to choose a period corresponding to the life of the options considered in the previous section. In fact, we would like to see whether the options are *predicting* the underlying asset dynamics correctly during their life. However, this provides us with one year of daily data, or 252 points, which as we know from the previous chapter is highly insufficient for time-series estimators. In order to obtain more reliable results, we use various filters (EKF, EPF, etc.) and take the average optimal parameter set. For a period of 12 years ending on January 2004 (which includes the options' life) and applying the filters studied in Chapter 2, we obtain the average results given in Table 3.2.

The results in Table 3.2 show a lower (ξ, ρ) and therefore a lower implied skewness and kurtosis—lower than the ones obtained from the options markets.

Robustness Issues for the Time-Series Method Given the above results, it would be instructive to test the sensitivity of the observations to the drift parameters (ω, θ) on the one hand, and to the volatility parameters (ξ, ρ) on the

TABLE 3.2 Average Optimal Heston Parameter Set (Under the Statistical Distribution) Obtained via Filtered MLE Applied to SPX between January 1992 and January 2004. Various filters were used in the MLE.

ω	θ	ξ	ρ
0.018620	0.523947	0.096389	−0.132527

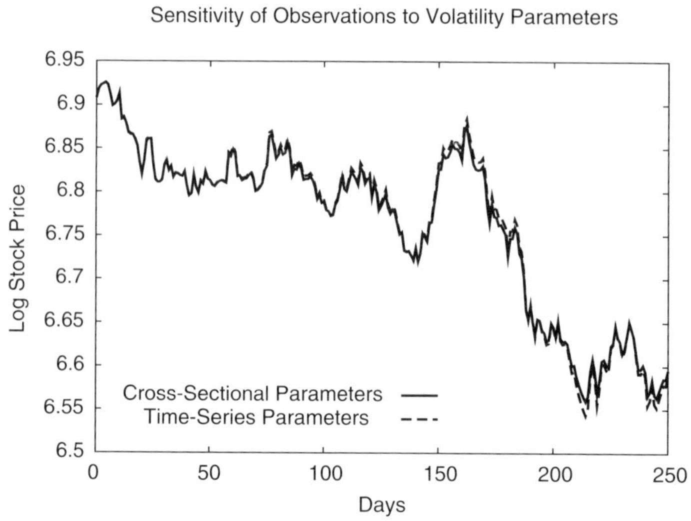

FIGURE 3.2 The Observations Have Little Sensitivity to the Volatility Parameters. One-year simulation with $\sqrt{v_0} = 0.20$, $\omega = 0.04$, $\theta = 0.5$. Cross-sectional uses $\xi = 0.036$ and $\rho = 0.50$, whereas time series uses $\xi = 0.09$ and $\rho = -0.80$. This is consistent with what we had seen previously.

other.[6] The point is that even if the state v_k itself is greatly affected by these volatility parameters, the impact of these parameters on the observations is small. However, the impact of the drift parameters is quite large. This could explain why the cross-sectional and time-series volatility-of-volatility parameters are not close. This point can be observed in the simulations represented in Figures 3.2 through 3.5. Note that this issue is related to the discussion in Chapter 2 on the sampling distribution. As previously stated, ξ and ρ have a lesser effect on the observations because they affect the "noise of the noise."

Financial Interpretation

The current financial econometrics consensus is the following: No matter which case we consider, the cross-sectional parameters ξ and ρ are always greater (in absolute value) than the time-series ones. This means that the skewness and the kurtosis implied from options are stronger than those implied from the time series. As we will see in the following paragraphs, this could suggest a trade to take advantage of this inconsistency, supposing that

[6] Note that we could *not* have done this separation in a nonparametric model, such as in [6].

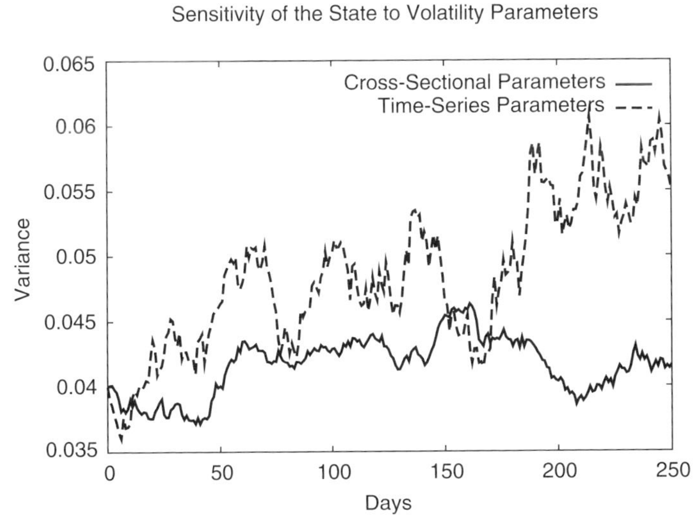

FIGURE 3.3 The State Has a Great Deal of Sensitivity to the Volatility Parameters. One-year simulation with $\sqrt{v_0} = 0.20$, $\omega = 0.04$, $\theta = 0.5$. Cross-sectional uses $\xi = 0.036$ and $\rho = 0.50$, whereas time series uses $\xi = 0.09$ and $\rho = -0.80$.

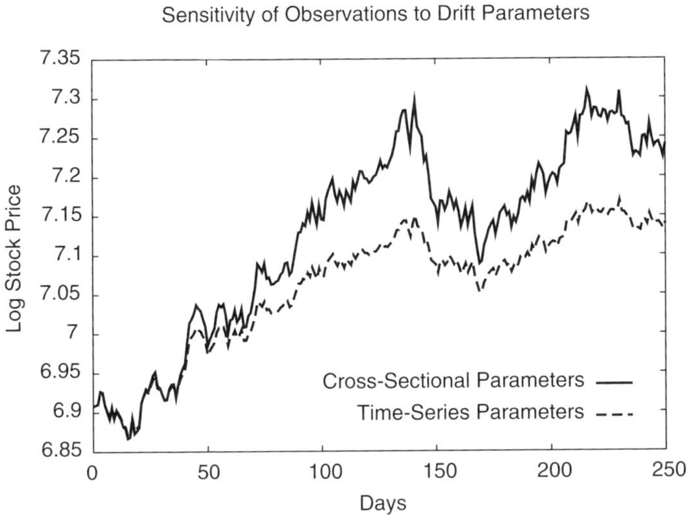

FIGURE 3.4 The Observations Have a Great Deal of Sensitivity to the Drift Parameters. One-year simulation with $\sqrt{v_0} = 0.20, \xi = 0.036, \rho = 0.50$. Cross-sectional uses $\omega = 0.04$ and $\theta = 0.50$ whereas time series uses $\omega = 0.08$ and $\theta = 5.0$.

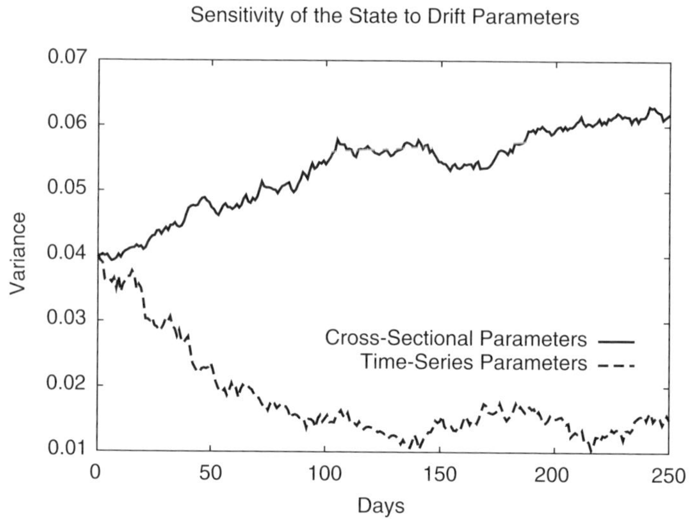

FIGURE 3.5 The State Has a Great Deal of Sensitivity to the Drift Parameters. One-year simulation with $\sqrt{v_0} = 0.20$, $\xi = 0.036$, $\rho = 0.50$. Cross-sectional uses $\omega = 0.04$ and $\theta = 0.50$, whereas time series uses $\omega = 0.08$ and $\theta = 5.0$.

the options are misjudging the spot movements. We can observe the above statement graphically by plotting the SPX volatility smile from the options market prices on the one hand, and from the time-series implied parameters on the other. Note that we need no calibration for the options because we are using the usual Black-Scholes implied volatility. Figure 3.6 shows the difference between the two slopes. Again, the options curve has a stronger (negative) slope, which is consistent with a stronger negative product $\xi\rho$.

As explained in [69], the higher moments of the stock-price return can be calculated from the stochastic-volatility model parameters. Indeed, for a given parameter set $\Psi = (\omega, \theta, \xi, \rho)$, we have

$$skewness = \left(\frac{3\xi\rho e^{\frac{1}{2}\theta T}}{\sqrt{\theta}}\right)\left[\frac{\frac{\omega}{\theta}\left(2 - 2e^{\theta T} + \theta T + \theta T e^{\theta T}\right) - v_0\left(1 + \theta T - e^{\theta T}\right)}{\left(\frac{\omega}{\theta}[(1 - \theta T + \theta T e^{\theta T}) + v_0(e^{\theta T} - 1)]\right)^{\frac{3}{2}}}\right]$$

and

$$kurtosis = 3\left[1 + \xi^2\left(\frac{\frac{\omega}{\theta}A_1 - v_0 A_2}{B}\right)\right]$$

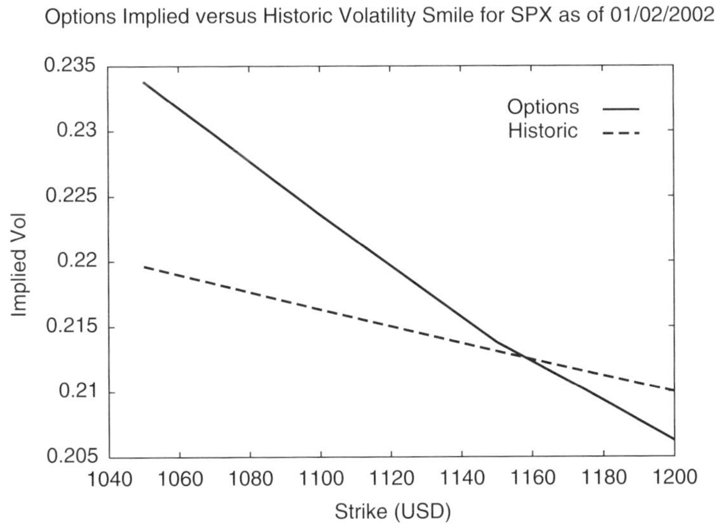

FIGURE 3.6 Comparing SPX Cross-Sectional and Time-Series Volatility Smiles (with Historic ξ and ρ) as of January 2, 2002. The spot is at \$1154.67.

with $y = \theta T$ and

$$\begin{aligned} A_1 &= \left[1 + 4e^y - 5e^{2y} + 4ye^y + 2ye^{2y}\right] + 4\rho^2 \\ &\quad \left[6e^y - 6e^{2y} + 4ye^y + 2ye^{2y} + y^2e^y\right] \\ A_2 &= 2\left[1 - e^{2y} + 2ye^y\right] + 8\rho^2\left[2e^y - 2e^{2y} + 2ye^y + y^2e^y\right] \\ B &= 2\theta\left[\frac{\omega}{\theta}\left(1 - e^y + ye^y\right) + v_0(e^y - 1)\right]^2 \end{aligned}$$

Without entering into the details of the calculations, we can see that for given ω and θ, higher $(\xi, |\rho|)$ correspond to higher skewness and kurtosis. As we said in the previous chapter, the skewness depends on ω, θ and the product $\xi\rho$, which has a more reliable estimation than the separate values of ξ and ρ. This makes the estimation of the skewness more trustworthy.

THE PESO THEORY

Background

As [6] mentions, one possibility regarding the cross-sectional versus time-series observed differences is the following. As we know, the time series corresponds to *one* realization of the stock-return stochastic process. Now supposing that the true stock stochastic differential equation (SDE) contains jumps, there is a possibility that the historic path we are observing does *not* contain any of these jumps.[7] This is referred to as the *peso* theory. As mentioned in [12], this term goes back to Milton Friedman in his analysis of Mexican peso during the early 1970s. The Mexican interest rates remained significantly above the U.S. interest rates, although the peso was pegged at 0.08 dollar per peso. Friedman argued that the interest rates reflected an *expectation* about a future devaluation of the peso. In August 1976, the peso was devaluated by 37.5% to a new rate of 0.05 dollar per peso, thus validating the previous interest rate differential.

This assumption seems reasonable because, as we saw in the previous tests, the cross-sectional method usually provides *higher* volatility parameters (ξ, ρ) and therefore *higher* skewness (in absolute value) and kurtosis. Introducing a jump component in the options pricing model should lower these optimal parameters.

Note that in [3], Aït-Sahalia tries to find out whether the discrete observations of S&P 500 come from a diffusion, or from a distribution containing jumps. He derives a criterion for continuity of the paths

$$\frac{\partial^2}{\partial x \partial y} \ln\left(p(\Delta t, y = X_{t+\Delta t} | x = X_t)\right) > 0$$

for every $\Delta t > 0$ and given (x, y). Based on the implied cross-sectional distribution, he finds that S&P 500 options *do consider jumps* in the paths.

Using the jump diffusion model, as we did in Chapter 2

$$d \ln S_t = \left(\mu_S - \frac{1}{2}v_t + \lambda j\right) dt + \sqrt{v_t} dB_t + \ln(1 - j) dN_t$$

$$dv_t = (\omega - \theta v_t) dt + \xi \sqrt{v_t} dZ_t$$

we may very well see no difference introduced from the parameters (λ, j) for the time series and we can even disregard them. However, this does not mean that the stock process does not contain jumps but rather that this *specific path* happens to contain none.

The options, by contrast, always include the possibility of jumps in their pricing. Adding (λ, j) will affect the resulting (ξ, ρ) from the cross-sectional method.

[7] Jackwerth and Rubinstein [155] refer to this phenomena as *crash-o-phobia*.

Numeric Results

We use the same options and time series as in the previous section. As shown in Merton's paper [190], we have for a given volatility path $\sigma = \sqrt{v}$

$$Call = \sum_{n=0}^{+\infty} e^{-\lambda(1-j)T} \frac{(\lambda(1-j)T)^n}{n!} C_{BS}(S, K, T, \sigma, r_n)$$

with

$$r_n = r + \lambda j + \frac{n}{T} \ln(1-j)$$

We then take the expectation upon the volatility stochastic process as we usually do in a mixing algorithm.[8]

We find for the parameter set $\hat{\Psi} = (\omega, \theta, \xi, \rho, \lambda, j)$ the values

$$\begin{aligned}\hat{\Psi}_{options} &= (\omega, \theta, \xi, \rho, \sqrt{v_0}, \lambda, j) = (0.032648, 1.165598, 0.360646, \\ &\quad -0.585302, 0.218333, 0.008982, 0.913772)\end{aligned}$$

instead of the previous pure-diffusion parameter set

$$\begin{aligned}\hat{\Psi}_{options-mid-call-put} &= (\omega = 0.043224, \theta = 1.144957, \xi = 0.482009, \\ &\quad \rho = -0.661427, \sqrt{v_0} = 0.224659)\end{aligned}$$

As we see even with the addition of jump parameters (λ, j), the cross-sectional volatility parameters (ξ, ρ) remain significantly above the time-series parameters. This is in agreement with the findings of Bakshi, Cao, and Chen [20]. We have a small λ and a j close to one. This means that options are expecting a large but infrequent jump; that is, they are factoring in the possibility of a *crash*.

TRADING STRATEGIES

Supposing that the model we are dealing with is correct, and if the options are mistaken in evaluating the stock distribution *during their lifetime*, there should be an arbitrage opportunity to take advantage of. The ninth chapter of the Härdle et al. book [128] has a description of these strategies. Note that both these strategies are *European* and cannot be changed[9] until maturity.

---

[8]Note that an alternative method would be to use a Fourier inversion of the known characteristic function, as Lewis does in [178] or [180].

[9]As we will see further, we *could* unwind the deal prior to expiration. However, we would then be subject to the movements of options prices.

At this point we should reiterate that the profit and loss of this trade could be used as an empirical and model-free measure of how consistent or inconsistent the information embedded in the options is with the one in the underlying stocks.

Skewness Trades

To capture an undervalued third moment, we can buy OTM calls and sell OTM puts. Note that Aït-Sahalia [6] says that the options are overly skewed, which means that the options skew is *larger in absolute value*. However, given the negative sign of the skew, the cross-sectional skew is actually *lower* than the one implied by the time series, hence the described strategy.

Note that in order to be immune to parallel shifts of the volatility curve, we should make the trade as vega-neutral as possible. The correspondence between the call and the put is usually not one-to-one. Therefore, calling $\mathcal{V}$ the vega, Δ's the hedge ratios for C the call and P the put option, then the hedged portfolio Π will be

$$\Pi = C(S_t, K_C) - \frac{\mathcal{V}_C}{\mathcal{V}_P} P(S_t, K_P) - \left(\Delta_C - \frac{\mathcal{V}_C}{\mathcal{V}_P} \Delta_P \right) S_t$$

and the positions in the options should be dynamically adjusted in theory. However, that would cause too much transaction cost and exposure to the bid-ask spread.

As we shall see in the paragraph on "exact replication," more-elaborate strategies are available to better exploit the third-moment differences.

Kurtosis Trades

To capture an overvalued fourth moment, we need to use the "fat tails" of the distribution. For this we can, for instance, sell ATM and far OTM options, and buy close OTM options.

Directional Risks

Despite the delta-hedging, the skewness trade applied to an undervalued third moment has an exposure to the direction of the markets. A bullish market is favorable to it, and a bearish one unfavorable. The kurtosis trade applied to an overvalued fourth moment generates a profit if the market stays at one point and moves sideways but loses money if there are large movements.

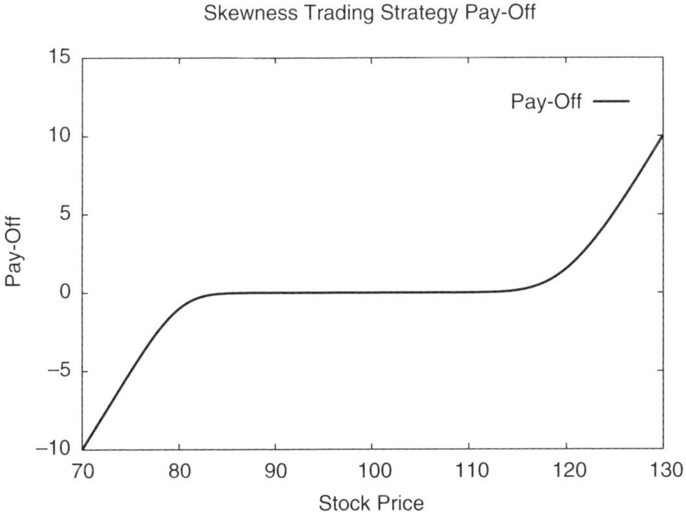

FIGURE 3.7 A Generic Example of a Skewness Strategy to Take Advantage of the Undervaluation of the Skew by Options. This strategy could be improved upon by trading additional OTM puts and calls.

This exposure to market conditions is consistent with the peso theory. The skewness and kurtosis trading strategies above are profitable given the options' implied moments, *unless* the options were actually *right* in factoring in a large and sudden downward movement. This also makes sense because the way the options were priced changed only *after* the crash of 1987. Prior to that, the volatility negative skew was practically absent altogether. Figures 3.7 and 3.8 show generic examples of the strategies described above.

Note that as the skew formula in [69] shows, the volatility-of-volatility ξ affects the skew as much as the correlation ρ does. This explains why sudden upward movements can hurt us as well. If the overall correlation is negative but there are large movements in both directions, we will have large third (in absolute value) and fourth moments, which would make the options expectations correct. In fact, as we will see in the following example, a large upward movement can make us lose on our hedge account.

As many, such as [32] and [128], have mentioned, it is possible to interpret this trade as an *insurance selling* strategy. The trade will generate moderate and consistent profits *if* no crash happens. But if the crash does happen we could suffer a large loss.

Skewness vs. Kurtosis The skewness trade seems to be a simpler one and has a better chance to be realized. Indeed, in order to have a large negative skew,

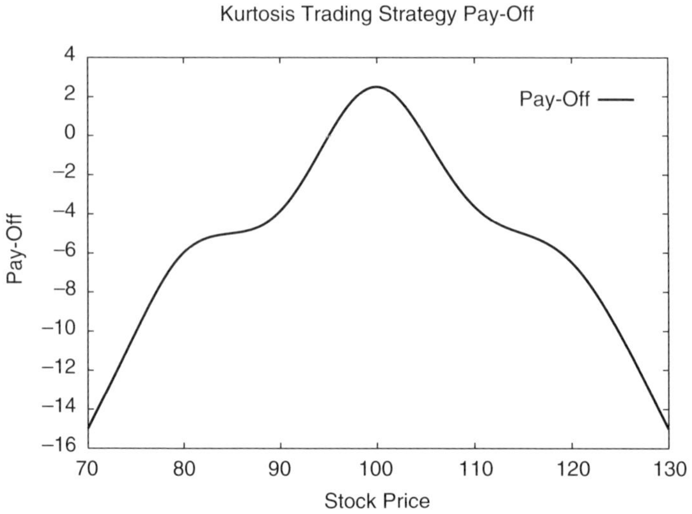

FIGURE 3.8 A Generic Example of a Kurtosis Strategy to Take Advantage of the Overvaluation of the Kurtosis by Options. This strategy could be improved upon by trading additional puts and calls.

we need a large volatility-of-volatility ξ (as we do for the kurtosis trade) *and* a large negative correlation ρ. In other words, if for a given stock time series we have a large volatility-of-volatility but a weak correlation, we will not have a kurtosis trade opportunity but we will have a skewness trade opportunity. The historic skew will be small and the historic kurtosis high. Graphically, we could have the following interpretation. For these assets, the historic distribution does have fat tails, but remains symmetric, whereas the implied distribution has a fatter *left* tail. This is why we have a skewness trade opportunity, even if we do not have a kurtosis trade opportunity. Finally, as we previously mentioned, the estimation of the skewness from a time series is more reliable because it depends only on the *product* of the volatility-of-volatility and the correlation.

An Exact Replication

These trading strategies can be refined using a Carr-Madan replication. As explained in [50], we have for *any* payoff function $f()$ the following identity

$$\begin{aligned}\mathbf{E}[f(S_T)] &= f(F) + e^{rT}\int_0^F f''(K)P(S_0, K, t=0, T)dK \\ &+ e^{rT}\int_F^{+\infty} f''(K)C(S_0, K, t=0, T)dK\end{aligned}$$

with $F = S_0 e^{rT}$ the forward price.

In order to get the Das [69] skew and kurtosis calculations, we need to take for the nth moment

$$f(S_T) = (Z_T - \mathbf{E}(Z_T))^n$$

with

$$Z_T = \ln(S_T/S_0)$$

However, this trade will clearly have a much higher transaction cost than the one described in the previous paragraph.

The Mirror Trades

Should we see the opposite conditions in the market, that is, having the skew (in absolute value) or kurtosis *undervalued* by the options given a historic path, we could obviously put on the mirror trades. The inverse of the peso theory would be as follows. The stock in question has already had a crash and the options are supposing there probably will *not* be another one in the near future. Setting up the overvalued kurtosis trade in the previous paragraph, we picked up a premium and made an immediate profit and hoped that there would not be a sudden movement. Here we start by losing money and hope a crash will happen within the life of the option so that we can generate a profit. Because jumps and crashes are rare by nature, this trade does not seem very attractive. Moreover, if there was a recent crash, the possibility of another one is indeed reduced and we should believe the options prediction. However, these mirror trades could be considered as *buying insurance* and therefore as a protection against a possible crash.

An Example of the Skewness Trade

The algorithm is as follows. For a given date t_0 we have S_0 and choose the closest maturity to $T = t_0 + 0.25$ in order to have a three-month trade, we then take the call and put strikes K_C and K_P as the closest ones to $1.10S_0$ and $0.90S_0$, respectively.

The original cost is therefore

$$options(0) = Call_{Ask}(S_0, K_C, t_0, T) - Put_{Bid}(S_0, K_P, t_0, T)$$

Note that we buy a call at the offer price and sell the put at the market bid price. At maturity, the position is worth

$$options(T) = MAX(0, S_T - K_C) - MAX(0, K_P - S_T)$$

During the trade, we have a delta-hedging cash flow of

$$hedge = -\sum_{t=0}^{T-1} \Delta(S_t, t, T)(S_{t+1} - S_t)$$

with

$$\Delta(S_t, t, T) = \Delta_{Call}(S_t, K_C, t, T, \sigma_{imp}(t_0, K_C)) - \Delta_{Put}(S_t, K_P, t, T, \sigma_{imp}(t_0, K_P))$$

where the implied volatilities used in the hedge ratios are using the mid prices (between bid and ask prices). The interest-rate cash flow is

$$interest = \sum_{t=0}^{T-1} \Delta(S_t, t, T)(e^{r_t \Delta t} - 1)S_t$$

Our final profit or loss (PnL) is therefore

$$PnL = options(T) - options(0) + hedge + interest$$

If the options' implied skew is indeed higher than justified by the stock movements, then this trade should be profitable. However, in case of a sudden large movement, this will not be true anymore.

We consider the case of the S&P 500 between 04/04/2002 and 06/22/2002. At that point in time, $S_0 = \$1126.34$, which means we can take $K_C = \$1250$ and $K_P = \$1050$. We also have $Call_{Ask}(t_0, K = 1250) = \$3.20$ and $Put_{Bid}(t_0, K = 1050) = \$14.20$, as well as the mid implied volatilities of $\sigma_{imp}(K_C) = 0.154$ and $\sigma_{imp}(K_P) = 0.214$.

As can be seen in Figures 3.9 and 3.10, the sudden spot movements generate most of the loss (for instance, around day 50). We have at the end of the trade

$$\begin{aligned} S_T &= \$989.14 \\ hedge &= \$50.39 \\ interest &= \$1.32 \end{aligned}$$

Therefore, the final PnL (in dollars) is

$$PnL = [0 - (1050 - 989.14)] + (14.20 - 3.20) + 50.39 + 1.32 = 1.85$$

As we can see, we *hardly* generated a profit, given the "jumps" occurring in the middle of the trade.

Note that we generated a profit in the beginning by selling an OTM put that was more expensive than the OTM call we bought. We lost a large amount because the spot ended *below* the put strike. However, we compensated that via the hedge.

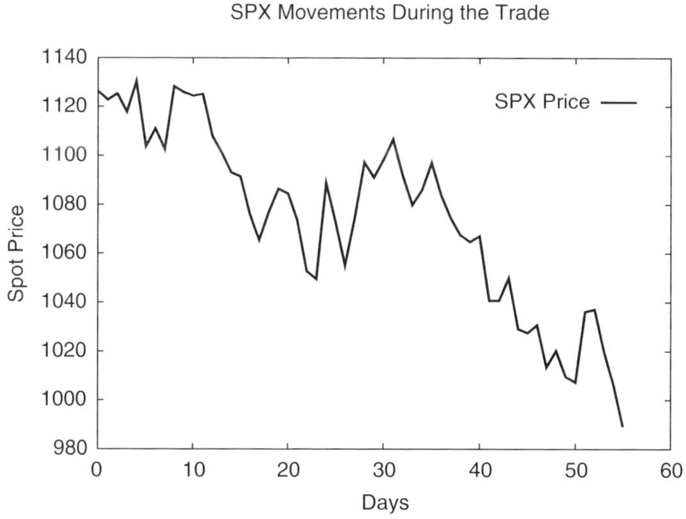

FIGURE 3.9 Historic Spot Level Movements During the Trade Period.

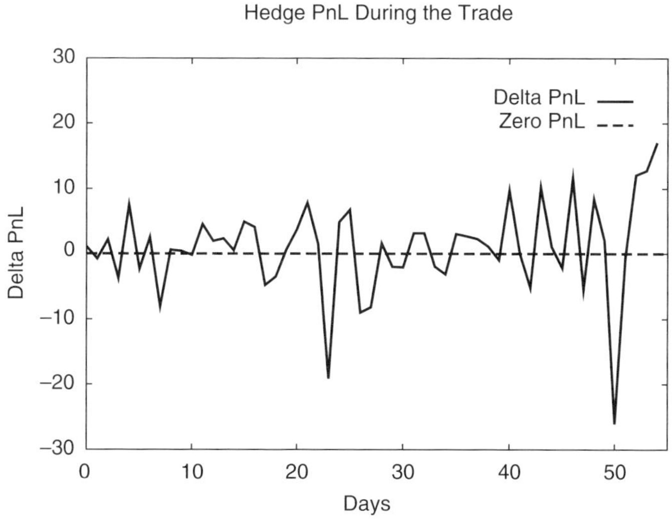

FIGURE 3.10 Hedging PnL Generated During the Trade Period. As we can see, losses occur upon jumps.

The Options Bid–Ask Spread It is important to know where we are buying the call and selling the put on the start date. Are we buying the call at the offer price and selling the put at the bid price? If so, we can lose the bid–ask spread, as compared to the case in which we would buy and sell both options at the

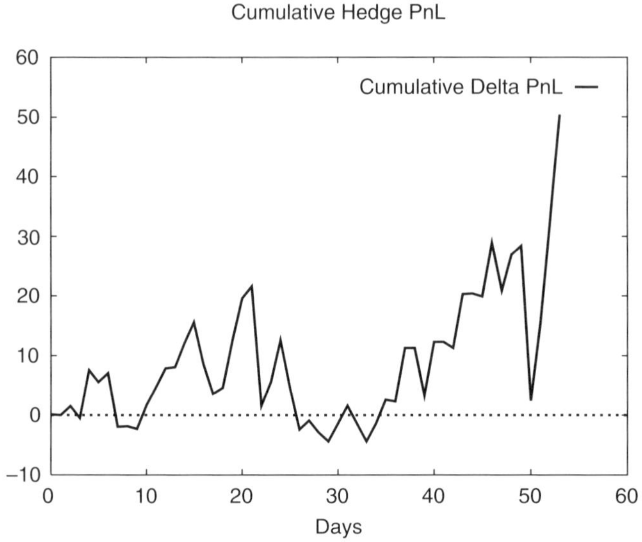

FIGURE 3.11 Cumulative Hedging PnL Generated During the Trade Period. This positive PnL will be offset by the option premiums and payoffs.

mid market. This spread averages approximately $1 for 10% OTM SPX options.

Early Termination We also should consider an early unwinding of the trade. Indeed as we get closer to maturity, our hedge-ratio might be close to one, which will make our hedge account extremely sensitive to adverse stock movements. In order to have a smoother PnL, we can buy back the put and sell the call at a date (e.g. one month) prior to maturity. Again, it is important to know whether we are unwinding the trade by selling the call at the bid and buying back the put at the offer. If so, we will have suffered from the bid–ask spread *twice*: once on the start date and once on the unwinding (termination) date.

This is not just a small detail, indeed having the right execution (at mid-market) can change the average sign of the PnL altogether. Furthermore, regardless of the bid–ask spread, we are subject to the movements of the options prices. By contrast, if we hold the positions until expiration, we will have a pure strategy between the original options prices and the spot price movements.

Implied Volatility Term Structure Yet another issue to take into account is that, in our back-testing, we used *fixed* implied volatilities in order to calculate the hedge ratios during the life of the trade. In reality, the implied

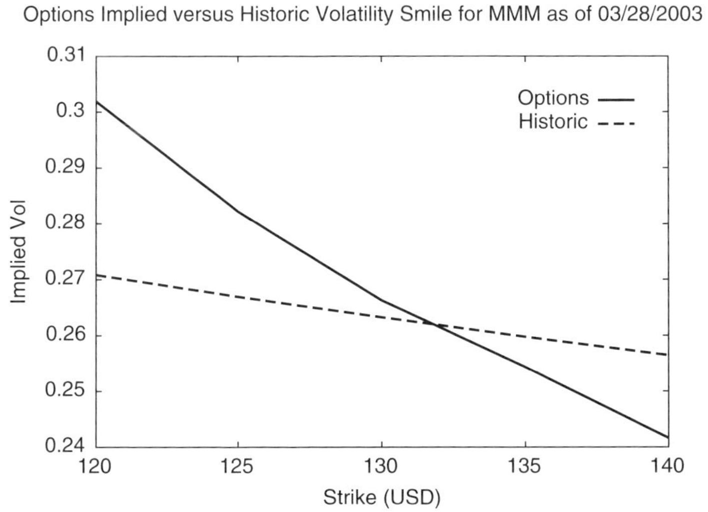

FIGURE 3.12 A Strong Option-Implied Skew: Comparing MMM (3M Co) Cross-Sectional and Time-Series Volatility Smiles as of March 28, 2003. The spot is at \$131.66.

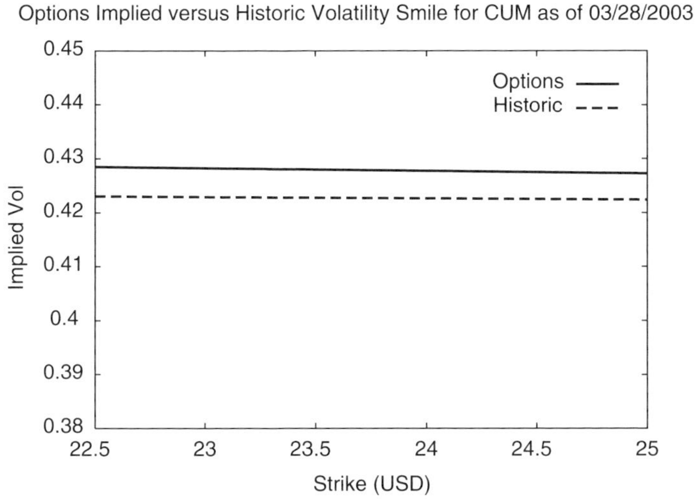

FIGURE 3.13 A Weak Option-Implied Skew: Comparing CMI (Cummins Inc) Cross-Sectional and Time-Series Volatility Smiles as of March 28, 2003. The spot is at \$24.59.

volatilities change every day even if we assume a sticky strike regime, in which the stock price will not affect the implied volatility level. Even if our strikes are fixed, the time-to-maturities of the options decreases, and this will make the implied volatilities vary. For S&P 500 the term structure of implied volatility is upward sloping, which means that *theoretically* all implied volatilities should come down from their original levels at the unwinding date.

Which Hedge Ratio should we use? In the hedging of our skew portfolio, which Δ should we apply? In other words, we ask which implied volatility should we use in the usual

$$e^{-q(T-t)}N(d_1(S_t, K, t, T, \sigma_{imp}))$$

If we believe that the volatility predicted by the options is wrong and the historic levels are correct, we should then use

$$\sigma_{stocks}^{imp}(K, T) = C_{BS}^{-1}\left(C_{model}(S_0, t_0, K, T, \hat{\Psi}_{stocks})\right)$$

where

$$\hat{\Psi}_{stocks} = (\hat{\omega}_{opts}, \hat{\theta}_{opts}, \hat{\xi}_{stocks}, \hat{\rho}_{stocks})$$

Note that this might give us a mismatch in terms of mark-to-market with the existing option levels in the market. However, if the time series is actually correct, the skew should eventually *collapse* before the options mature.[10] We should note, however, that using the options' implied volatilities makes better practical sense because those are the ones at which the options are actually traded.

Multiple Trades

The next natural step would be to repeat the previous trade in order to see whether the trade would be *statistically* profitable. We use SPX puts and calls between 01/02/2002 and 02/01/2003 on the expiration month such that the

[10] Bates [29] suggests the use of an adjusted delta as

$$\Delta \approx \Delta_{BS} - \frac{K}{S}\mathcal{V}\frac{\partial \sigma}{\partial K}$$

where $\mathcal{V}$ represents the option vega. However, as he points out, this is the hedge ratio as perceived by the options market and this perception could very well be wrong. After all, this is what we are trying to take advantage of: the mispricing of the skew by the options, supposing that the historic time series has the same dynamics as the future spot movements.

original life of the trade is around three months. We systematically unwind the trades around 20 business days to expiration. Once again, we buy 10% OTM calls and we sell 10% OTM puts.

We cover in this manner forty different cases. We calculate the PnL's as previously described and take their average.

> *The results are mixed: If we put the trade on and unwind at the bid and ask levels, we will actually suffer a loss. However, if we can execute at the mid, then we will generate a profit.*

This shows a lack of decisive proof on an inconsistency between the options and stock markets.[11] Indeed we have used the PnL of this trade as a measure of discrepancy.[12]

High Volatility-of-Volatility and High Correlation

As previously discussed, many stocks do have a high historic volatility-of-volatility ξ; however, given a weak (or even positive) spot-volatility correlation ρ, the historic skew is still very low. This is especially true of "penny" stocks. Indeed, when these stocks increase in price, in some sense they "come back to life" and therefore become more volatile. This means that the historic skew is actually positive, which seems to indicate an even stronger case for a skewness trade. However, given that we are dealing with penny stocks, the possibility of a crash for these stocks is high, and that is precisely what causes the negative option–implied skew! The stock GW (Grey Wolf Inc.) in Figure 3.14 is a good example for this case. This presents a trading opportunity as shown in Figure 3.15. By contrast, there are cases, such as MSFT (Microsoft), where we do have a strong historic negative correlation as well as a high volatility-of-volatility. As the stock price goes down, the asset becomes riskier and therefore more volatile. We can see this in Figure 3.16. This justifies the option-implied skew observable in Figure 3.17 and means that there is no trade opportunity. The safest trade therefore seems to be an

---

[11]Note that this trade generates a regular and stable profit and sudden large losses. This is in agreement with the interpretation of *selling insurance* and collecting the premiums. It is very profitable until there is a "disaster."

[12]There is a case where a skew trade should be considered. Even if we have an inefficient estimate of ξ and ρ, we do have their sampling distributions, as seen in Chapter 2. If, for instance, the average estimate of ξ is 0.03, supposing the lowest and highest estimates are respectively -0.20 and 0.20, and if $\xi_{opt} = 0.40$, then there is an inconsistency in a conclusive manner. We would then have our cross-sectional volatility-of-volatility far superior to its highest possible time-series estimate.

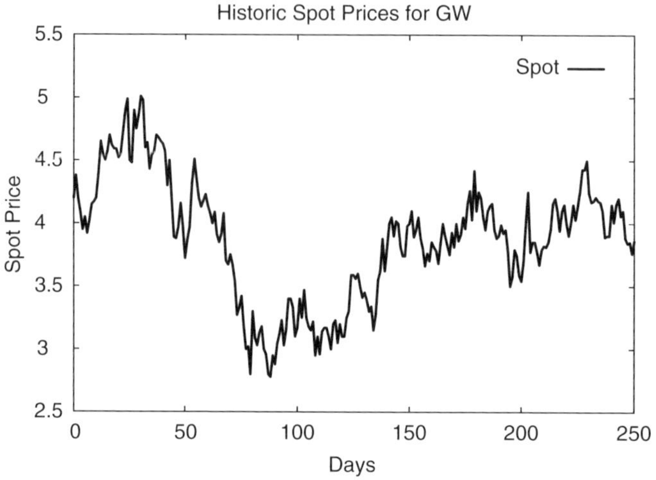

FIGURE 3.14 GW (Grey Wolf Inc.) Historic Prices (03/31/2002–03/31/2003) Show a High Volatility-of-Volatility But a Weak Stock-Volatility Correlation. The resulting negative skew is low.

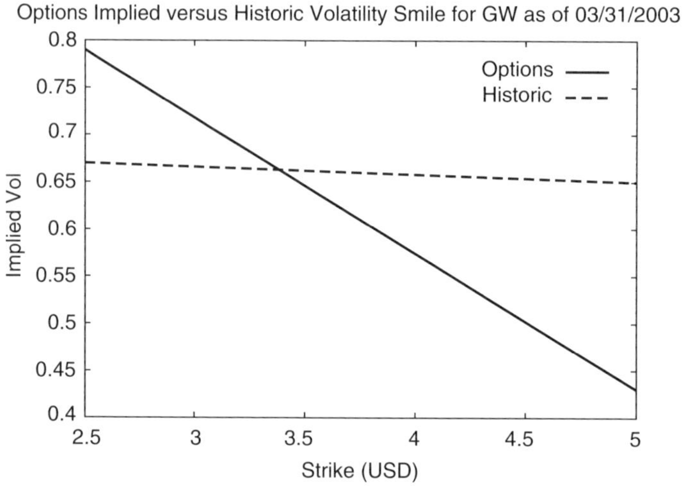

FIGURE 3.15 The Historic GW (Grey Wolf Inc.) Skew Is Low and Not in Agreement with the Options Prices. There is a skew trading opportunity here.

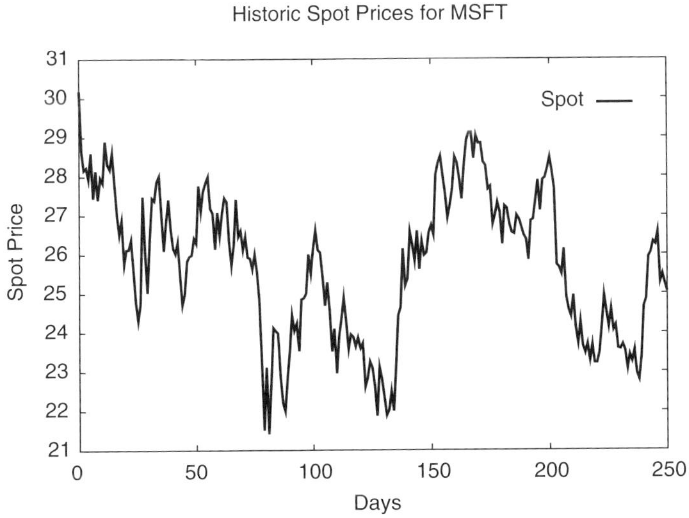

FIGURE 3.16 MSFT (Microsoft) Historic Prices (03/31/2002–03/31/2003) Show a High Volatility-of-Volatility and a Strong Negative Stock-Volatility Correlation. The resulting negative skew is high.

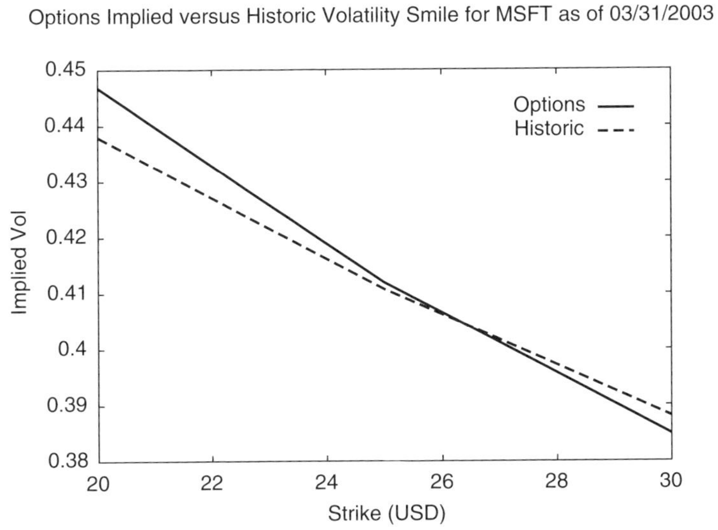

FIGURE 3.17 The Historic MSFT (Microsoft) Skew Is High and in Agreement with the Options Prices. There is no skew trading opportunity here.

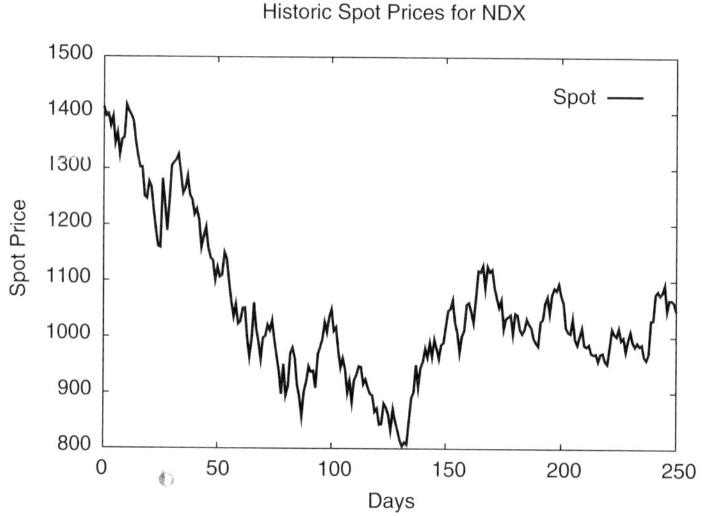

FIGURE 3.18 NDX (Nasdaq) Historic Prices (03/31/2002–03/31/2003) Show a High Volatility-of-Volatility and a Strong Negative Stock-Volatility Correlation. The resulting negative skew is high.

index skewness trade, given that the likelihood of a crash is lower thanks to the diversification effect.

Note that the strong negative historic skew is not limited to individual stocks. Taking the case of the NDX index in Figures 3.18 and 3.19, we can see that there is no trading opportunity available and the historic skewness is in line with the one implied by the options prices.

Therefore we have *two* possible reasons[13] why a skewness trade opportunity may exist.

1. Weak historic volatility-of-volatility (e.g., SPX [S&P 500])
2. Weak Historic Correlation (e.g., GW [Grey Wolf Inc.])

If neither of the above is verified (e.g., NDX [Nasdaq] or MSFT [Microsoft]), there is no skew trading opportunity.

The graphical interpretation seen in Figures 3.12 through 3.19 is based on the comparison of the observable options-implied skew

$$\sigma^{imp}_{options}(K, T) = C^{-1}_{BS}\left(C_{mkt}(S_0, t_0, K, T)\right)$$

and the skew implied from historic stock-price movements

$$\sigma^{imp}_{stocks}(K, T) = C^{-1}_{BS}\left(C_{model}(S_0, t_0, K, T, \hat{\Psi}_{stocks})\right)$$

[13]These tests were performed around the end of March 2003.

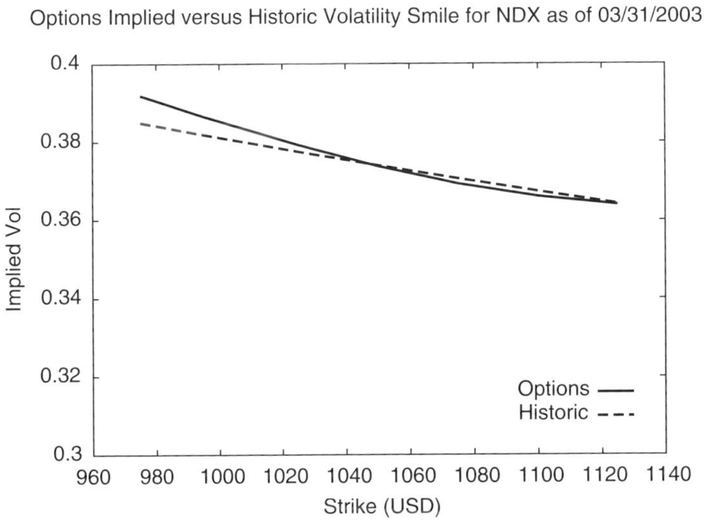

FIGURE 3.19 The Historic NDX (Nasdaq) Skew is High and in Agreement with the Options Prices. There is no skew trading opportunity here.

where C_{BS} corresponds the usual Black-Scholes pricing function.

Again we use the option-implied volatility-drift parameters $\hat{\omega}_{options}$, $\hat{\theta}_{options}$ in $\hat{\Psi}_{stocks}$. The only assumption here would be that of diffusion in the processes. Then, according to the Girsanov theorem, the volatility-of-volatility and the correlation should be the same for the continuous statistical and risk-neutral processes.

NON-GAUSSIAN CASE

As previously discussed, once we start dealing with some of the pure-jump models, such as VGG, we will no longer have the Girsanov theorem and cannot compare the parameters directly. However, no matter what the arrival process is, we still have the VG parameters (σ, ν, θ) as in

$$d \ln S_t = (\mu_S + \omega)dt + X(dt; \sigma, \nu, \theta)$$

where, as before, μ_S is the real-world statistical drift of the stock log-return and $\omega = \frac{1}{\nu}\ln(1 - \theta\nu - \sigma^2\nu/2)$. As for $X(dt; \sigma, \nu, \theta)$, it has the following meaning

$$X(dt; \sigma, \nu, \theta) = B(\gamma(dt, 1, \nu); \theta, \sigma)$$

where $B(dt;\theta,\sigma)$ would be a Brownian motion with drift θ and volatility σ. In other words

$$B(dt;\theta,\sigma)=\theta dt+\sigma\sqrt{dt}N(0,1)$$

where $N(0,1)$ is a standard Gaussian realization.

Further, we know what the centralized third and fourth moments (skewness and kurtosis) are

$$skewness=\left(2\theta^3\nu^2+3\sigma^2\theta\nu\right)t$$
$$kurtosis=\left(3\sigma^4\nu+12\sigma^2\theta^2\nu^2+6\theta^4\nu^3\right)t+\left(3\sigma^4+6\sigma^2\theta^2\nu+3\theta^4\nu^2\right)t^2$$

We therefore can always compare the skewness and kurtosis implied from time series with those implied from options. However, a mismatch between the two does *not* indicate an arbitrage opportunity because once again we are comparing them under two different measures. Having said this, the determination of the statistical density $p()$ and the risk-neutral density $q()$ is still useful in the sense that it could allow us to determine the optimal position we would take in the derivatives market given a utility function, as described in [52] and [53].

Indeed, having an increasing concave utility function $U()$, the idea is to find the optimal payoff $\phi(S)$, maximizing the expected utility at a given horizon T, and among all possible payoffs $f(S)$

$$\phi=argmax\int_0^{+\infty}U[f(S_T)]p(S_T)dS_T$$

In addition to this, we have the initial budget W_0, which imposes a constraint: The discounted *risk-neutral* expected value of the payoff cannot be greater than this initial budget.

$$\exp(-rT)\int_0^{+\infty}f(S_T)q(S_T)dS_T\le W_0$$

This can be seen by using a "self-financing" portfolio argument, as was done by Black and Scholes. Using the two foregoing equations, we can write the Lagrangian

$$\mathcal{L}(f)=\int_0^{+\infty}U\big[f(S_T)\big]p(S_T)dS_T-\lambda\exp(-rT)\int_0^{+\infty}f(S_T)q(S_T)dS_T$$

where λ is the Lagrange multiplier. We then can differentiate with respect to the payoff $f()$ and obtain the optimal payoff satisfying

$$\exp(rT)\frac{p(S)}{q(S)}U'[\phi(S)]=\lambda$$

or equivalently

$$\phi(S) = (U')^{-1}\left(\lambda \exp(-rT)\frac{q(S)}{p(S)}\right)$$

and the constant λ could be determined by a normalization, such as

$$\exp(-rT)\int_0^{+\infty}(U')^{-1}\left(\lambda \exp(-rT)\frac{q(S)}{p(S)}\right)q(S_T)dS_T = W_0$$

This would provide us with the optimal payoff function that we would need to choose in the derivatives market, and therefore motivates the estimation of the statistical and risk-neutral densities p and q even for the non-Gaussian case.

VGSA

Unlike VGG and many other pure-jump models, VGSA has a conditionally Gaussian arrival rate. This means that the volatility of the arrival-rate λ *should remain the same* under the statistical and risk-neutral measures. We therefore do have an approach that is analogous to the diffusion-based models for VGSA.

VGSA vs. VG In their original paper [182], Carr, Madan, and Chang found comparable results for the VG model applied to the S&P 500 for the period 1992–1994. As previously discussed, the VG model has an integrated density, and therefore the MLE could be performed without any filtering. The statistical (historical) parameters are

$$(\sigma = 0.117200, \theta = 0.0056, \nu = 0.002)$$

And their risk-neutral parameters are

$$(\sigma = 0.1213, \theta = -0.1436, \nu = 0.1686)$$

Again we can see that the historical estimate for θ is close to zero, whereas the risk-neutral one is significantly negative. This negative θ is what creates the negative skewness observed in cross-sectional estimations.

We can try to reproduce the foregoing parameters with the VGSA model. The resulting time-series parameter set is

$$(\kappa = 79.499687, \eta = 3.557702, \lambda = 0.000000)$$
$$(\sigma = 0.049656, \theta = 0.006801, \nu = 0.008660, \mu = 0.030699)$$

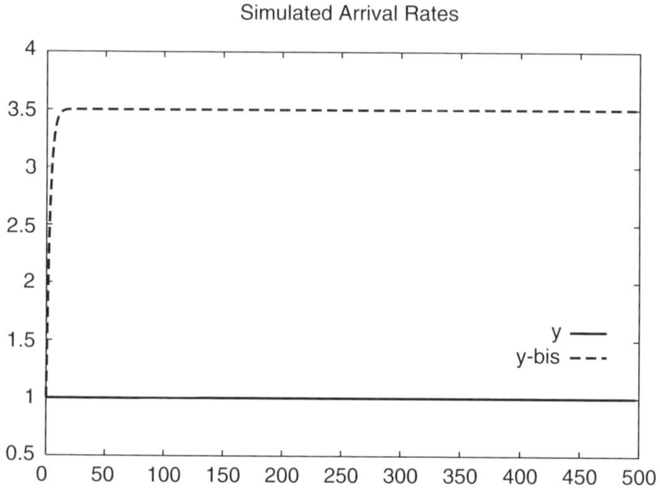

FIGURE 3.20 Arrival Rates for Simulated SPX Prices Using $\Psi = (\kappa = 0.0000, \eta = 0.0000, \lambda = 0.000000, \sigma = 0.117200, \theta = 0.0056, \nu = 0.002)$ and $\Psi = (\kappa = 79.499687, \eta = 3.557702, \lambda = 0.000000, \sigma = 0.049656, \theta = 0.006801, \nu = 0.008660, \mu = 0.030699)$. We can see that they are quite different.

Although the results seem to be very different, upon simulation we can see that even if the resulting arrival rates and gamma variables *are* different, the log stock prices are close. This can be seen in Figures 3.20, 3.21, and 3.22.

An alternative would be to use the EPF algorithm with the VGSA model over the same period, in which case we would obtain

$$(\kappa = 190.409721, \eta = 3.459288, \lambda = 5.430759)$$
$$(\sigma = 0.050243, \theta = 0.002366, \nu = 0.007945, \mu = 0.032576)$$

Once again the most unstable parameters are (κ, η, λ), or the ones corresponding to the arrival rate. We have seen this many times; the estimation of the parameters affecting the noise is less reliable. This is in agreement with what we had observed in Chapter 2 and shows the limitations of these inference tools.

Cross-Sectional vs. Time-Series VGSA Applying the particle filtering algorithm described in Chapter 2 to S&P 500, we find for 2001–2003 period the *statistical* parameter set

$$(\kappa = 55.01778, \eta = 3.721583, \lambda = 8.666717,$$
$$\sigma = 0.118637, \theta = 0.060053, \nu = 0.00103)$$

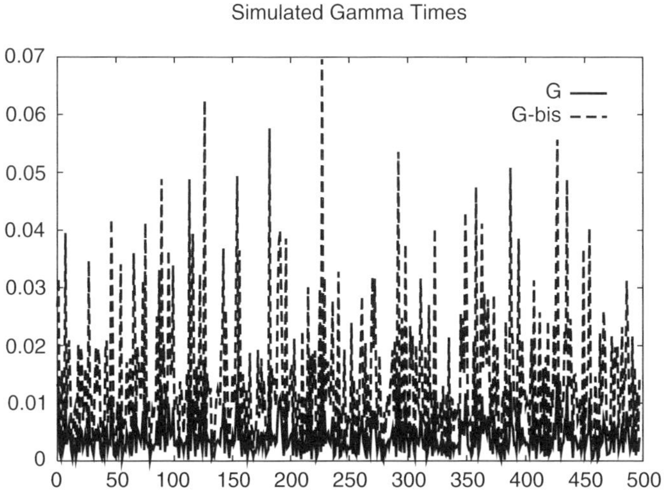

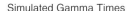

FIGURE 3.21 Gamma Times for Simulated SPX Prices Using $\Psi = (\kappa = 0.0000, \eta = 0.0000, \lambda = 0.000000, \sigma = 0.117200, \theta = 0.0056, \nu = 0.002)$ and $\Psi = (\kappa = 79.499687, \eta = 3.557702, \lambda = 0.000000, \sigma = 0.049656, \theta = 0.006801, \nu = 0.008660, \mu = 0.030699)$.

$$\mu_S = -0.2910$$

and for the 1995–1999 period

$$(\kappa = 1.151952, \eta = 5.418226, \lambda = 2.840461, \sigma = 0.055811,$$
$$\theta = 0.008626, \nu = 0.006021)$$
$$\mu_S = 0.249051$$

A typical cross-sectional *risk-neutral* parameter set

$$(\kappa = 2.72, \eta = 2.18, \lambda = 5.68, \sigma = 0.21, \theta = -0.41, \nu = 0.06)$$

As we can see, the implied skew and kurtosis are stronger for the cross-sectional method compared with the statistical one. This is consistent with results observed with other diffusion-based models.

We perform more recent parameter estimations corresponding to 06/10/1999–06/10/2003 and 09/10/1999–09/10/2003 (via PF based on 1000 particles) for S&P 500. The results are reported in Table 3.3. As we can see, the algorithm for the estimation of the statistical parameters seems fairly stable *provided that the initial parameters are chosen sufficiently close to the optimal ones.*

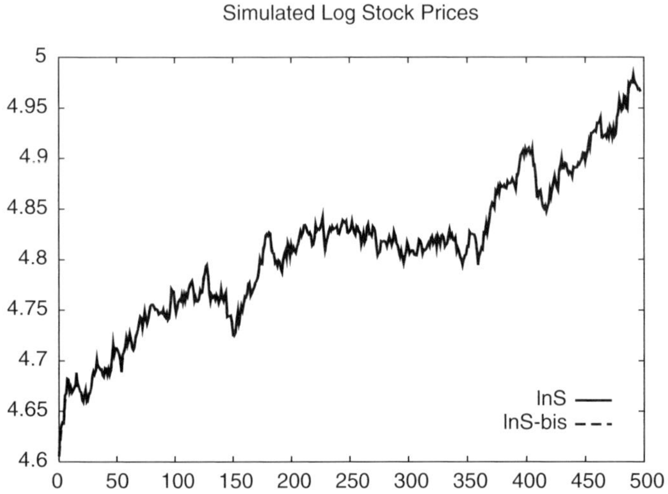

FIGURE 3.22 Log Stock Prices for Simulated SPX Prices Using $\Psi = (\kappa = 0.0000, \eta = 0.0000, \lambda = 0.000000, \sigma = 0.117200, \theta = 0.0056, \nu = 0.002)$ and $\Psi = (\kappa = 79.499687, \eta = 3.557702, \lambda = 0.000000, \sigma = 0.049656, \theta = 0.006801, \nu = 0.008660, \mu = 0.030699)$. Unlike arrival rates, the spot prices are hard to distinguish. This is consistent with our previous observations.

TABLE 3.3 VGSA Statistical Parameters Estimated via PF. The stock drifts μ_S are -0.009999 and -0.010000 respectively.

period	κ	η	λ	σ	θ	ν
990910-030910	5.131967	6.499669	**4.360002**	0.087000	−0.024862	0.002000
990610-030610	6.514068	6.500001	**4.360000**	0.085000	−0.025000	0.001800

The cross-sectional results could be computed in the same way as for diffusion-based models. Quoting the results of Carr et al. [48], we have Table 3.4. As shown, for some periods the risk-neutral implied λ is much larger than the statistical one. This implies the possibility of a skewness trade, as previously discussed.

It therefore seems that, depending on the period, the statistical and risk-neutral parameters λ may or may not be consistent.

A WORD OF CAUTION

Accuracy issues of the inference tools aside, there are practical considerations we need to bear in mind. We are applying basic models, such as Heston or

TABLE 3.4 VGSA Risk-Neutral Arrival-Rate Parameters Estimated from Carr et al. [48]

period	κ	η	λ
Mar 2000	4.08	15.99	16.52
Jun 2000	7.24	32.15	24.81
Sep 2000	0.25	0.00	3.76
Dec 2000	2.18	5.71	5.67

VGSA, to a complex and constantly changing market. The true dynamics of the stock and option markets are unknown, and, even if the above models approximate them fairly well, there is no guarantee that there will not be a mutation in future dynamics. The best we can do is to use the information hitherto available and hope that the future behavior of the assets is not too different from the past.

Needless to say, as time passes by and new information becomes available, we need to update our models and parameter values. This could be done within either a Bayesian or classical framework. Therefore, detecting an inconsistency between the stock and option markets does not allow us to make a riskless profit, because we simply do not know what the future is reserving for us. Once again, the skewness transaction described in this chapter is more similar to selling insurance than to an arbitrage.

FOREIGN EXCHANGE, FIXED INCOME, AND OTHER MARKETS

Foreign Exchange

It is important to note that everything discussed in this book can be applied to time series from other asset classes. A popular asset class to which the Heston and Bates models are often applied is the foreign exchange (FX). Bates [27] applies his jump diffusion model to the USD/deutsche Mark (now euro) exchange rate.

Calling X_t the FX rate process, for a Heston model, we would have under the real-world measure P

$$d\ln X_t = \left(\mu_X - \frac{1}{2}v_t\right)dt + \sqrt{v_t}dB_t$$

$$dv_t = (\omega - \theta v_t)dt + \xi\sqrt{v_t}\left(\rho dB_t + \sqrt{1-\rho^2}dZ_t\right)$$

TABLE 3.5 The Volatility and Correlation Parameters for the Cross-Sectional and Time-Series Approaches.

Method	ξ	ρ
Cross-Sectional	0.45	−0.05
Time-Series	0.11	−0.09

with $< dB_t, dZ_t >= 0$. We could therefore apply any of the previously used filters to the discretization of the above SDE and obtain the optimal parameters via MLE.

Under the risk-neutral measure Q, the FX drift is the difference between the domestic and the foreign interest rates r_D and r_F. Therefore, we would have

$$d \ln X_t = \left[r_D(t) - r_F(t) - \frac{1}{2}v_t\right]dt + \sqrt{v_t}dB_t^{(r)}$$
$$dv_t = (\omega^{(r)} - \theta^{(r)}v_t)dt + \xi\sqrt{v_t}\left(\rho dB_t^{(r)} + \sqrt{1-\rho^2}dZ_t^{(r)}\right)$$

with $< dB_t^{(r)}, dZ_t^{(r)} >= 0$. Note that the usual Heston closed-form option-pricing expression is valid for the FX process.

As previously discussed, according to the Girsanov theorem, (ξ, ρ) should be the same under the two measures. It is well known that compared with equities, FX options markets have a much lower correlation ρ and have a more symmetric smile. A skewness trade would therefore be more difficult to carry out in this market, but a kurtosis trade taking advantage of the high volatility-of-volatility ξ embedded in the options markets could be appropriate (Table 3.5).

Similarly to what we did for the equities, we estimate the model parameters from the three-month EUR/USD options cross-sectionally via a least-squares method on January 2004. And we estimate the time-series parameters (January 2000 to January 2005) via our second chapter filters. As before, adding jumps to the Heston model will help lower the cross-sectional volatility-of-volatility, but it remains insufficient to reconcile them.

Fixed Income

The Time Series The same principles could be applied to the interest-rate models with stochastic volatility. Using, for instance, a generalization of the extended-Vasicek [146] short-rate model[14], we would have under P

$$dr_t = a[\mu(t) - r_t]dt + \sqrt{v_t}dB_t$$
$$dv_t = (\omega - \theta v_t)dt + \xi\sqrt{v_t}\left(\rho dB_t + \sqrt{1-\rho^2}dZ_t\right)$$

with $< dB_t, dZ_t >= 0$. The difference between this first SDE and the corresponding ones in FX or equities is that the short-rate process is not directly observable. What *is* observable is the bond yield, which has a closed-form expression as a function of r_t. In an extended Vasicek model, for a given path of v_t the price of a forward starting zero-coupon bond is

$$P(t,T) = A(t,T)e^{-B(t,T)r(t)}$$

with

$$B(t,T) = \frac{1 - e^{-a(T-t)}}{a}$$

$$\ln A(t,T) = \ln\frac{P(0,T)}{P(0,t)} - B(t,T)\frac{\partial \ln P(0,t)}{\partial t}$$
$$-\frac{1}{2}\left(B(t,T)\frac{\partial B(0,t)}{\partial t}\right)^2 \int_0^t \left(1/\frac{\partial B(0,u)}{\partial u}\right)^2 v_u du$$

and the bond yield is

$$R(t,T) = -\frac{\ln P(t,T)}{T-t}$$

From the foregoing expressions we can fairly easily deduce that at a given time t, the short rate simply becomes

$$r(t) = R(t,t) = -\frac{\partial \ln P}{\partial t}(t,t)$$

Therefore, we can observe the current short rate as the (negative) initial slope of the yield curve, and we are back to the same framework as for equities and FX processes.

The Cross Section For the option pricing under Q we would have

$$dr_t = a^{(r)}\left[\mu^{(r)}(t) - r_t\right]dt + \sqrt{v_t}dB_t^{(r)}$$
$$dv_t = (\omega^{(r)} - \theta^{(r)}v_t)dt + \xi\sqrt{v_t}\left(\rho dB_t^{(r)} + \sqrt{1-\rho^2}dZ_t^{(r)}\right)$$

---

[14]In what follows we consider the speed of mean reversion a fixed. One could estimate it via a global calibration, for instance.

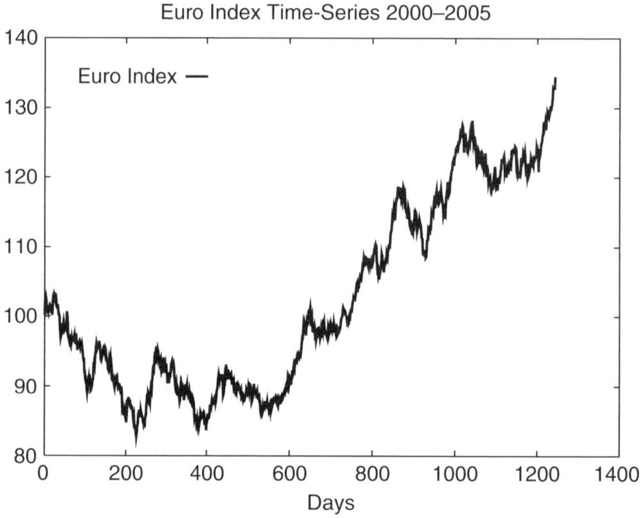

FIGURE 3.23 A Time Series of the Euro Index from January 2000 to January 2005.

with $< dB_t^{(r)}, dZ_t^{(r)} >= 0$. Naturally because of the randomness of the volatility, we would lose the closed-form expressions for the options on bonds (or caps or swaptions). However, we can still value them via a two-factor Monte Carlo algorithm. Indeed, we have for an option with maturity U on a zero-coupon bond with maturity $T > U$

$$c = \mathbf{E}_0\left[\left(\exp(-\int_U^T r_t dt) - 1\right)^+\right]$$
$$= \int_0^{+\infty}\int_0^{+\infty}\left(\exp(-\int_U^T r_t dt) - 1\right)^+ q(r_U, v_U)dr_U dv_U$$

where $q(r, v)$ represents the joint density of the short rate and its volatility.

Once again, the Girsanov theorem would require the same (ξ, ρ) parameters under the real-world and risk-neutral measures. A more negative correlation in the cross-sectional options market would therefore favor a skewness trade, and a higher volatility-of-volatility, a kurtosis trade.

One noticeable point is that, for a given level of option maturity U, we can have many bond maturities. It is known that a swaption can be modeled and priced as an option on a coupon bond.[15] However, there may be many swap *tenors* for the same option expiration, which introduces an

[15] See [146] for instance.

extra dimension. But nothing stops us from using many tenors and option maturities at once for a cross-sectional calibration.

The choice of the time-series period is still to be questioned. Do we consider the period beginning at our cross-sectional date, or do we consider a start date before this date? The latter would provide us with more data points; however, these points would be historic. As we saw, we probably would need the longer time series in order to have more reliable estimations.

References

[1] Ackerberg D. A. (2000) "Importance Sampling and the Method of Simulated Moments" *Department of Economics, Boston University and NBER.*

[2] Aihara S., Bagchi A. (2000) "Estimation of Stochastic Volatility in the Hull-White Model" *Applied Mathematical Finance*, 7.

[3] Aït-Sahalia Y. (2001) "Telling from Discrete Data Whether the Underlying Continuous-Time Model Is a Diffusion" *Journal of Finance*, Vol. 57, No. 5.

[4] Aït-Sahalia Y. (2002) "Maximum Likelihood Estimation of Discretely Sampled Diffusions: A Closed-Form Approximation Approach" *Econometrica*, Vol. 70, No. 1.

[5] Aït-Sahalia Y. (2003) "Disentangling Volatility from Jumps" *Working Paper, Princeton University.*

[6] Aït-Sahalia Y., Wang Y., Yared F. (2001) "Do Option Markets Correctly Price the Probabilities of Movement of the Underlying Asset?" *Journal of Econometrics*, 101.

[7] Alexander C. (1999) "A Primer on the Orthogonal GARCH Model" *ISMA Center, University of Reading.*

[8] Alexander C. (2000) "Principles of Skew" *RISK.*

[9] Alexander C. (2001) "Market Models: A Guide to Financial Data Analysis" *John Wiley & Sons, Ltd.*

[10] Alizadeh S., Brandt M. W., Diebold F. X. (2002) "Range-Based Estimation of Stochastic Volatility Models" *Journal of Finance*, Vol. 57, No. 3.

[11] Amin K. I., Ng V. (1993) "Option Valuation with Systematic Stochastic Volatility" *Journal of Finance*, Vol. 48, Issue 3.

[12] Andersen A. B. (2000) "Quantifying the *Peso Problem* Bias: A Switching Regime Approach" *Department of Finance, The Aarhus Schools of Business, Denmark.*

[13] Andersen L. B. G., Brotherton-Ratcliffe R. (1997) "The Equity Option Volatility Smile: An Implicit Finite Difference Approach" *Journal of Computational Finance*, Vol. 1(2).

[14] Arulampalam S., Maskell S., Gordon N., Clapp T. (2002) "A Tutorial on Particle Filters for On-line Non-linear/ Non-Gaussian Bayesian Tracking" *IEEE Transactions on Signal Processing*, Vol. 50. No. 2.

[15] Avellaneda M. (2002) "Empirical Aspects of Dispersion Trading in U.S. Equity Markets" *Slides from Presentation at Le Petit Dejeuner de la Finance, Paris.*

[16] Avellaneda M., Friedman C., Holmes R., Samperi D. (1997) "Calibrating Volatility Surfaces via Relative-Entropy Minimization" *Applied Mathematical Finance*, 4(1).

[17] Avellaneda M., Levy A., Paras A. (1995) "Pricing and Hedging Derivative Securities in Markets with Uncertain Volatilities" *Applied Mathematical Finance*, 2.

[18] Bachelier L. (1900) "Théorie de la Spéculation" *Annales Scientifiques de l'École Normale Supérieure, Troisième Série*, 17.

[19] Bagchi A. (2004) "Volatility Estimation under Heston's Framework" *Supervisor, University of Twente Working Paper.*

[20] Bakshi G., Cao C., Chen Z. (1997) "Empirical Performance of Alternative Option Pricing Models" *Journal of Finance*, Vol. 52, Issue 5.

[21] Balland P. (2002) "Deterministic Implied Volatility Models" *Quantitative Finance*, Vol. 2.

[22] Barle S., Cakici N. (1995) "Growing a Smiling Tree" *RISK Magazine*, Vol. 8, No. 10.

[23] Barndorff-Nielsen O. E., Nicolato E., Shephard N. (2002) "Some Recent Developments in Stochastic Volatility Modeling" *Quantitative Finance*, 2.

[24] Barndorff-Nielsen O. E., Shephard N. (2001) "Non-Gaussian Ornstein-Uhlenbeck-based Models and Some of Their Uses in Financial Economics" *Royal Statistical Society*, 63, Part 2.

[25] Barndorff-Nielsen O. E., Shephard N. (2002) "Econometric Analysis of Realized Volatility and Its Use in Estimating Stochastic Volatility Models" *Journal of the Royal Statistical Society*, Series B, Vol. 64.

[26] Bates D. S. (1991) "The Crash of 87: Was It Expected? The Evidence from Options Markets" *Journal of Finance*, Vol. 46, Issue 3.

[27] Bates D. S. (1996) "Jumps and Stochastic Volatility: Exchange Rate Processes Implicit in Deutsche Mark Options" *Review of Financial Studies*, 9.

[28] Bates D. S. (1998) "Pricing Options Under Jump Diffusion Processes" *The Wharton School, University of Pennsylvania.*

[29] Bates D. S. (1998) "Hedging the Smirk" *University of Iowa & NBER.*

[30] Bates D. S. (2000) "Post-87 Crash Fears in the S&P 500 Futures Option Market" *Journal of Econometrics*, 94.

[31] Bates D. S. (2002) "Maximum Likelihood Estimation of Latent Affine Processes" *University of Iowa & NBER.*

[32] Bates D. S. (2002) "Empirical Option Pricing: A Retrospection" *Forthcoming in Journal of Econometrics.*

[33] Bensoussan A., Crouhy M. and Galai D. (1995) "Stochastic Equity Volatility Related to the Leverage Effect I: Equity Volatility Behavior" *Applied Mathematical Finance*, 1.

[34] Bernardo J., Smith A. F. M. (2001) "Bayesian Theory" *John Wiley and Sons.*

[35] Bertsekas D. P. (2000) "Dynamic Programming and Optimal Control" (2nd Edition, Vols. 1 and 2), *Athena Scientific.*

[36] Blacher G. (1998) "Local Volatility" *RISK Conference Presentation.*

[37] Black F. (1976) "Studies in Stock Price Volatility Changes" *Proceedings of the 1976 Meeting of the Business and Economics Statistics Section, American Statistical Association.*

[38] Black F., Scholes M. (1973) "The Pricing of Options and Corporate Liabilities" *Journal of Political Economy*, 81.

[39] Blinnikov S., Moessner R. (1998) "Expansion for Nearly Gaussian Distributions" *Astronomy and Astrophysics Supplement Series*, 130.

[40] Bollerslev T. (1986) "Generalized Autoregressive Conditional Heteroskedasticity" *Journal of Econometrics*, 31.

[41] Bouchaud J. P., Perelló J., Masoliver J. (2003) "Multiple Time-Scales in Volatility and Leverage Correlations: A Stochastic Volatility Model" *Working Paper, Centre d'Etudes de Saclay and Universitat de Barcelona.*

[42] Bouchouev I. (1998) "Derivatives Valuation for General Diffusion Processes" *The International Association of Financial Engineers (IAFE) Conferences.*

[43] Brandt M. W., Santa-Clara P. (2002) "Simulated Likelihood Estimation of Diffusions with an Application to Exchange Rate Dynamics in Incomplete Markets" *Journal of Financial Economics*, 63.

[44] Breeden D. T., Litzenberger R. H. (1978) "Prices of State-Contingent Claims Implicit in Option Prices" *Journal of Business*, Vol. 51, No. 4.

[45] Brockhaus O., Long D. (2000) "Volatility Swaps Made Simple" *RISK*, January 2000.

[46] Buraschi A., Jackwerth A. C. (2001) "The Price of a Smile: Hedging and Spanning in Option Markets" *Review of Financial Studies*, 14.

[47] Carr P., Geman H., Madan D., Yor M. (2002) "The Fine Structure of Asset Returns" *Journal of Business*, Vol. 75, No. 2.

[48] Carr P., Geman H., Madan D., Yor M. (2003) "Stochastic Volatility for Lévy Processes" *Mathematical Finance*, Vol. 13, No. 3.

[49] Carr P., Lewis K. (2002) "Corridor Variance Swaps" *Research Papers, Courant Institute of Mathematical Sciences, New York University.*

[50] Carr P., Madan D. (1998) "Toward a Theory of Volatility Trading" *Research Papers, Courant Institute of Mathematical Sciences, New York University.*

[51] Carr P., Madan D. (1998) "Option Valuation Using the Fast Fourier Transform" *Morgan Stanley and University of Maryland.*

[52] Carr P., Madan D. (2001) "Optimal Positioning in Derivative Securities" *Quantitative Finance*, Vol. 1.

[53] Carr P., Madan D. (2001) "Optimal Investment in Derivative Securities" *Finance and Stochastics*, Vol. 5.

[54] Carr P., Wu L. (2003) "Time-Changed Lévy Processes and Option Pricing" *Journal of Financial Economics.*

[55] Casella G., George E. I. (1992) "Explaining the Gibbs Sampler" *The American Statistician*, Vol. 46, No. 3.

[56] Chernov M., Ghysels E. (2000) "A Study Toward a Unified Approach to the Joint Estimation of Objective and Risk-Neutral Measures for the Purpose of Option Valuation" *Journal of Financial Economics*, 56.

[57] Chib S., Nadari F., Shephard N. (1998) "Markov Chain Monte-Carlo Methods for Generalized Stochastic Volatility Models" *Washington University and The University of Oxford.*

[58] Chib S., Greenberg E. (1995) "Understanding the Metropolis-Hastings Algorithm" *The American Statistician*, Vol. 49, No. 4.

[59] Chourdakis K. M. (2001) "Volatility Persistence, Regime Switches and Option Pricing" *Department of Economics, University of London.*

[60] Chriss N. A. (1997) "Black Scholes and Beyond: Option Pricing Models" *Irwin/McGraw Hill.*

[61] Corradi V. (2000) "Reconsidering the Continuous Time Limit of the GARCH(1,1) Process" *Journal of Econometrics*, 96.

[62] Corrado C. J., Su T. (1997) "Implied Volatility Skews and Stock Index Skewness and Kurtosis Implied by S&P 500 Index Option Prices" *University of Missouri at Columbia, University of Miami at Coral-Gables.*

[63] Corrado C. J., Su T. (1997) "Implied Volatility Skews and Stock Return Skewness and Kurtosis Implied by Stock Option Prices" *The European Journal of Finance*, 3.

[64] Cox J. C. (1996) "The Constant Elasticity of Variance Option Pricing Model" *Journal of Portfolio Management*, Special Issue.

[65] Cox J. C., Ross S. (1976) "The Valuation of Options for Alternative Stochastic Processes" *Journal of Financial Economics*, 3.

[66] Cox J. C., Ross S., Rubinstein M. (1979) "Option Pricing: A Simplified Approach" *Journal of Financial Economics*, 7.

[67] Cox J. C., Rubinstein M. (1985) "Options Markets" *Prentice Hall.*

[68] Crosbie P. J. (1999) "Modeling Default Risk" *KMV Working Papers.*

[69] Das S. R., Sundaram R. K. (1997) "Taming the Skew: Higher-Order Moments in Modeling Asset-Price Processes in Finance" *National Bureau of Economic Research.*

[70] Demeterfi K., Derman E., Kamal M., Zou J. (1999) "More than You Ever Wanted to Know About Volatility Swaps" *Goldman Sachs Quantitative Strategy Papers.*

[71] Dempster M. A. H., Gotsis G. Ch. (1998) "On the Martingale Problem for Jumping Diffusions" *University of Cambridge and Hellenic Capital Market Commission.*

[72] Deng S. (2000) "Stochastic Models for Energy Commodity Prices and Their Applications: Mean-Reversion with Jumps and Spikes" *Industrial and Systems Engineering, Georgia Institute of Technology.*

[73] Derman E. (1999) "Regimes of Volatility: Some Observations on the Variations of S&P 500 Implied Volatilities" *Goldman Sachs Quantitative Strategy Papers.*

[74] Derman E., Kani I. (1994) "Riding on a Smile" *RISK Magazine*, 7.

[75] Derman E., Kani I. (1994) "The Volatility Smile and Its Implied Tree" *Goldman Sachs Quantitative Strategy Papers.*

[76] Derman E., Kani I. (1998) "Stochastic Implied Trees: Arbitrage Pricing with Stochastic Term and Strike Structure of Volatility" *International Journal of Theoretical and Applied Finance*, 1.

[77] Derman E., Kani I., Chriss N. (1996) "Implied Trinomial Trees of the Volatility Smile" *Goldman Sachs Quantitative Strategy Papers.*

[78] Derman E., Kani I., Zou J. (1995) "The Local Volatility Surface: Unlocking the Information in Index Option Prices" *Goldman Sachs Quantitative Strategy Papers.*

[79] Doucet A., De Freitas N., Gordon N. (2001) "Sequential Monte-Carlo Methods in Practice" *Springer-Verlag.*

[80] Doucet A., Gordon N., Krishnamurthy V. (2001) "Particle Filters for State Estimation of Jump Markov Linear Systems" *IEEE Transactions on Signal Processing*, Vol. 49, No. 3.

[81] Dragulescu A. A., Yakovenko V. M. (2002) "Probability Distribution of Returns in the Heston Model with Stochastic Volatility" *Department of Physics, University of Maryland.*

[82] Duan J. C. (1995) "The GARCH Option Pricing Model" *Mathematical Finance*, 5.

[83] Duan J. C. (1996) "Cracking the Smile" *RISK Magazine*, 9.

[84] Duan J. C. (1996) "A Unified Theory of Option Pricing Under Stochastic Volatility: From GARCH to Diffusion" *Hong Kong University of Science and Technology.*

[85] Duan J. C. (1997) "Augmented GARCH(p,q) Process and Its Diffusion Limit" *Journal of Econometrics*, 79.

[86] Duan J. C. (2001) "Risk Premium and Pricing of Derivatives in Complete Markets" *Rotman School of Management, University of Toronto.*

[87] Dufresne Daniel (2001) "The Integrated Square-Root Process" *Center for Actuarial Studies, The University of Melbourne.*

[88] Dumas B., Fleming J., Whaley R. E. (1998) "Implied Volatility Functions: Empirical Tests" *Journal of Finance*, Vol. 53, Issue 6.

[89] Dupire B. (1994) "Pricing with a Smile" *RISK Magazine*, 7.

[90] Durrett R. (1996) "Stochastic Calculus: A Practical Introduction" *CRC Press, Boca Raton, Florida.*

[91] El-Karoui N., Quenez M. C. (1995) "Dynamic Programming and Pricing of Contingent Claims in Incomplete Markets" *SIAM Journal of Control and Optimization*, 33(1).

[92] Elerian O., Chib S., Shephard N. (2001) "Likelihood Inference for Discretely Observed Nonlinear Diffusions" *Econometrica.*

[93] Elliott R. J., Lahaie C. H., Madan D. (1997) "Filtering Derivative Security Valuations from Market Prices" *University of Alberta, University of Maryland.*

[94] Engle R. F. (1982) "Autoregressive Conditional Heteroskedasticity with Estimates of the Variance of United Kingdom Inflation" *Econometrica*, Vol. 50, No. 4.

[95] Engle R. F., Ishida I. (2002) "The Square-Root, the Affine, and the CEV GARCH Models" *Working Paper, New York University and University of California, San Diego.*

[96] Engle R. F., Mezrich J. (1995) "Grappling with GARCH" *RISK Magazine*, 9.

[97] Engle R. F., Ng V. (1993) "Measuring and Testing the Impact of News on Volatility" *Journal of Finance*, Vol. 48, Issue 5.

[98] Eraker B., Johannes M., Polson N. (2003) "The Impact of Jumps in Equity Index Volatility and Returns" *Journal of Finance*, 58.

[99] Fama E. (1965) "The Behavior of Stock Market Prices" *Journal of Business*, 38.

[100] Fan J., Yao Q. (2003) "Nonlinear Time Series: Nonparametric and Parametric Methods" *Springer.*

[101] Fleming J., Kirby C. (2003) "A Closer Look at the Relation Between GARCH and Stochastic Autoregressive Volatility" *Journal of Financial Econometrics*, Vol. 1, December.

[102] Follmer H., Sondermann D. (1986) "Hedging of Non-Redundant Contingent-Claims" *Contributions to Mathematical Economics, North-Holland.*

[103] Forbes C. S., Martin G. M., Wright J. (2002) "Bayesian Estimation of a Stochastic Volatility Model Using Option and Spot Prices" *Department of Econometrics and Business Statistics, Monash University, Australia.*

[104] Fouque J. P., Papanicolaou G., Sircar K. (2000) "Derivatives in Financial Markets with Stochastic Volatility" *Cambridge University Press.*

[105] Fouque J. P., Papanicolaou G., Sircar K. (2000) "Mean Reverting Stochastic Volatility" *International Journal of Theoretical and Applied Finance*, 3(1).

[106] Fouque J. P., Tullie T. A. (2002) "Variance Reduction for Monte-Carlo Simulation in a Stochastic Volatility Environment" *Quantitative Finance*, 2.

[107] Frey R. (1997) "Derivative Asset Analysis in Models with Level-Dependent and Stochastic Volatility" *Department of Mathematics, ETH Zurich.*

[108] Fridman M., Harris L. (1998) "A Maximum Likelihood Approach for Non-Gaussian Stochastic Volatility Models" *Journal of Business and Economic Statistics.*

[109] Gallant A. R., Tauchen G. (2001) "Efficient Method of Moments" *University of North Carolina and Duke University.*

[110] Galli A. (2000) "Variograms and Cross-Variograms" *Ecole des Mines de Paris*, Working Paper.

[111] Galli A., Lautier D. (2001) "Un Modèle de Structure par Terme des Prix des Matières Premières avec Comportement Asymétrique du Rendement d'Opportunité" *École des Mines de Paris & CEREG, Université Paris IX.*

[112] Garcia R., Ghyseles E., Renault E. (2002) "The Econometrics of Option Pricing" *Université de Montreal and University of North Carolina.*

[113] Gatheral J. G. (2001) "Stochastic Volatility and Local Volatility" *Courant Institute of Mathematical Sciences, New York University.*

[114] Gatheral J. G. (2001) "Fitting the Volatility Skew" *Courant Institute of Mathematical Sciences, New York University.*

[115] Gatheral J. G. (2001) "Asymptotics and Dynamics of the Volatility Skew" *Courant Institute of Mathematical Sciences, New York University.*

[116] Gatheral J. G. (2001) "Volatility and Variance Swaps" *Courant Institute of Mathematical Sciences, New York University.*

[117] Geman H., El-Karoui N., Rochet J. C. (1995) "Changes of Numeraire, Changes of Probability Measure and Option Pricing" *Journal of Applied Probability*, 32(2).

[118] Geman H., Madan D., Yor M. (2001) "Stochastic Volatility, Jumps and Hidden Time Changes" *Finance and Stochastics.*

[119] Geske R. (1979) "The Valuation of Compound Options" *Journal of Financial Economics*, 7.

[120] Gilks W. R., Richardson S., Spiegelhalter D. J. (1995) "Markov Chain Monte Carlo in Practice" *Chapman & Hall/ CRC.*

[121] Gondzio J., Kouwenberg R., Vorst T. (2003) "Hedging Options Under Transaction Costs and Stochastic Volatility" *Journal of Economic Dynamics and Control*, 27.

[122] Gordon N. J., Salmond D. J. Smith A. F. M. (1993) "Novel Approach to Nonlinear/Non-Gaussian Bayesian State Estimation" *IEE Proceedings-F*, Vol. 140, No. 2.

[123] Gourieroux C., A. Monfort, Renault E. (1993) "Indirect Inference" *Journal of Applied Econometrics*, 8.

[124] Gourieroux C., Jasiak J. (2001) "Financial Econometrics" *Princeton University Press*.

[125] Grabbe J. O. (1983) "The Pricing of Put and Call Options on Foreign Exchange" *Journal of International Money and Finance*, December.

[126] Hamilton J. D. (1989) "A New Approach to the Econometric Analysis of Non-stationary Time Series and the Business Cycle" *Econometrica*, Vol. 57, No. 2.

[127] Hamilton J. D. (1994) "Time Series Analysis" *Princeton University Press*.

[128] Härdle W., Kleinow T., Stahl G. (2002) "Applied Quantitative Finance" *Springer-Verlag*.

[129] Harvey A. C. (1989) "Forecasting, Structural Time Series Models, and the Kalman Filter" *Cambridge University Press*.

[130] Harvey A. C., Ruiz E., Shephard Neil (1994) "Multivariate Stochastic Variance Models" *Review of Economic Studies*, Vol. 61, Issue 2.

[131] Harvey C. R., Whaley R. E. (1991) "S&P 100 Index Option Volatility" *Journal of Finance*, Vol. 46, Issue 4.

[132] Haug E. G. (1997) "The Complete Guide to Option Pricing Formulas" *McGraw-Hill, New York*.

[133] Haykin S. (2001) "Kalman Filtering and Neural Networks" *Wiley Inter-Science*.

[134] Heston S. (1993) "A Closed-Form Solution for Options with Stochastic Volatility with Applications to Bond and Currency Options" *Review of Financial Studies*, 6.

[135] Heston S. (2000) "Derivatives on Volatility: Some Simple Solutions Based on Observables" *Federal Reserve Bank of Atlanta*, Working Paper.

[136] Heston S., Christoffersen P., Jacobs K. (2004) "Option Valuation with Conditional Skewness" *University of Maryland and McGill University*.

[137] Heston S., Nandi S. (1997) "A Closed Form GARCH Option Pricing Model" *Federal Reserve Bank of Atlanta*, Working Paper 97-9.

[138] Hipp C., Taksar M. (2000) "Hedging in Incomplete Markets and Optimal Control" *University of Karlsruhe and SUNY at Stony-Brook*.

[139] Hirsa A., Javaheri A. (2003) "A Particle Filtering Algorithm for the VGSA Model" *Working Paper, Morgan Stanley and RBC Capital Markets*.

[140] Hobson D. G. (1996) "Stochastic Volatility" *School of Mathematical Sciences, University of Bath*.

[141] Hobson D. G., Rogers L. C. G. (1998) "Complete Models with Stochastic Volatility" *Mathematical Finance*, 8.

[142] Honoré P. (1998) "Pitfalls in Estimating Jump-Diffusion Models" *Department of Finance, The Aarhus School of Business, Denmark.*

[143] Howison S. D., Rafailidis A., Rasmussen H. O. (2000) "A Note on the Pricing and Hedging of Volatility Derivatives" *The University of Oxford, Kings College London.*

[144] Hughston L. P. (2004) "International Models for Interest Rates and Foreign Exchange: A General Framework for the Unification of Interest Rate Dynamics and Stochastic Volatility" *Global Derivatives and Risk Management*, May 2004.

[145] Hughston L. P., Rafailidis A. (2004) "A Chaotic Approach to Interest Rate Modeling" *Finance and Stochastic.*

[146] Hull J. (1999) "Options, Futures, and Other Derivative Securities" *Englewood Cliffs*, 4th Edition.

[147] Hull J., Suo W. (2002) "A Methodology for Assessing Model Risk and its Application to the Implied Volatility Function Model"*Journal of Financial and Quantitative Analysis.*

[148] Hull J., Suo W. (2002) "Modeling the Volatility Surface" *University of Toronto and Queen's University.*

[149] Hull J., White A. (1987) "The Pricing of Options on Assets with Stochastic Volatility" *Journal of Finance*, Vol. 42, Issue 2.

[150] Hull J., White A. (1988) "An Analysis of the Bias in Option Pricing Caused by a Stochastic Volatility" *Advances in Futures and Options Research*, 3.

[151] Ito K., Xiong K. (1999) "Gaussian Filters for Nonlinear Filtering Problems" *Center for Research in Scientific Computation, North Carolina State University.*

[152] Jackel P. (2002) "Monte-Carlo Methods in Finance" *Wiley Series in Finance.*

[153] Jackson N., Suli E., Howison S. (1998) "Computation of Deterministic Volatility Surfaces" *Journal of Computational Finance* Vol. 2(2).

[154] Jackwerth J. C. (2000) "Option-Implied Risk-Neutral Distributions and Implied Binomial Trees: A Literature Review" *Journal of Derivatives*, 7.

[155] Jackwerth J. C., Rubinstein M. (1996) "Recovering Probability Distributions from Option Prices" *Journal of Finance*, Vol. 51, Issue 5.

[156] Jacquier E., Polson N. G., Rossi P. E. (1994) "Bayesian Analysis of Stochastic Volatility Models" *Journal of Business and Economic Statistics*, Vol. 12, No, 4.

[157] Jarrow R., Rudd A. (1982) "Approximate Option Valuation for Arbitrary Stochastic Processes" *Journal of Financial Economics*, 10.

[158] Javaheri A., Wilmott P., Haug E. G. (2002) "GARCH and Volatility Swaps" *Wilmott*, January 2002.

[159] Javaheri A., Lautier D., Galli A. (2003) "Filtering in Finance" *Wilmott*, Issue 5.

[160] Javaheri A. (2004) "Inference and Stochastic Volatility" *Wilmott*, Issue 11.

[161] Jex M., Henderson R., Wang D. (1999) "Pricing Exotics Under the Smile" *RISK Magazine.*

[162] Jiang G. J., Van der Sluis P. J. (2000) "Index Option Pricing with Stochastic Volatility and Stochastic Interest Rates" *Center for Economic Research.*

[163] Johannes M., Polson N. (2002) "MCMC Methods for Financial Econometrics" *The Handbook of Financial Econometrics*.
[164] Johannes M., Polson N., Stroud J. (2002) "Nonlinear Filtering of Stochastic Differential Equations with Jumps" *Working Paper, Columbia University, University of Chicago and University of Pennsylvania*.
[165] Jones C. S. (2001) "The Dynamics of Stochastic Volatility: Evidence from Underlying and Options Markets" *Simon School of Business, University of Rochester*.
[166] Julier S. J., Uhlmann J. K. (1997) "A New Extension of the Kalman Filter to Nonlinear Systems" *The University of Oxford, The Robotics Research Group*.
[167] Karatzas I., Shreve S. (1991) "Brownian Motion and Stochastic Calculus" *Springer-Verlag*, 2nd Edition.
[168] Kennedy P. (1998) "A Guide to Econometrics" *MIT Press*, 4th Edition.
[169] Kim S., Shephard N., Chib S. (1998) "Stochastic Volatility: Likelihood Inference and Comparison with ARCH Models" *Review of Economic Studies*, Vol. 65.
[170] Kitagawa G. (1987) "Non-Gaussian State Space Modeling of Non-Stationary Time Series" *Journal of American Statistical Association*, 82.
[171] Kitagawa G. (1996) "Monte-Carlo Filter and Smoother for Non-Gaussian Nonlinear Sate Space Models" *Journal of Computational and Graphical Statistics*, Vol. 5, No. 1.
[172] Kou S. (2000) "A Jump Diffusion Model for Option Pricing with Three Properties: Leptokurtic Feature, Volatility Smile, and Analytical Tractability" *Econometric Society World Congress 2000 Contributed Papers*.
[173] Kushner H. J. (1967) "Approximations to Optimal Nonlinear Filters" *IEEE Transactions on Automatic Control*, Vol. 12.
[174] Kushner H. J., Budhiraja A. S. (2000) "A Nonlinear Filtering Algorithm Based on an Approximation of the Conditional Distribution" *IEEE Transactions on Automatic Control*, Vol. 45. No. 3.
[175] Lagnado R., Osher S. (1997) "A Technique for Calibrating Derivative Security Pricing Model: Numerical Solution of an Inverse Problem" *Journal of Computational Finance*, Vol. 1(1).
[176] Lee D. S., Chia N. K. K (2002) "A Particle Algorithm for Sequential Bayesian Parameter Estimation and Model Selection" *IEEE Transactions on Signal Processing*, Vol. 50, No. 2.
[177] Lewis A. L. (2000) "Option Valuation under Stochastic Volatility" *Finance Press*.
[178] Lewis A. L. (2001) "A Simple Option Formula for General Jump-Diffusion and Other Exponential Levy Processes" *OptionCity.net Publications*.
[179] Lewis A. L. (2002) "The Mixing Approach to Stochastic Volatility and Jump Models" *Wilmott*, March 2002.
[180] Lewis A. L. (2002) "Fear of Jumps" *Wilmott*, Issue 2.
[181] Li Y. (2000) "A New Algorithm for Constructing Implied Binomial Trees: Does the Implied Model Fit Any Volatility Smile?" *Journal of Computational Finance*, Vol. 4(2).

[182] Madan D., Carr P., Chang E. C. (1998) "The Variance-Gamma Process and Option Pricing" *European Finance Review*, Vol. 2, No. 1.

[183] Maes K. (2001) "Panel Data Estimating Continuous-Time Arbitrage-Free Affine Term-Structure Models with the Kalman Filter" *International Economics, Leuven University*.

[184] Maheu J. M., McCurdy T. H. (2003) "News Arrival, Jump Dynamics, and Volatility Components for Individual Stock Returns" *University of Toronto*.

[185] Markowiz H. M. (1990) "Mean-Variance Analysis in Portfolio Choice and Capital Markets" *Basil Blackwell*.

[186] Matacz A. (1997) "Financial Modeling and Option Theory with the Truncated Levy Process" *School of Mathematics and Statistics, University of Sidney*.

[187] Matytsin A. (1999) "Modeling Volatility and Volatility Derivatives" *Columbia Practitioners Conference on the Mathematics of Finance*.

[188] Merton R. C. (1973) "The Theory of Rational Option Pricing" *Bell Journal of Economics and Management*, 7.

[189] Merton R. C. (1974) "On the Pricing of Corporate Debt: The Risk Structure of Interest Rates" *Journal of Finance*, Vol. 29, Issue 2.

[190] Merton R. C. (1976) "Option Pricing When the Underlying Stock Returns Are Discontinuous" *Journal of Financial Economics*.

[191] Meyer R., Fournier D. A., Berg A. (2003) "Stochastic Volatility: Bayesian Computation Using Automatic Differentiation and the Extended Kalman Filter" *Econometrics Journal*, Vol. 6.

[192] Muzzioli S., Torricelli C. (2001) "Implied Trees in Illiquid Markets: A Choquet Pricing Approach" *Universita degli Studi di Modena e Reggio Emilia, Dipartimento di Economia Politica*.

[193] Neftci S. N. (1996) "An Introduction to the Mathematics of Financial Derivatives" *Academic Press, San Diego, CA*.

[194] Nelson D. B. (1990) "ARCH Models as Diffusion Approximations" *Journal of Econometrics*, 45.

[195] Nelson D. B. (1990) "Conditional Heteroskedasticity and Asset Returns: A New Approach" *Econometrica*, 59.

[196] Nelson D. B., Foster D. P. (1994) "Asymptotic Filtering Theory for Univariate ARCH Models" *Econometrica*, Vol. 62, Issue 1.

[197] Oksendal B. (1998) "Stochastic Differential Equations: An Introduction with Applications" *Springer-Verlag New York*, 5th Edition.

[198] Pan G. (2001) "Equity to Credit Pricing" *RISK* November 2001.

[199] Pan J. (2002) "The Jump Risk-Primia Implicit in Options: Evidence from an Integrated Time-Series Study" *Journal of Financial Economics*, 63.

[200] Parkinson M. (1980) "The Extreme Value Method for Estimating the Variance of the Rate of Return" *Journal of Business*, 53.

[201] Pedersen A. R. (1995) "A New Approach to Maximum Likelihood Estimation for Stochastic Differential Equations Based on Discrete Observations" *Scandinavian Journal of Statistics*, 22.

[202] Pham H. (2001) "Smooth Solutions to Optimal Investment Models with Stochastic Volatilities and Portfolio Constraints" *CNRS and Université Paris 7*.

[203] Pitt M. K., Shephard N. (1999) "Filtering via Simulation: Auxiliary Particle Filters" *Journal of the American Statistical Association*, 94.

[204] Press W. H., Teukolsky S. A., Vetterling W. T., Flannery B. P. (1997) "Numerical Recipes in C: The Art of Scientific Computing" *Cambridge University Press*, 2nd Edition.

[205] Reif K., Gunther S., Yaz A. (1999) "Stochastic Stability of the Discrete-Time Extended Kalman Filter" *IEEE Transactions on Automatic Control.*

[206] Renault E., Touzi N. (1996) "Option Hedging and Implied Volatilities in a Stochastic Volatility Model" *Mathematical Finance*, 6.

[207] Ribiero C., Webber N. (2002) "Valuing Path-Dependent Options in the Variance-Gamma Model by Monte-Carlo with a Gamma Bridge" *Working Paper, University of Warwick and City University of London.*

[208] Ritchken P., Trevor R. (1997) "Pricing Options under Generalized GARCH and Stochastic Volatility Processes" *CMBF Papers, Macquarie University*, 19.

[209] Romano M., Touzi N. (1997) "Contingent Claims and Market Completeness in a Stochastic Volatility Model" *Mathematical Finance*, 7.

[210] Rubinstein M. (1983) "Displaced Diffusion Option Pricing" *Journal of Finance*, Vol. 38, Issue 1.

[211] Samuelson P. A. (1965) "Rational Theory of Warrant Pricing" *Industrial Management Review*, 6, 2.

[212] Sandmann G., Koopman S. J. (1998) "Estimation of Stochastic Volatility Models via Monte-Carlo Maximum Likelihood" *Journal of Econometrics*, 87.

[213] Schonbucher P. J. (1998) "A Market Model for Stochastic Implied Volatility" *Department of Statistics, Bonn University.*

[214] Scott L. O. (1987) "Option Pricing when the Variance Changes Randomly: Theory, Estimation, and Application" *Journal of Financial and Quantitative Analysis*, Dec.

[215] Scott L. O. (1997) "Pricing Stock Options in a Jump-Diffusion Model with Stochastic Volatility and Interest Rates: Applications of Fourier Inversion Methods" *Mathematical Finance*, 7.

[216] Shimko D. (1993) "Bounds on Probability" *RISK*, 6.

[217] Shimko D., Tejima N., Van Deventer D. R. (1993) "The Pricing of Risky Debt when Interest Rates are Stochastic" *Journal of Fixed Income*, September 1993.

[218] Shreve S., Chalasani P., Jha S. (1997) "Stochastic Calculus and Finance" *Carnegie Mellon University.*

[219] Silva A. C., Yakovenko V. M. (2002) "Comparison Between the Probability Distribution of Returns in the Heston Model and Empirical Data for Stock Indices" *Department of Physics, University of Maryland.*

[220] Sin C. A. (1998) "Complications with Stochastic Volatility Models" *Advances in Applied Probability*, 30.

[221] Smith A. F. M., Gelfand A. E. (1992) "Bayesian Statistics Without Tears: A Sampling-Resampling Perspective" *The American Statistician*, Vol. 46, No. 2.

[222] Srivastava A., Grenander U., Jensen G. R., Miller M. I. (2002) "Jump-Diffusion Markov Processes on Orthogonal Groups for Object Recognition" *Journal of Statistical Planning and Inference*, Special Issue.

[223] Stein E. M., Stein J. (1991) "Stock Price Distributions with Stochastic Volatility: An Analytic Approach" *Review of Financial Studies*, 4.

[224] Storvik G. (2002) "Particle Filters in State Space Models with Presence of Unknown Static Parameters" *IEEE Transactions on Signal Processing*, 50.

[225] Taleb N. (1996) "Dynamic Hedging: Managing Vanilla and Exotic Options" *John Wiley & Sons, Ltd.*

[226] Tavella D., Klopfer W. (2001) "Implying Local Volatility" *Wilmott*, August 2001.

[227] Tavella D., Randall C. (2000) "Pricing Financial Instruments: The Finite Difference Method" *John Wiley & Sons, Ltd.*

[228] Toft K. B., Prucyk B. (1997) "Options on Leveraged Equity: Theory and Empirical Tests" *Journal of Finance* Vol. 52, Issue 3.

[229] Van der Merwe R., Doucet A., de Freitas N., Wan E. (2000) "The Unscented Particle Filter" *Oregon Graduate Institute, Cambridge University, and UC Berkeley.*

[230] Varadhan S. R. S. (2000) "Probability Theory" *Courant Institute of Mathematical Sciences, New York University.*

[231] Wan E. A., Van der Merwe R. (2000) "The Unscented Kalman Filter for Nonlinear Estimation" *Oregon Graduate Institute of Science and Technology.*

[232] Wan E. A., Van der Merwe R., Nelson A. (2000) "Dual Estimation and the Unscented Transformation" *Oregon Graduate Institute of Science and Technology.*

[233] Welch G., Bishop G. (2002) "An Introduction to the Kalman Filter" *Department of Computer Science, University of North Carolina at Chapel Hill.*

[234] Wells C. (1996) "The Kalman Filter in Finance (Advanced Studies in Theoretical and Applied Econometrics), Vol. 32" *Kluwer Academic Publishers.*

[235] Whitt W. (2001) "Stochastic Process Limits: An Introduction to Stochastic Process Limits and Their Application to Queues" *AT&T Labs Research, Springer.*

[236] Wiggins J. B. (1987) "Option Values under Stochastic Volatility" *Journal of Financial Economics*, 19.

[237] Wilmott P. (2000) "Paul Wilmott on Quantitative Finance" *John Wiley & Sons, Ltd.*

[238] Wilmott P., Dewynne J., Howison S. (1993) "Option Pricing: Mathematical Pricing and Computations" *Oxford Financial Press.*

[239] Wilmott P., Rasmussen H. O. (2002) "Asymptotic Analysis of Stochastic Volatility Models" *Wilmott Associates.*

[240] Zellner A. (2000) "Bayesian and Non-Bayesian Approaches to Scientific Modeling and Inference in Economics and Econometrics" *University of Chicago.*

[241] Zhang L., Mykland P. A., Aït-Sahalia Y. (2003) "A Tale of Two Time-Scales: Determining Integrated Volatility with Noisy High-Frequency Data" *Working Paper. Carnegie Melon University, University of Chicago, and Princeton University.*

[242] Zhou C. (1997) "A Jump-Diffusion Approach to Modeling Credit Risk and Valuing Defaultable Securities" *Federal Reserve Board, Washington, DC.*

Index